Data Protection
for Software
Development
and IT

Ralf Kneuper

Data Protection for Software Development and IT

A Practical Introduction

 Springer

Ralf Kneuper
Darmstadt, Germany

ISBN 978-3-662-70638-1   ISBN 978-3-662-70639-8   (eBook)
https://doi.org/10.1007/978-3-662-70639-8

Translation from the German language edition: "Datenschutz für Softwareentwicklung und IT" by Ralf Kneuper, © Springer-Verlag GmbH Deutschland, ein Teil von Springer Nature 2021. Published by Springer Berlin Heidelberg. All Rights Reserved.

This Springer imprint is published by the registered company Springer-Verlag GmbH, DE, part of Springer Nature.
The registered company address is: Heidelberger Platz 3, 14197 Berlin, Germany

If disposing of this product, please recycle the paper.

Preface

Data protection has received a great deal of public attention over the last couple of years, in particular since the introduction of the European General Data Protection Regulation (GDPR), which has become applicable on 25 May 2018. However, this attention has been far from always positive, caused, among other things, by sometimes extravagant interpretations and scaremongering that have been published since then.

A major aim of this book is to provide a realistic introduction to the subject of data protection. Contrary to what the name suggests, data protection is not concerned with the protection of data, but with the protection of individuals from *misuse* of their personal data. Furthermore, it is about the right to determine for oneself which personal data may be communicated to others and used by them. In everyday life, people constantly give personal data to third parties, be it their employer, a doctor, an online retailer or a social network. This is usually done in the confidence that these data will be used appropriately (only for the agreed purpose) and will not be misused, although there are very different opinions as to what exactly this means. Data protection regulations such as the GDPR make these expectations more specific and define what constitutes "appropriate use" and what constitutes "misuse" of personal data.

Since the processing of such personal data is, by its very nature, largely performed by software and IT, software development and IT operations bear a considerable part of the responsibility for how this is done. This book is intended to help implement this responsibility appropriately and competently.

The book's target groups therefore primarily includes software developers, IT consultants, requirements analysts, IT operations personnel and project managers in IT projects, but also data protection managers and data protection officers in the context of software development and IT. However, a clear demarcation between data protection topics that affect these target groups and other topics is not possible, as software development can affect almost all business processes of an organisation. Nevertheless, the focus of this book will be on the topics of particular relevance to these target groups, concentrating on the direct impact of data protection on software development, for example, in the form of functional requirements for software systems resulting from data protection. The subsequent operation of the software is also considered but has less importance, since the main data protection aspects are determined during development. The most important contribution of IT operation is to ensure IT security for the software under consideration and the entire infrastructure.

In this context, it is important to distinguish between the development of customised software, by or on behalf of a user organisation, and the development of standard software. In the case of standard software, the development organisation bears a significantly greater share of the responsibility for ensuring that the software complies with the relevant legal regulations, i.e. data protection in this context, whereas in the case of customised software, more responsibility lies with the user organisation.

This book was originally published in 2021 in German language. It has now been translated into English, updated and adapted for an international audience. The main legal basis used is the GDPR, which is directly relevant for countries in the European Union (EU) and the European Economic Area (EEA), but in some cases also needs to be complied to in other countries, in particular when providing cloud or other services to EU or EEA customers. Independent of that, data protection legislation in countries outside the EU and EEA is often based on the same concepts as GDPR, and many of the explanations in this book will apply for those countries as well. Additionally, the book provides a summary of national data protection legislation for some selected countries both within and outside the EU and EEA. The goal in this case is not to provide a complete overview but a first understanding of the differences and similarities of data protection regulation in different legislations.

Legal Note As this book builds on the GDPR in many places, it is advisable to have a copy of this regulation handy when reading the book.[1] Individual excerpts of the GDPR that are particularly important in this context are also included in Appendix A of this book. In addition, the book also deals at relevant points with essential aspects of national legislation in a number of other countries. The reference in all these cases is the state of the law valid at the time of writing in 2024.

Aligned with the target group, the description is based on the GDPR, but the focus is on the fundamental concepts of data protection and is therefore largely independent of the details of the current legal situation. On the contrary, many statements are applicable beyond Europe, but of course, this is not true for all statements.

In addition, it is not always clear how legal regulations are to be interpreted, and the decision on this ultimately lies with the competent courts. Therefore, the author can of course not assume any liability for the legal statements, but only for the fact that they were compiled to the best of his knowledge and belief on the basis of the current state of information and that open questions are named as such where possible.

---

[1] The GDPR is available free of charge in electronic format directly from the EU in the various EU languages at https://eur-lex.europa.eu/legal-content/AUTO/?uri=CELEX:32016R0679&qid=1661354935368&rid=1.

In case of doubt, an IT lawyer or other data protection specialist should therefore be consulted to discuss the specific situation. In this case, however, this book hopefully helps to at least ask the right questions and to understand and implement the legally formulated answers correctly.

Case Studies and Examples For a better understanding of the content covered, the following case studies are used throughout the book, each describing a specific company and its implementation of data protection. Even though these companies do not exist in exactly this form, their descriptions are strongly based on actual existing companies.

> **Case Study 1 (Online Retail Company)** The company considered here is an online retailer with a Web site, a customer management system in the back office and an external service provider for warehousing and shipping.

It should be noted that software development forms only a small part of online marketing in its many variants, and this topic is therefore only considered superficially in this book. In particular, the interpretation of legal requirements is also more in flux than with other topics. In order to delve deeper here, current legal literature or the advice of specialised data protection experts or IT lawyers should therefore be sought.

> **Case Study 2 (Software House)** The second company considered is a software house that develops applications and tools for data analysis for client companies. In some cases, the corresponding applications and tools are provided to the respective customer; in other cases, the analyses themselves are carried out at the software house. The software house has its headquarters in Germany and a legally independent small subsidiary in Austria.

In addition to the case studies, there are a number of examples of the topics covered in each case, which are also displayed in grey boxes and which are also based on companies that actually exist, even if they are described in a slightly different way to make them anonymous.

> **Example 1 (Example of Topic)** This is an example of the current topic, independent of the two case-study companies.

Structure of the Book Chapter 1 introduces the topic and provides an initial overview of the basic concepts of data protection and its legal foundations.

Chapter 2 delves deeper into the GDPR, covering in particular the basic concepts, terminology and requirements, but still does so in general terms and without looking at their specific interpretation in the context of software and IT.

This specific implementation and interpretation of the GDPR requirements in software and IT will be dealt with from Chap. 3 onwards, starting with the principles of data protection defined in the GDPR (Chap. 3) and the rights of data subjects (Chap. 4).

In many cases, several organisations are involved in the processing of data, each taking on a different role. The organisations exchange data with each other as needed, for example, in the case of processing by a service provider. Chapter 5 discusses data transfer, including the relevant constellations, the legal framework and its practical implementation.

While the discussion so far has focused on the consideration of individual regulations and their implementation, Chap. 6 looks more generally at the technical and organisational design of data protection, in particular its embedding in the software life cycle, as well as the concept of *privacy/data protection by design* required by the GDPR.

An essential basis for the implementation of data protection is information security. Chapter 7 provides a first overview of this topic, naturally with a focus on those aspects relevant to data protection.

However, software development and IT are not only shapers of data protection for other organisations but also data subjects themselves, whose data are collected and processed in development tools and who must implement data protection for their own organisation. This topic is dealt with in Chap. 8.

The annexes contain the most important extracts from the Charter of Fundamental Rights of the EU and the GDPR in this context, a collection of links to relevant laws and supervisory authorities as well as a glossary of the most important terms used.

About the Author Ralf Kneuper has a first degree in mathematics, a PhD in computer science and an LLM in "IT and Law". He has worked in industry for more than 20 years in various positions, mainly in software quality management, process improvement and data protection. Today, he is a professor of data protection and IT security in the distance learning branch of IU International University of Applied Sciences. In addition, he advises companies and other organisations on data protection and is a certified external data protection officer.

Acknowledgements Finally, I would like to thank all those who contributed to this book. My colleagues Petra Beenken, Frank Müller and Brian Gannon reviewed preliminary versions, helping to clarify the book and correct errors. All remaining errors are of course my own responsibility.

Darmstadt, Germany   Ralf Kneuper
October 2024

Contents

1   **Introduction** 1
  1.1   Basic Concepts of Data Protection 1
  1.2   Legal Foundations of Data Protection Within the European Union
      and the European Economic Area 6
      1.2.1   The General Data Protection Regulation (GDPR) 6
      1.2.2   The ePrivacy Directive of the EU 8
      1.2.3   Data Protection in Germany 9
      1.2.4   Data Protection in Austria 10
      1.2.5   Data Protection in Ireland 10
      1.2.6   Data Protection in Estonia 11
      1.2.7   Data Protection in Norway 11
  1.3   Legal Foundations of Data Protection Outside the European
      Economic Area 12
      1.3.1   Data Protection in Switzerland 12
      1.3.2   Data Protection in the United Kingdom 12
      1.3.3   Data Protection in the USA 13
      1.3.4   Data Protection in Brazil 14
      1.3.5   Data Protection in India 15
      1.3.6   Data Protection in China 16
  1.4   Alternative Reference Models 17
  1.5   Data Protection and Software Requirements 19
  References 20

2   **Foundations of Data Protection According to GDPR** 21
  2.1   The European General Data Protection Regulation (GDPR) 21
      2.1.1   Basic Terminology and Structure 21
      2.1.2   Scope of Application of GDPR 23
  2.2   Personal Data 25
      2.2.1   Definition of Personal Data 25
      2.2.2   Special Categories of Personal Data 26
      2.2.3   Metadata 27

2.3   Identifiability, Pseudonymisation and Anonymisation   28
2.4   Roles in Data Protection   34
2.5   Data Protection Principles According to GDPR   37
        2.5.1   Lawfulness, Fairness and Transparency   37
        2.5.2   Purpose Limitation   42
        2.5.3   Data Minimisation   43
        2.5.4   Accuracy   43
        2.5.5   Storage Limitation   43
        2.5.6   Integrity and Confidentiality   44
        2.5.7   Accountability   45
2.6   Rights of the Data Subjects   45
2.7   Further Requirements for Data Protection According to GDPR   49
        2.7.1   Technical and Organisational Measures (TOM)   49
        2.7.2   Data Protection by Design   50
        2.7.3   Data Protection by Default   50
        2.7.4   Cooperation of Multiple Parties   51
        2.7.5   Records of Processing Activities (RoPA)   51
        2.7.6   Reporting of Personal Data Breaches   54
        2.7.7   Data Protection Impact Assessment (DPIA)   54
        2.7.8   Data Protection Officer   57
        2.7.9   Certification   59
        2.7.10   Supervisory Authorities   60
2.8   Consequences of Non-conformance   61
2.9   Data Protection, AI and the EU AI Act   62
References   65

3   Data Protection Principles and Their Implementation   67
3.1   Lawfulness, Fairness and Transparency   67
        3.1.1   Lawfulness of Processing   68
        3.1.2   Consent   68
        3.1.3   Other Legal Bases   73
        3.1.4   Lawfulness of Processing Personal Data in Machine Learning ...   74
        3.1.5   Fair Processing   75
        3.1.6   Transparency   76
        3.1.7   Lawfulness and Transparency in the Case of Web Sites and
                 Online Marketing   76
3.2   Purpose Limitation   83
        3.2.1   Requirements   83
        3.2.2   Checklist for Purpose Changes   84
        3.2.3   Legal Basis for Further Processing After Purpose Change   84
        3.2.4   Software Test Using Production Data   85

        3.2.5   Changing Purpose: Data Analysis, Big Data and Machine
                 Learning   89
    3.3   Data Minimisation   90
    3.4   Accuracy   92
    3.5   Storage Limitation   93
        3.5.1   Implementation of Storage Limitation   93
        3.5.2   Retention Periods and Erasure Concepts   96
        3.5.3   Example: Blockchain   102
    3.6   Integrity and Confidentiality   103
    3.7   Accountability   104
    References   105

4   **Rights of Data Subjects and Their Implementation**   107
    4.1   Transparency Rights and Obligations   107
        4.1.1   Information to Be Provided and Right of Access   108
        4.1.2   Authentication of Data Subjects   112
        4.1.3   Transparency and Data Protection Policies of Web Sites   113
    4.2   Right to Rectification   114
    4.3   Right to Erasure   115
    4.4   Right to Restriction of Processing   117
    4.5   Notification Obligation in Case of Rectification, Erasure or
           Restriction of Processing   119
    4.6   Right to Data Portability   119
    4.7   Right to Object   121
    4.8   Automated Individual Decision-Making   123
    References   124

5   **Data Transfer**   125
    5.1   Basic Rules for the Transfer of Personal Data   125
    5.2   Commissioned Processing   128
    5.3   Joint Controllership   129
    5.4   Transfer of Personal Data to Third Countries   131
    5.5   Use of Cloud Services   134
    Reference   136

6   **Technical and Organisational Implementation of Data Protection**   137
    6.1   Technical and Organisational Measures (TOM)   137
    6.2   Internal Regulations   138
        6.2.1   Basic Rules   138
        6.2.2   Handling of Data Breaches   139
        6.2.3   Training and Commitment of Employees   142

6.3   Anonymisation of Data.. 143
        6.3.1   Basic Concepts.. 143
        6.3.2   Anonymisation Procedure 147
        6.3.3   Anonymity Models 150
        6.3.4   *k*-Anonymity 151
        6.3.5   Differential Privacy 152
6.4   Privacy-Enhancing Technologies (PET)..................................... 155
        6.4.1   Confidential Computing and Trusted Execution Environments ... 156
        6.4.2   Synthetic Data Generation 156
        6.4.3   Secure Multi-party Computation................................. 157
        6.4.4   Federated Learning 158
6.5   Data Protection by Design and by Default 159
        6.5.1   Data Protection by Design.. 159
        6.5.2   Data Protection by Default 160
        6.5.3   Privacy by Design According to Cavoukian...................... 161
6.6   Embedding Data Protection into the Software Life Cycle................. 161
        6.6.1   Analysis 162
        6.6.2   Design and Architecture... 163
        6.6.3   Implementation 165
        6.6.4   Test and Acceptance 166
        6.6.5   Transition to Operations 166
        6.6.6   IT Operations 167
        6.6.7   Change Control 169
        6.6.8   Withdrawal 169
        6.6.9   Agile Development 169
6.7   Data Protection in Platforms and Software Ecosystems 171
6.8   Developing and Operating AI Systems...................................... 173
6.9   Tools for Implementing Data Protection 174
References 176

7   **Basic Concepts of Information Security** 179
7.1   Information Security 179
7.2   Information Security Management 181
7.3   Identification, Authentication and Authorisation 182
        7.3.1   Identification 182
        7.3.2   Authentication 182
        7.3.3   Authorisation... 187
7.4   Cryptology 187
        7.4.1   Foundations 188
        7.4.2   Security of Encryption... 188
        7.4.3   Symmetric and Asymmetric Encryption........................... 189
        7.4.4   Cryptographic Hash Functions 192

	7.4.5	Long-Term Protection of Personal Data	193
	7.4.6	Secure Data Exchange	193
	7.4.7	The Way Ahead: Quantum Computing and Post-quantum Cryptography	195
	References		197

8   Data Protection Within IT Organisations 199

8.1	Software Developers and IT Considered as Data Subjects	199
8.2	Implementing Data Protection Within an IT Organisation	202
8.3	Protecting Your Own Data	203

A   Excerpts from Important Data Protection Legislation 205

A.1	Charter of Fundamental Rights of the European Union	205
A.2	General Data Protection Regulation (GDPR)	205
A.3	Links to Relevant Laws and Supervisory Bodies	209

Glossary 211

Index 213

Acronyms

CJEU	Court of Justice of the European Union
CMDB	Configuration Management Database
CPO	Chief Privacy Officer
DPA	Data Protection Agreement
DPIA	Data Protection Impact Assessment
DPO	Data Protection Officer
ECJ	European Court of Justice
EDPB	European Data Protection Board
EDPS	European Data Protection Supervisor
EEA	European Economic Area (EU plus Iceland, Liechtenstein and Norway)
EU	European Union
FTC	Federal Trade Commission
GDPR	General Data Protection Regulation
HIPAA	Health Insurance Portability and Accountability Act
ICT	Information and Communication Technology
ISMS	Information Security Management System
IT	Information Technology
NIST	(US) National Institute of Standards and Technology
PET	Privacy-Enhancing Techniques
PIMS	Personal Information Management System; Privacy Information Management System
ROPA	Records of Processing Activities
SW	Software
TOM	Technical and Organisational Measure(s)

Introduction

Abstract

Contrary to what the name suggests, data protection does not serve to protect data, but to protect individuals from misuse of their data. Nevertheless, data protection is often seen as a bureaucratic obstacle to be circumvented if it cannot be ignored. Spurred on by the European *General Data Protection Regulation* (GDPR), however, data protection has taken on a much higher profile in the EU and beyond since 2018. This also has implications for software development and IT, on the one hand in their role as shapers of data protection and on the other hand as they themselves are affected by data protection. This chapter provides an introduction to the basic ideas of data protection and the role and responsibility of software development and IT in this context. This introduction is supplemented by an initial overview of the relevant legal foundations, in particular the GDPR, various national legislations and also some other reference models for data protection.

1.1 Basic Concepts of Data Protection

Data protection is a topic that has gained a lot of importance and attention, especially since the introduction of the European GDPR. Before discussing the requirements of data protection and their implementation in the context of software development and IT, it is first important to understand what data protection is about and what goals it pursues. Unfortunately, the term "data protection" is misleading and accordingly often misinterpreted: Data protection is about the protection of *persons*[1] from inappropriate processing or misuse of their data and thus only indirectly about the protection of the data itself. At the core of data protection is the right of individuals to decide for themselves what happens to their personal data and who may use it and to what extent. Accordingly, data protection is also only concerned with *personal data* and not with other possibly also confidential data (such as technical design data or financial data), even if the protection mechanisms used are often identical and the implementation of data protection therefore usually serves to protect other confidential data at the same time. Therefore, when this book talks about "data" it means *personal* data, even if this is not always explicitly formulated.

Data protection has emerged as a manifestation of the *general right to privacy* and has been defined as a fundamental right in Art. 8 of the *Charter of Fundamental Rights of the European Union*.[2] Even if one has "nothing to hide" it is an important aspect of personal freedom not to be under constant observation, as already formulated in the well-known *Volkszählungsurteil* ("census ruling") of the German Federal Constitutional Court in 1983.[3]

Data protection is not a new concept that started with the proliferation of computers but has been around for a long time in various forms, e.g. confessional secrecy or banking secrecy. However, the need for limitation and protection against inappropriate use grew rapidly with the new possibilities of electronic data processing and the massively increasing scope of data use. In most cases, the processing of data leads to an imbalance of power between the organisations that process the data or at least decide about the processing that is performed, in GDPR called the controller, and the persons whose data are processed, in GDPR called data subjects, because, for example, they have bought a product, visited a Web site or work for the organisation.

Unfortunately, data protection also leads to some bureaucratic hurdles, especially for small and medium-sized enterprises. However, as the experience of the last few years has shown, relaxing these provisions does not really benefit these small and medium-sized enterprises but rather makes it easier for large monopolies to collect and use personal data, as it is easier for them to implement the data collection and other processing in a legally correct manner and to explore legal limits in the process. The Internet is subject to network effects, which lead to monopolies, and without regulation, this effect is strengthened further.

---

[1] In this book, the term "person" is always used in the sense of a *natural person* (human). Legally speaking, there are of course also *legal persons* such as companies or associations, but these are not relevant in the context of data protection under most relevant legislations including GDPR.

[2] See Appendix A.1 for the text of this article.

[3] Available at https://www.bundesverfassungsgericht.de/SharedDocs/Entscheidungen/EN/1983/12/rs19831215_1bvr020983en.html.

Principles of Data Protection The essential ideas of data protection are described by some principles which are—with some variations—included in all relevant sets of rules, for example, the "Fair Information Practice Principles" (FIPP).[4] As an alternative example, the following list summarises the principles as defined in ISO/IEC 29100 (cf. Sect. 1.4):

1. *Consent and choice*: data subjects have a fundamental choice as to whether their data are processed or not.
2. *Purpose legitimacy and specification* states that personal data are to be processed only for specified and legally authorised purposes.
3. *Collection limitation*: data are only collected to the extent that is legally permitted and necessary for the respective purposes.
4. *Data minimisation* extends the collection limitation principle and requires that further processing of the data is also limited to what is necessary.
5. *Use, retention and disclosure limitation*: the use, retention and disclosure of data shall be limited to what is necessary.
6. *Accuracy and quality*: ensure that the data processed are accurate, complete and up to date.
7. *Openness, transparency and notice*: data subjects are provided with open and transparent information about how and why their data are processed.
8. *Individual participation and access*: data subjects shall have access to their data and shall be able to verify it and, where appropriate, request corrections, additions or deletion of such data.
9. *Accountability*: appropriate work processes are documented and communicated in order to comply with data protection requirements and to act accordingly in the event of incidents and to inform the data subjects.
10. *Information security*: confidentiality, integrity and availability of data are protected against external influences or attacks.
11. *Privacy compliance*: compliance with data protection requirements is demonstrated and verified through appropriate audit mechanisms.

These general expectations on data protection were then expressed as laws, of which the EU's GDPR is certainly the most important at present and will therefore comprise the focus of this book. In addition, there are many other relevant laws, such as the national data protection laws existing in each EU state, which supplement and concretise the GDPR in selected points. Sections 1.2 and 1.3 provide an initial overview of these legal foundations within the EU and beyond.

Regulations to Enforce Implementation of the Data Protection Principles While the principles above describe *what* needs to be done regarding data protection, most legislation

---

[4] The principles contained in the GDPR will be dealt with in more detail in Sect. 2.5.

on this topic also includes some regulations that aim to ensure that these principles are implemented adequately. This includes the setup of some *national supervisory authority* and the requirement, at least for organisations with large-scale and/or risky processing of personal data, to nominate organisational *data protection officers* (DPO), who have the task to support and supervise such processing. Additionally, some form of documentation is often required, for example, in the form of records of the processing performed (e.g. the *records of processing activities* (RoPA)) as required by GDPR or in the form of a national register of relevant processing as, under certain conditions, is the case in Switzerland.

Data Protection vs. Privacy In addition to the term "data protection" as used here, the similar term "privacy" is also used widely. These terms are not identical, although a strict distinction is rarely made. In Europe, the term "data protection" is commonly used, while in the USA, the term "privacy" is commonly used. Furthermore, "privacy" mostly focuses on safeguarding of confidentiality, going beyond personal data and including, for example, the privacy of the home. "Data Protection", on the other hand, obviously refers only to data but goes beyond their confidentiality and includes the rights of the data subjects, for example, to be informed about the processing of one's data. However, this is not a strict demarcation; for example, ISO/IEC 29100, from which the data protection principles listed above originate, uses the term "privacy" rather than "data protection".

Threats to Data Protection When it comes to data protection, many people initially only think of personal data becoming known to unauthorised persons, i.e. that the confidentiality of the data is at risk. However, there are many other threats to data protection, as Solove describes in the taxonomy shown in Fig. 1.1. (Note that Solove talks about threats to "privacy" rather than "data protection". Apart from the threat of "invasion" discussed below, this taxonomy is equally applicable to data protection.) Data protection thus has the task of protecting against all these threats.

Invasion While most of the terms used by Solove are fairly self-explanatory, the term "invasion" needs a bit more explanation here: in contrast to the other groups of threats, invasion does not necessarily refer to information (and thus includes privacy threats that are not, in a narrow sense, data protection threats). These privacy threats thus include, for example, intrusion to the home and interfering with decisions that are considered private.

Data Analysis Data analysis can affect individuals without considering or even knowing their individual personal data: For example, if data analysis shows that residents of a certain region have on average a low income and a high likelihood of not repaying loans, this may have an impact on individuals in that region who were not considered in the data analysis and for whom these findings do not apply.

The legitimacy of such aggregated analyses, which can lead to various forms of discrimination, is certainly an important ethical and legal issue. However, it is considered

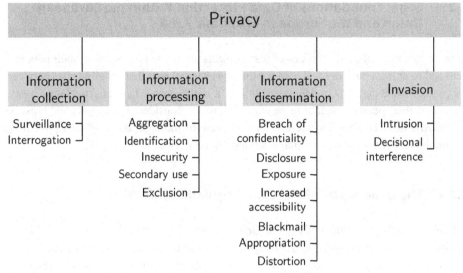

Fig. 1.1 Taxonomy of privacy threats according to Solove [Sol06]

a separate issue from data protection in this book, in line with the usual view used in legal regulations such as the GDPR.

Data Protection and Artificial Intelligence   In recent years, artificial intelligence (AI), in particular machine learning and generative artificial intelligence, has gained in importance considerably. Since this approach is largely based on the use of data on a large scale, often including personal data, data protection needs to be taken into account when training or using AI systems.[5] This leads to specific challenges, for example, the correct assignment of data protection responsibilities to the different parties involved, which is discussed in the relevant sections of this book.[6]

---

[5] See, for example, the study on "The impact of the General Data Protection Regulation (GDPR) on artificial intelligences", published by the European Parliament, available under https://www.europarl.europa.eu/thinktank/en/document/EPRS_STU(2020)641530.

[6] For an overview of the relevance of the AI Act for data protection, including the definition of roles and the assignment of responsibilities, see Sect. 2.9. Automated individual decision-making with the help of AI is addressed on p. 49. There are some specific challenges of AI regarding transparency which are discussed in Sect. 3.1.6. Finally, Sect. 6.8 gives some guidance on how to address data protection when developing AI systems.

1.2   Legal Foundations of Data Protection Within the European Union and the European Economic Area

In order to specify the expectations of data subjects about the processing of their personal data and to at least partially make up for the power imbalance that usually exists between data subjects and data processing organisations, many countries have enacted laws on data protection that specify which of these expectations are considered legitimate and must be complied with.[7] This section presents an overview of the legal bases of data protection within the EU, followed by a similar overview for countries outside the EU.

1.2.1   The General Data Protection Regulation (GDPR)

Within the European Union (EU), the *General Data Protection Regulation* (GDPR) is the main law on data protection. Although it is an EU law, it has a strong effect on data protection beyond the EU and even beyond Europe. This is true because it applies not only if data are processed within the EU but under certain conditions outside the EU, as discussed in Sect. 2.1.2. In addition, several other countries have taken the GDPR as a blueprint when setting up their own data protection law, for example, Brazil (see Sect. 1.3.4) and Saudi Arabia.[8]

The GDPR was enacted in 2016 after long discussions as the successor to the European Data Protection Directive 95/46/EC and came into force after a 2-year preparation period in 2018. Note that there is a fundamental difference between the two types of laws: EU directives such as the aforementioned Data Protection Directive contain legal requirements that address the respective legislators of all EU states and must be transposed by them into national laws. EU regulations such as the GDPR, on the other hand, contain law that is directly applicable in all EU states. An EU regulation takes precedence over national laws of individual member states. Occasionally, this raises questions, as it is not always clear to what extent certain national regulations are considered applicable or whether they are superseded by the GDPR.

As the GDPR has been adopted in the different EU languages, there are different names and abbreviations of this regulation. In English, this law is called the "General Data Protection Regulation". In German, the same law is known as the "Datenschutz-grundverordnung" (DSGVO), while in French, it is known as the "Règlement Général sur la Protection des Données" (RGPD).

Although the GDPR is an EU law and was enacted by the EU, it is also directly applicable in the European Economic Area (EEA), which, in addition to the EU, includes

---

[7] See Appendix A.3 for links collections covering national data protection and privacy legislation within the EU as well as almost all other countries worldwide.

[8] See https://iapp.org/news/a/saudi-arabia-publishes-final-personal-data-protection-law/.

the European Free Trade Association (EFTA) states Liechtenstein, Norway and Iceland. In addition, under certain conditions, the GDPR also applies outside the EU/EEA, as described in Sect. 2.1.2.

The remainder of this section introduces the core ideas of GDPR. An extensive discussion of the law and its main requirements is contained in Chap. 2.

Principles of Data Protection In Art. 5, the GDPR contains a set of explicitly stated principles of data protection very similar to those in ISO/IEC 29100. Since it is often difficult to identify how to interpret these principles in any given case, additional articles of the law provide more detail. For example, Art. 12 to 15 describe data subjects' right to information and access to personal data, thus detailing the principle of transparency. Similarly, other rights of data subjects help implement the principles, for example, the right to rectification (Art. 16) and the right to erasure (Art. 17).

Prohibition with Reservation of Permission A fundamental concept of the GDPR, which was already contained in Directive 95/46/EC, is called the "prohibition with reservation of permission". This is a strengthened version of the purpose legitimacy and specification principle described above and states that the processing of personal data is prohibited unless it is expressly permitted.

Opening Clauses Although in general the GDPR defines uniform rules on data protection applicable in all EU states, it leaves some opportunity for specific national provisions via so-called opening clauses,[9] for example, to define the age limit for young people to consent to the processing of their data (Art. 8 No. 1 GDPR). Additionally, some issues are explicitly left open by the GDPR, which need to be filled by national legislation, such as the definition of the national supervisory body. Each EU member state thus has its own national data protection law which implements the GDPR and modifies it only to the extent allowed by the GDPR. The GDPR as EU law always takes precedence over national data protection legislation.

The legal provisions on data protection have thus become more uniform throughout the EU compared to the situation before the GDPR, but are still not completely harmonised—with all the advantages and disadvantages involved.

The GDPR and the EU AI Act In 2024, the EU passed the *AI Act* to regulate the development and use of AI and thereby to minimise the risks of this new technology. To some extent, these risks concern the processing of personal data. However, the AI Act does not contain clauses explicitly relating to the processing of personal data but instead refers to the GDPR for this purpose (Art. 2 (7) AI Act). The AI Act concentrates on general risks

---

[9] From a strictly legal point of view, however, most of these are not really opening clauses since they allow additions and refinements, but no deviations from the GDPR.

involved with AI systems and on setting up fairly strict regulations about managing the use of high-risk systems.

1.2.2   The ePrivacy Directive of the EU

The second major EU law regarding data protection and privacy is the ePrivacy Directive,[10] which addresses electronic communication and its privacy. This refers to all forms of electronic communication, including older forms such as telephone and telefax. The motivation for this law is the importance of confidential communication for a functioning society as can be seen, for example, in long-standing concepts such as the secrecy of correspondence and telecommunications. Although the ePrivacy Directive addresses similar topics to the GDPR, there are some differences: for example, the ePrivacy Directive discusses the protection of data and metadata by communication service providers such as email providers.

Furthermore, the ePrivacy Directive addresses the fact that techniques such as setting a cookie by a Web site not only leads to processing of the user's data but additionally affects the privacy of the user's device. Using cookies involves writing to the user's device by setting the cookies and later reading from it by reading the cookies.

The ePrivacy Directive was originally planned to be updated and upgraded to an ePrivacy Regulation in parallel with the GDPR. However, no agreement could be reached among the parties involved regarding core questions such as the extent to which tracking of visitors to a Web site should be possible without their explicit consent. On the one hand, the requirement for such consent fits well with the GDPR's way of thinking that, as a matter of principle, data subjects should have control over the processing of their data. On the other hand, this approach would severely restrict online marketing in its current form. Due to these unresolved conflicts of interest, it is currently not foreseeable when a new ePrivacy Regulation will be enacted.

As a result (as of October 2024), the ePrivacy Directive is still in force, though it was supplemented in 2009 by a directive colloquially known as the "Cookie Directive",[11] according to which users' explicit consent is required to set cookies.[12]

---

[10] Officially titled Directive 2002/58/EC, "Directive on privacy and electronic communications", available at https://eur-lex.europa.eu/legal-content/EN/ALL/?uri=CELEX%3A32002L0058.

[11] Directive   2009/136/EC: https://eur-lex.europa.eu/legal-content/EN/TXT/?uri=CELEX:32009L0136.

[12] Note that as EU Directives, both these laws do not have a direct impact on data protection but, unlike an EU Regulation, must first be transferred into national laws.

1.2.3   Data Protection in Germany

Until the GDPR came into effect, the German *Federal Data Protection Act*, like the data protection laws in all EU countries, was an independent law that determined the main rules of data protection applicable in Germany, based on the EU *Data Protection Directive* discussed above. Once the GDPR became applicable, most of these provisions were superseded or incorporated into the GDPR, so that a completely revised version of the act was introduced in parallel to the GDPR. This new act primarily has the task of addressing the opening clauses of the GDPR and thus only represents a small supplement to the GDPR, not an independent set of rules.

In addition to the *Federal Data Protection Act*, there are a number of other German laws concerning certain aspects of data protection, which, however, have far less practical significance and will therefore not be considered any further. These include, for example, the state data protection laws of the individual federal states, which define the legal framework for the work of the state data protection authorities and also define details on data protection analogous to the federal act but with state authorities and municipal authorities as regulatory addressees. As a result, Germany is the only EU country that does not only have one data protection authority but a total of 18 such authorities, with different areas of responsibility.

Another important specifically German adaptation of the GDPR concerns the need for defining data protection officers (DPO). While the GDPR contains fairly vague rules about when an organisation needs to designate a DPO which apply mainly to large organisations (cf. Sect. 2.7.8), the German act in § 38 states that private organisations must designate a DPO if at least twenty persons within the organisation regularly handle personal data. Although there are repeated discussions whether this rule might lead to too much bureaucracy, proponents point out that the DPO actually causes hardly any bureaucracy at all but instead helps understand and efficiently implement the various data protection requirements which exist independently of the DPO.[13]

For selected areas of application, there are also special data protection regulations, for example, for social data in the *Tenth Social Code* (SGB X) and for digital services and telecommunication in the TDDDG,[14] which mainly transfers the ePrivacy Directive into national law. As a matter of fact, there were several hundred national laws in Germany that contained at least minor statements concerning data protection and had to be adapted as a consequence of the GDPR.

---

[13] The author's personal experience as a DPO for some small organisations (that are not obliged to appoint a DPO under GDPR) is that such organisations would struggle to implement complex GDPR rules without specialist advice.

[14] *Telekommunikation-Digitale-Dienste-Datenschutz-Gesetz.*

1.2.4   Data Protection in Austria

The Austrian *Data Protection Act* (DPA) also had to be substantially revised and adapted when the GDPR came into force. In terms of content, however, this mainly meant that provisions were moved from a national law to an EU regulation, while the real changes remained rather small.

Data Protection for Legal Persons   A difference in content between the GDPR and the DPA concerns the rule that according to the DPA, the right to data protection applies to "everyone" and thus also to legal persons such as corporations or associations. There was a lengthy dispute whether this was a permitted addition to the data protection law for Austria or whether this regulation was annulled by the restriction of the GDPR to natural persons. According to a decision of the Austrian data protection authority of 2020,[15] legal persons also have a fundamental right to data protection, even if many individual provisions do not apply in this case.

The Data Protection Deregulation Act of 2018   There was also a heated debate on the *Data Protection Deregulation Act* of 2018,[16] which has been described by critics as a "dilution" of the GDPR. In particular, there are differing opinions on the explicit regulation that warnings rather than fines should be issued for first-time data protection infringements, and it is argued that this is not compatible with the GDPR objective of uniform assessment and sanctioning of data protection infringements across Europe.

1.2.5   Data Protection in Ireland

The Irish data protection law, called the *Data Protection Act* (DPA), was first introduced in 1988 and, similar to the data protection laws in other EU countries, adapted to the GDPR regulations in 2018. Overall, the DPA does not contain any unusual regulations, apart from section 26A as described below.

Although Ireland is a comparatively small country, many large international players such as Microsoft, Google/Alphabet and Facebook/Meta have located their European headquarters there. As a result, the lead supervisory authority for GDPR compliance for these companies is the Irish Data Protection Commission (DPC). The DPC is often criticised for not enforcing the GDPR adequately, and it is the only EU data

---

[15] GZ   2020-0.191.240,   Nr.   62–64;   see   https://www.ris.bka.gv.at/Dokumente/Dsk/
DSBT_20200525_2020_0_191_240_00/DSBT_20200525_2020_0_191_240_00.pdf (in German).
[16] Available at https://www.parlament.gv.at/PAKT/VHG/XXVI/BNR/BNR_00027/fname_691190.
pdf (in German).

protection authority whose decisions have repeatedly been overruled by the *European Data Protection Board* (EDPB).[17]

In 2022, the new section 26A was introduced into the DPA, which allows the DPC to declare information about its procedures as confidential, making it an offence to communicate any such information. There is considerable concern that this may be used to silence any criticism about the DPC's procedures and is a reaction to the fight by various NGOs as well as other European supervisory authorities to force the DPC to enforce the GDPR adequately.[18]

1.2.6 Data Protection in Estonia

Estonia is a fairly small country that has put a strong emphasis on the digitalisation of its economy and on e-government, resulting in almost all its public services being available online. This implies a strong need for protecting the personal data involved.

As a member of the EU, the GDPR applies in Estonia, and a national *Personal Data Protection Act* has been passed to address the GDPR opening clauses and a *Data Protection Inspectorate* has been set up. As in most EU countries, this act only includes very minor variations of the GDPR regulations that data processors need to consider beyond the GDPR itself.

1.2.7 Data Protection in Norway

Norway is not a member of the EU but of the EEA, and the GDPR therefore applies in Norway. Furthermore, the Norwegian data protection authority *Datatilsynet* is a member of the EDPB, though without voting rights, and actively cooperates with other data protection authorities.

As for all other EU/EEA countries, there is a national *Personal Data Act* to address the GDPR opening clauses, but this mainly contains specific regulations such as the nomination of the national data protection authority and only very minor variations of the regulations that concern controllers.

---

[17] See https://www.iccl.ie/digital-data/iccl-2023-gdpr-report/.

[18] See, e.g. https://edri.org/wp-content/uploads/2023/06/Open-letter-Irish-DPA-gag-law.pdf and https://noyb.eu/en/irish-gov-makes-critizising-big-tech-and-irish-dpc-crime.

1.3   Legal Foundations of Data Protection Outside the European Economic Area

This section discusses examples of legal foundations of data protection in countries where the GDPR is not directly applicable, i.e. outside the EU and the EEA. In GDPR, such countries are called "third countries", and additional restrictions apply for the transfer of personal data to such third countries, as discussed in Sect. 5.4. The purpose of the following discussion is to provide an overview of how different countries implement data protection.

GDPR is often called the "gold standard" of data protection, and many other legislations have taken it as guidance for their own regulations. Additionally, the GDPR to some extent also applies outside the EU/EEA (see Sect. 2.1.2), and there are restrictions regarding the data transfer from the EU/EEA to countries with a different approach to data protection. Setting up similar standards therefore makes it easier for organisations in those countries to process personal data of EU citizens.

1.3.1   Data Protection in Switzerland

Switzerland is neither part of the EU nor the EEA, and therefore, the GDPR is not immediately applicable there. Due to the close economic ties, personal data of EU citizens are however often processed in Switzerland. The GDPR must therefore be complied with in Switzerland in such cases (Art. 3 GDPR).

Switzerland also has its own legal regulations on data protection, in particular the Swiss *Data Protection Act* (DPA), as well as the *Ordinance to the Federal Act on Data Protection* (VDSG), which contains some supplementary regulations. After the GDPR came into effect, the DPA was revised, and the new version came into force in September 2023.

In terms of content, the previous version of the DPA largely corresponded to the original EU Data Protection Directive, and Switzerland had therefore been granted adequacy by the EU (see Sect. 5.4). The goal of the revision was both to update the data processing regulations and also to align it with the GDPR so that this adequacy decision will continue to hold. For example, according to the old DPA, processing of personal data was allowed unless it was explicitly forbidden, while the revised DPA is based on the principle of prohibition with reservation of permission as described above for GDPR.

1.3.2   Data Protection in the United Kingdom

While the United Kingdom (UK) was part of the EU, the GDPR also applied, but this changed when the UK left the EU. Thereafter, the provisions of GDPR were incorporated into UK law as the *UK GDPR*, in combination with the *Data Protection Act 2018* (DPA).[19] Because British data protection law currently is very similar to EU data protection law, the EU commission in 2021 decided, in a so-called adequacy decision, that the resulting level of data protection in the UK is adequate and controllers within the EU may transfer personal data to the UK based on the same rules as within the EU (see Sect. 5.4).

1.3.3   Data Protection in the USA

Many cloud services, social networks and other services are located in the USA, which leads to an extensive exchange of data between the USA and other countries, including the EU countries. The US data protection law is therefore quite important for data processing in the EU.

In the USA, data protection law is largely divided into sector-specific regulations, for example, for health-related personal data in the *Health Insurance Portability and Accountability Act* (HIPAA) or for the education sector in the *Family Educational Rights and Privacy Act* (FERPA). In addition, there is a rapidly growing number of state data protection laws (as opposed to federal laws that apply to the entire USA), partly initiated by the introduction of GDPR in the EU, with more than a third of the states having introduced comprehensive data protections laws (as of October 2024) and others having introduced laws on privacy of biometric or on facial recognition. One of the first of these state laws was the *California Consumer Privacy Act* (CCPA), which in 2020 introduced relatively strict regulations compared to other states. These differences in regulations pose a problem for cross-regional companies in particular. Therefore, in 2022, an *American Data Privacy and Protection Act (ADPPA)* was proposed, which however faced considerable opposition and did not get passed. A revised *American Privacy Rights Act (APRA)* was proposed in 2024, and it remains to be seen whether this will eventually be passed.

There are some conceptual differences between the data protection regulations in the USA and in the EU:

- In the USA, the right to *free speech* is often given more weight than data protection, which leads to conflicts between the two rights.
- Promises made to consumers play an important role in the USA. Even if certain protections of personal data are not required by law, if a company makes any promises about protecting their customers' data, they must then keep these promises, and non-compliance can lead to sanctions by the *Federal Trade Commission* (FTC). For example, if a company announces that it will conform to the *Trans-Atlantic Data Privacy Framework*, which will ease any data transfer from the EU to that company

---

[19] The UK GDPR is available under https://www.legislation.gov.uk/eur/2016/679/contents; the DPA is available under https://www.legislation.gov.uk/ukpga/2018/12/data.pdf.

(see Sect. 5.4), then such conformance becomes binding, and deviations are punishable by law.

- In Europe, data protection checks and controls by supervisory authorities or data protection commissioners have a certain weight, whereas in the USA, there are fewer such controls. However, if non-compliances are detected in a company, there is a tendency towards harsher penalties in the USA. Additionally, private litigation plays a much larger role in the USA compared to the EU and can become very expensive for organisations, in particular if a non-compliance affects many data subjects.

In spite of these differences, more states are introducing data protection laws that are based on data protection principles similar to those defined by ISO/IEC 29100 or GDPR.

The *CLOUD Act* and Similar Legislation In the USA, security and intelligence agencies have broad powers to monitor electronic communications, especially when no US citizens are involved in the communication.[20]

From the perspective of the GDPR, it is at least questionable whether an adequate level of data protection exists in the USA and whether or on what basis personal data may be transferred from EU countries to the USA, for example, in the context of cloud computing. This topic of data transfer to the USA as well as to other countries is examined in more detail in Sect. 5.4.

The *CLOUD Act* in particular causes considerable difficulties with regard to data protection, as it obliges companies based in the USA, including Internet companies and IT service providers, to guarantee US authorities access to stored data, even if the storage does not take place in the USA but, for example, within the EU. In certain contexts, the requirements of the GDPR and the *CLOUD Act* move in opposite directions, and it becomes difficult for the companies involved to comply with both laws at the same time— a dilemma which the EU and the USA are trying to address with the *Trans-Atlantic Data Privacy Framework* (see Sect. 5.4).

1.3.4   Data Protection in Brazil

The Brazilian *Lei Geral de Proteção de Dados* (LGPD) (General Data Protection Law) was passed in 2018 and became enforcable law in 2020. It was strongly inspired by the GDPR and contains very similar terminology, definitions and regulations. In particular, core contents such as the set of principles (Art. 6), the set of conditions under which processing of personal data is allowed (Art. 7) and the set of data subjects' rights (Art. 18) in LGPD are all very similar to those in GDPR. Also similar to GDPR, the LGPD applies not only

---

[20] Relevant legal regulations here are in particular the *Foreign Intelligence Surveillance Act (FISA) Amendments Act of 2008*, the *Executive Order 12333*, the *Clarifying Lawful Overseas Use of Data Act* (CLOUD Act) and the *USA Patriot Act*.

within Brazil but under certain conditions beyond that (extraterritorial applicability), for example, if the processing is aimed at offering goods or services in Brazil or if the data to be processed were originally collected in Brazil (Art. 3 LGPD).

A difference between the LGPD and the GPDR concerns the requirement to designate data protection officers, which in Brazil is required for all controllers responsible for the processing of personal data (see Sect. 2.7.8).

1.3.5   Data Protection in India

Many providers of outsourcing services are based in India, and therefore Indian data protection law plays a considerable role beyond that country. India does not have a long tradition of data protection legislation but only enacted its first data protection law, the *Digital Personal Data Protection Act* (DPDPA), in 2023 after several years of discussion and three very different drafts of this act. The DPDPA uses a slightly different terminology to GDPR. In particular, the controller is called "data fiduciary" in DPDPA, and the data subject is called the "data principal" (see Table 1.2).

The DPDPA implements basic principles for data protection similar to those described above and applicable in most other countries. Like GDPR, the Act defines a set of legal bases (also called lawful bases) as conditions for the processing of personal data to be allowed (Sect. 7), with a strong focus on consent, while, for example, contractual obligations as well as legitimate interest are not acceptable bases for processing according to the DPDPA.

Furthermore, the DPDPA defines a set of rights of the data principals, quite similar to the data subjects' rights defined in GDPR, for example, the right to access or information on personal data, the right to rectification and the right to erasure (Sects. 11–14 DPDPA). Quite an unusual concept in DPDPA is that data principals do not only have data protection rights but also duties, for example, the duty not to impersonate another person, not to suppress information when providing their personal data and not to register a false grievance or complaint (Sect. 15 DPDPA). Although these duties, to some extent, apply in other legislations as well, they are not usually part of the data protection law.

The (material) scope of the DPDPA is somewhat smaller compared to the GDPR: the DPDPA only covers the automated processing of *digital* personal data, and it does not protect data that have been made public by the relevant data principal himself (Sect. 3 (a))), which implies that data collected by scraping them from Web pages or social networks, as often done for training of machine learning systems, in most cases are not subject to data protection according to the DPDPA (Sect. 3 (c)).

Similar to GDPR, the DPDPA contains some extraterritorial regulations. More specifically, it applies to the processing of personal data outside India if that processing is related to offering goods and services inside India (Sect. 3 (b) DPDPA).

The DPDPA allows considerable discretionary powers to the Indian government regarding data protection and the applicability of the act. For example, it allows the government to define that the Act does not apply to certain types of processing if this is considered in the interest of the state (Sect. 17 DPDPA). On the other hand, the DPDPA does not define any specific requirements about when personal data may be transferred abroad, but it allows the government to restrict, by notification, the transfer of personal data to a country outside India (Sect. 16 DPDPA). Furthermore, the government is entitled to nominate data fiduciaries as "significant", in which case additional regulations apply, in particular the need to nominate a data protection officer and an independent data auditor and to perform periodic data protection impact assessments and audits (Sect. 10 DPDPA).

According to the DPDPA, a *Data Protection Board* is to be set up, which will act as a supervisory authority, although there is some criticism that the rules how it is set may not ensure sufficient independence and objectivity in its work.

DPDPA does not require data fiduciaries to nominate a DPO unless they are declared to be a *significant* data fiduciary. However, data fiduciaries are required to nominate a "consent manager" who acts as the contact person for data principals that want to give, manage, review or withdraw their consent (Sect. 6 No. 7–9) and who has to register with the board.

1.3.6 Data Protection in China

The Chinese *Personal Information Protection Law (PIPL)*[21] came into effect in 2021 and is closely based on the concepts used in the GDPR. This law contains a set of principles similar to those of the GDPR, and controllers (here called personal information handlers) need a legal basis for processing (here called handling) personal data again similar to those of the GDPR, except that there is no "legitimate interest", but there is a legal basis that allows processing if the personal information has been disclosed by the persons themselves (Art. 13 PIPL). In Art. 52, PIPL introduces the obligation to nominate a *personal information protection officer*, a similar role to a DPO, which did not exist before and which applies to organisations whose processing reaches a threshold to be defined by the national cybersecurity administration authority.

The PIPL applies to data processing activities within China by handlers both in the public and private sector. Additionally, the law has extra-territorial applicability and, under certain conditions such as processing for providing products or services to Chinese residents, also applies to the processing of Chinese residents' data outside of China.

All these regulations in PIPL are supported by the threat of serious penalties for non-compliance going up to 5% of the previous year's annual revenue.

An aspect of data protection in China that is often discussed in the Western world is the Chinese social scoring system. This originally was developed for scoring creditworthiness,

---

[21] An English version of the PIPL is available from http://en.npc.gov.cn.cdurl.cn/2021-12/29/c_694559.htm.

as is widely used in other countries as well but to some extent goes beyond that and deals with general trustworthiness of individuals based on their social behaviour and thus on a large amount of personal data. However, contrary to what is often stated, such a social scoring system is not in general use, and the data collected differ considerably between different regions [Yan22].

There is no direct conflict between this social scoring system and the PIPL, which, like most data protection laws, allows the processing of data for purposes defined by law. Data protection legislation in China is very similar to that in Western Europe, but there is somewhat more processing of personal data explicitly allowed in China.

1.4   Alternative Reference Models

In addition to the GDPR and other legal regulations, there are a number of other reference models for data protection. This section provides a brief overview of the most important of these models.

ISO Norms on Data Protection and Privacy International standards such as those published by ISO and IEC are not legally binding. Nevertheless, some of them are of considerable importance because they standardise terms and concepts internationally and in some cases also form a basis for certification by defining specific requirements. Table 1.1 gives an overview of the ISO standards on data protection.

Table 1.1 Overview of the main ISO/IEC norms on data protection and privacy

ISO/IEC 27001 Information technology – Security techniques – Information security management systems – Requirements
ISO/IEC 27018 *Information technology – Security techniques – Code of practice for protection of personally identifiable information (PII) in public clouds acting as PII processors*
ISO/IEC 27701 *Security techniques – Extension to ISO/IEC 27001 and ISO/IEC 27002 for privacy information management – Requirements and guidelines*
ISO/IEC 29100 *Information technology – Security techniques – Privacy framework*
ISO/IEC 29134 *Information technology – Security techniques – Guidelines for privacy impact assessment*
ISO/IEC 29151 *Information technology – Security techniques – Code of practice for personally identifiable information protection*

ISO/IEC 29100 Privacy Framework The ISO/IEC 29100 norm itself does not set any requirements for data protection but defines the essential concepts and principles of data protection, which are then used in other standards on data protection. The names of the concepts differ somewhat from GDPR (see Table 1.2), but the underlying concepts as

well as the defined principles of data protection are very similar. The terms defined in
ISO/IEC 29100 are also used in other ISO standards and partly referenced from there, for
example, in ISO/IEC 27701.

Table 1.2 Different terminology for data protection

GDPR	ISO/IEC 29100	Digital Personal Data Protection Act, (India)
Data protection	Privacy	Data protection
Personal data	Personally identifying information (PII)	Personal data
Special categories of personal data	Sensitive PII	(Not applicable)
Data subject	PII principal	Data principal
Controller	PII controller	Data fiduciary
Processor	PII processor	Data processor

In addition, ISO/IEC 29100 describes an approach to identifying data protection risks
using the following four factors as a starting point:

- Legal and regulatory factors, such as the GDPR
- Contractual factors, in particular contractual agreements with business partners
- Business factors, where a company determines from a business perspective to comply
  with certain data protection requirements
- Other factors

Independent of other uses of ISO/IEC 29100, this approach thus describes a useful procedure for clarifying which regulations must be complied with in any given environment.

ISO/IEC 27701   The ISO/IEC 27701 standard describes a so-called Privacy Information
Management System (PIMS) as a supplement to an information security management
system according to ISO/IEC 27001. In the case of certification for information security in
accordance with ISO/IEC 27001, data protection can thus also be taken into account.[22]
In accordance with its role as a definition of a management system, ISO/IEC 27701
places particular emphasis on the definition of the relevant processes and responsibilities
in the organisation needed to implement the data protection requirements. In addition,
the standard contains an appendix with a mapping of the standard requirements to the
requirements of the GDPR.

---

[22] However, this is not a certification of compliance with the GDPR requirements as defined in
Art. 42 GDPR.

ISO/IEC 29134   This standard describes a procedure for conducting data protection impact assessments (DPIAs). These are used to identify and assess data protection risks and are described in more detail in Sect. 2.7.7.

ISO/IEC 29151 and ISO/IEC 27018   These two standards describe measures and best practices for implementing data protection and are based on the principles contained in ISO/IEC 29100. The difference between the two standards is that ISO/IEC 29151 is generic, while ISO/IEC 27018 is specific to cloud computing.

The OECD Privacy Framework   The OECD's "Privacy Framework" [OEC13] describes data protection from a slightly different perspective and makes recommendations to legislators on what content their respective data protection legislation should include in order to facilitate the exchange of data between different countries.

The OASIS Privacy Management Reference Model and Methodology (PMRM)   The PMRM [DMS16] was published in 2016 by OASIS, a non-profit organisation for the development of open standards in IT. PMRM starts from principles of data protection, such as those defined in ISO/IEC 29100, in order to select suitable services and functions for implementing these principles in the next step. For this purpose, PMRM describes six phases with a total of 20 tasks, where the last phase initiates the iteration of the previous phases.

1.5   Data Protection and Software Requirements

What does all this mean for software development and IT?[23] Of course, software development and IT have a great influence on how (personal) data are processed and whether the data subjects are adequately protected. This creates a legal and moral responsibility for design, not only from the perspective of data protection. Specifically in software development, the following classes of requirements for implementing data protection arise:

- *Requirements for the software to be developed*, here mainly considered in Chaps. 3 and 4
- *Requirements for the development procedure*, here mainly considered in Sect. 6.6
- *Requirements for the development organisation*, here mainly considered in Chap. 8

Following [GvLSB24, p. 10], a distinction is made between functional requirements (identifiers of the form F-*nn*), quality requirements (identifiers Q-*nn*) and constraints

---

[23] When talking about "IT", this refers to the organisational unit operating the IT systems.

(identifiers C-*nn*) for the requirements, especially the requirements for the software. The formulation of the requirements including their identifiers is largely taken from [Kne20].

Requirements Template In order to achieve a formulation of the functional requirements that is as exact as possible, their formulation is oriented towards the phrase templates described in [GvLSB24, Sect. 3.3.1] with the basic structure

[<Condition>] <Subject> <Action> <Objects> [<Restriction>]

A distinction is made between "shall", "should" and "may" requirements. If the fulfilment of the requirement is necessary to comply with the GDPR, then it is a mandatory ("shall") requirement. If compliance with the requirement is strongly recommended as helpful, but there are also other ways to comply with the relevant legal requirements, then the requirement is formulated as a "should" requirement. A "may" requirement describes a suggestion and is optional.

However, many legal requirements for data protection describe which processing or other activities are *not* allowed. For this reason, some of the requirements in this book are also formulated in a negative way and specify what must *not* happen, although this is usually considered bad style for formulating requirements.

References

DMS16. Drgon, Michele, Magnuson, Gail, and Sabo, John: *Privacy management reference model and methodology (PMRM) version 1.0, committee specification 02.* Technical report, OASIS, May 2016. http://docs.oasis-open.org/pmrm/PMRM/v1.0/cs02/PMRM-v1.0-cs02.html.
GvLSB24. Glinz, Martin, Loenhoud, Hans van, Staal, Stefan, and Bühne, Stan: *CPRE Foundation Level Handbook, v. 1.2.0.* IREB International Requirements Engineering Board, 2024. https://cpre.ireb.org/en/knowledge-and-resources/downloads#cpre-foundation-level-handbook.
Kne20. Kneuper, Ralf: *Translating data protection into software requirements.* In Furnell, Steven, Mori, Paolo, Weippl, Edgar, and Camp, Olivier (editors): *Proceedings of the 6th International Conference on Information Systems Security and Privacy (ICISSP), Valetta, Malta,* pages 257–264. Scitepress, 2020. http://www.scitepress.org/DigitalLibrary/Link.aspx?doi=10.5220/0008873902570264.
OEC13. OECD Organisation for Economic Co-operation and Development: The *OECD Privacy Framework,* 2013. https://web-archive.oecd.org/2013-09-05/247484-oecd_privacy_framework.pdf.
Sol06. Solove, Daniel J.: *A taxonomy of privacy.* University of Pennsylvania Law Review, 154(3):477–560, January 2006. https://pennlawreview.com/2020/04/28/a-taxonomy-of-privacy/.
Yan22. Yang, Zeyi: *China just announced a new social credit law. Here's what it means.* MIT Technology Review, 2022. https://www.technologyreview.com/2022/11/22/1063605/china-announced-a-new-social-credit-law-what-does-it-mean/.

Foundations of Data Protection According to GDPR

2

Abstract

The most important, though not the only, legal instrument for data protection in Europe is the GDPR. This chapter provides an introduction to GDPR and its provisions, focusing on the content relevant to software development and IT as a foundation for their implementation. After an overview of the basic terminology used in the GDPR, the principles of data protection as formulated in the GDPR such as lawfulness, data minimisation and storage limitation are introduced. Another central component of the GDPR are the rights of data subjects defined therein, such as the right to information. The basic concepts of identifiability, pseudonymisation and anonymisation are then considered. The chapter concludes with an introduction to some of the other provisions of the GDPR that are relevant for software development and IT, such as the data protection impact assessment.

2.1 The European General Data Protection Regulation (GDPR)

To get started, this chapter provides an overview of the structure and application area of GDPR.

2.1.1 Basic Terminology and Structure

As was briefly explained in Sect. 1.2.1, the GDPR was adopted in 2016 after much discussion and debate. A two-year transition period then applied until the regulation became applicable law on May 25, 2018. The aim was primarily to harmonise data protection legislation across the EU (although "appropriate" naturally has very different meanings for different stakeholders).

Personal Data Data protection refers to personal data, defined in the GDPR (and similarly in other frameworks such as ISO/IEC 29100:2011) as "any information relating to an identified or identifiable natural person".[1] This is a key definition, as it determines whether or not the processing of certain data falls under data protection regulations or not. It is more difficult to interpret than is apparent at first glance and is therefore considered in more detail in Sects. 2.2 and 2.3.

Data Processing The second core concept of data protection is the *processing* of data, which is interpreted very broadly and includes, among other things, the collection, storage, adaptation or modification; reading, use and dissemination; and also the deletion of data. Figure 2.1 shows a simple life cycle for data, which forms a basis for the further discussion of data protection in this book.

Fig. 2.1 Typical life cycle of (personal) data

GDPR Structure The GDPR consists of two main parts: The first part contains the so-called recitals, which explain the motivation behind the articles and thus help with the interpretation. The second part contains the articles, divided into eleven chapters, which describe the provisions of the law, that is, what one must comply with when processing personal data.

In documentations of the GDPR, the recitals are therefore often not listed at the beginning as in the original text but assigned to the relevant articles as appropriate. The 99 articles of the GDPR are divided into eleven chapters, as shown in Table 2.1.

In the context of software development and IT, the important chapters are I to V. Other chapters have only minor or indirect influence and are therefore not considered in detail in this book.

Complex Wording One consequence of the lengthy discussions during the drafting of the GDPR are the complex and not always clear-cut formulations, with many exceptions and exceptions of exceptions, etc. This book deals with a few of these special cases and concentrates on describing the core ideas. As already pointed out in the preface, a specialist

---

[1] Note: For complete definitions of terms introduced here, see the glossary at the end of this book.

Table 2.1 Structure of GDPR

	Recitals	1–173
Ch. I	General provisions	Art. 1–4
Ch. II	Principles	Art. 5–11
Ch. III	Rights of the data subject	Art. 12–23
Ch. IV	Controller and processor	Art. 24–43
Ch. V	Transfers of personal data to third countries or international organisations	Art. 44–50
Ch. VI	Independent supervisory authorities	Art. 51–59
Ch. VII	Cooperation and consistency	Art. 60–76
Ch. VIII	Remedies, liability and penalties	Art 77–84
Ch. IX	Provisions relating to specific processing situations	Art. 85–91
Ch. X	Delegated acts and implementing acts	Art. 92–93
Ch. XI	Final provisions	Art. 94–99

should be consulted in cases of doubt, such as a data protection officer or a specialist lawyer.

2.1.2   Scope of Application of GDPR

With regard to the scope of application of GDPR, a distinction must be made between the *material* scope, defined in Art. 2 GDPR, and the *territorial* scope, defined in Art. 3 GDPR.

Material Scope of the GDPR The material scope of application includes the "processing of personal data wholly or partly by automated means ..." (Art. 2 No. 1 GDPR). Under certain conditions, manual processing is also covered by GDPR, but this is not relevant here.

There are some exceptions to this, such as the processing by *law enforcement, security and similar authorities*, which are explicitly not covered by the GDPR but by the separate Directives 2016/680 and 2016/681. These directives are similar to the GDPR and were published in parallel with it. Furthermore, processing "by a natural person in the course of a purely personal or household activity" (Art. 2 No. 2 lit c GDPR) is not covered by the GDPR. Other exceptions are not relevant in the context of this book.

Example 2.1 (WhatsApp Usage in a Sports Club) The members of a small sports club without commercial activities use WhatsApp to make appointments. From the perspective of the club members, these are "exclusively personal activities", which thus do not fall under the GDPR. However, if the club itself

(continued)

distributes such information via its own WhatsApp account, then it is no longer a case of processing "by natural persons" and the GDPR applies. A fortiori, this applies to the provision of the service by WhatsApp itself, i.e. WhatsApp is obliged to process the data in compliance with the GDPR.

Territorial Scope The GDPR is an EU law and therefore is first of all applicable in the EU. As mentioned before, the EFTA states Liechtenstein, Norway and Iceland have also decided to adopt the GDPR, and the GDPR thus applies in the entire *European Economic Area* (EEA), which consists of the EU and the EFTA states.

In contrast to the previous regulations, the GDPR is also applicable outside the EEA ("extraterritorial applicability") according to the *establishment criterion* and the *targeting criterion* as follows:

Establishment Criterion The principle of establishment specifies that the GDPR applies insofar as the processing is carried out in the context of the activities of an establishment of the controller or a processor in the EU or the EEA (Art. 3 No. 1 GDPR). This includes in particular all companies, public authorities and other organisations with their registered office within the EU/EEA.

Targeting Criterion The targeting criterion additionally defines that the GDPR applies if the processing is related to offering goods or services to data subjects in the EU, independent of whether these must be paid for (in money or data), or to monitoring the behaviour of individuals in the EU. So even if an organisation does not have an establishment in the EU but offers goods or services to customers in the EU, then that processing falls within the scope of the GDPR. The same applies if the behaviour of individuals in the EU is monitored, for example, by tracking visitors to a Web site.

This criterion makes it difficult for data controllers to know and apply all relevant data protection rules. At the same time, the strong interconnectedness via the Internet means that such extra-territorial regulation becomes necessary to adequately protect EU citizens, and there are comparable regulations in the USA and Japan.

Special Cases and Exceptions There are a number of special cases and exceptions to the applicability of the GDPR, which are briefly mentioned here, but are not discussed in any detail.

Media Privilege The GDPR requires a balancing between the right to protection of personal data and the right to freedom of expression and freedom of information, where the concrete regulations are to be determined individually by each EU Member State (Art. 85 GDPR).

Processing for Journalistic, Scientific, Artistic or Literary Purposes   Again, Art. 85 GDPR contains special provisions that require an individual determination in the respective member state. In addition, Art. 89 defines special rules for processing for archiving purposes in the public interest, for scientific or historical research purposes and for statistical purposes.

Churches and Religious Communities   Churches and religious communities may, under Art. 91 of the GDPR, adopt their own data protection regimes to some extent, as long as they are in line with the GDPR. For example, in Germany, both the Catholic and Protestant churches have their own data protection laws.

2.2 Personal Data

2.2.1 Definition of Personal Data

The concept of personal data is a central basis of data protection, as data protection only refers to personal data. In the GDPR, personal data are defined as "any information relating to an identified or identifiable natural person (hereinafter 'data subject') ..." (Art. 4 (1) GDPR; see Glossary). The main terms used in this definition and their meaning in data protection are considered in more detail below.

Data and Information   The GDPR uses the terms "data" and "information", as is also customary in IT. However, these terms are not really distinguished in the GDPR and are used as synonyms, as the definition of personal data as "all information ..." shows. Therefore, this distinction is also dispensed with here, and the designation used in the GDPR is adopted in each case as far as possible.

Identifiability   The distinction between identified and identifiable persons used in the definition is also not systematically used in the GDPR, so that the distinction remains unclear, but since both are treated the same way, this does not make any difference in practice. The decisive factor is that personal data, directly or indirectly, can each be assigned to a specific person. The opposite of personal data are *anonymous data*, which is characterised by the fact that it cannot be assigned to a specific person.

In addition to the name of a person, examples of personal data include identification numbers (e.g. a social security or tax number), online identifiers (e.g. an IP address or a cookie identifier), location data, photos or special characteristics that can be used to identify a person. On closer inspection, the definition of identifiability leaves much room for interpretation, because whether a person is identifiable depends significantly on the effort expended and the background knowledge available. Recital 26 of the GDPR therefore defines that in deciding whether a person is identifiable, "account should be taken of all the means reasonably likely to be used, such as singling out, either by the controller or by another person to identify the natural person directly or indirectly". Thus, a strict distinction between identifiable and non-identifiable, i.e. anonymous, persons is not possible in most cases, but this must be assessed in each case on the basis of the effort involved and the benefit achievable for an "attacker". It is therefore not surprising that in different jurisdictions and environments, the meaning of identifiability is sometimes interpreted differently, despite using the same definition. In Sect. 2.3, the topic of identifiability is considered in more detail from the perspective of anonymisation.

Persons The second aspect of the definition of personal data that needs a closer look is the meaning of the term "person". GDPR only refers to natural persons, i.e. human beings, while legal entities such as corporations and associations ("legal persons") are not covered.[2] Unborn or deceased persons are not legally considered persons and thus do not fall under data protection.[3]

It should be noted that many companies are organised in the form of a partnership (of natural persons), i.e. not a corporation, and thus do fall under data protection. As a result, even a database of companies usually contains personal data. In addition, it may contain personal data in the form of information about contact persons.

2.2.2   Special Categories of Personal Data

Some data are classified as needing more protection than others, for example, health data, data on ethnic or religious affiliation or on criminal convictions. In the GDPR, most of these are referred to as "special category personal data" and dealt with in Art. 9 of the GDPR (see Appendix A for a full list of these special categories). Data on criminal convictions and offences, on the other hand, are addressed in Art. 10 of the GDPR (see below).

Most legislations have some similar distinction between "normal" personal data and personal data with higher protection needs, with India being an exception, which only has one class of personal data.

The main difference compared to the processing of other kinds of personal data is that for the processing of personal data of special categories, the legal bases mentioned in Art. 6 GDPR are not sufficient, but additional stricter rules apply according to Art. 9 (2) GDPR. The main possible legal bases for the processing of personal data of special categories are consent, the implementation of legal rules on labour and social law as well as healthcare and health protection.

---

[2] In some legislations, this is regulated differently. For example, in Switzerland and in Austria, certain data protection requirements also apply to legal entities.

[3] Again, in some legislations, this is regulated differently. For example, in Estonia, processing of data about deceased persons is still restricted for a period of 10–20 years (§ 9 Personal Data Protection Act).

Biometric Data for Identification and Authentication According to the GDPR, special categories of personal data include biometric data that are used to uniquely identify (often also authenticate) individuals, such as fingerprints or facial recognition profiles. Apart from the well-known problems with biometric access data, such as the fact that they cannot be easily changed like a password in case of a breach, their use must also take into account the stricter data protection requirements for special categories of personal data (as defined in Art. 9 GDPR). This applies in particular to the legal basis, where, apart from exceptional cases, only consent is applicable in practice. Put differently, when using biometric data for authentication, one usually also needs an alternative form of authentication for those who do not give this consent.

Photos Although photos of persons usually contain information about the ethnic origin, often also health data (e.g. wearer of glasses) of the person, they are in general not that sensitive and therefore not considered data of special categories, as Recital 51 GDPR states. According to that recital, photos are only data of special categories "when processed through a specific technical means allowing the unique identification or authentication of a natural person". This seems quite adequate even though it creates the systematic difficulty that the same photo may be data of special categories or not, depending how it is processed.

Employee Data The data of employees in a company practically always contain personal data of special categories, as they include at least health data in the form of sick leave, possibly also religious affiliation (if required for tax purposes, as is the case in Germany).

At least the personal data of special categories that are *legally required* for the employment relationship including social security may be processed by the employer according to Art. 9 (2)(b) GDPR. This includes, for example, the administration of sick leave or religious affiliation (if required for tax purposes).

Criminal Convictions Data on criminal convictions must be handled even more restrictively than special category personal data. According to Art. 10 GDPR, they may only be processed under the control of official authorities or if there is a special legal regulation for this. In practice, processing of such data can be relevant, for example, for credit agencies, for journalistic purposes or, in some specific cases, for the processing of employee data. However, these are legally complex topics for whose implementation in software development and IT a specialist should be consulted if necessary and which will not be discussed in further detail here.

2.2.3   Metadata

The term metadata is not explicitly defined or considered in the GDPR but is (implicitly) regarded as a kind of data. Thus, if metadata have a personal reference, they fall under the same regulations as other personal data.

By "metadata", we mean data that represent attributes of other data. In the case of a message between different communication partners, metadata may include the names or identifiers of the communication partners, the time and the size of the message and the medium used. For database entries as well as for documents, metadata may include the authors and the time of creation and of changes.

These examples show why metadata play an important role in data protection and can themselves constitute data worth protecting. Information that describes with whom, how often and when a person communicates can also tell a lot about the person and even their communication partner. In addition, metadata are in many cases more structured than the data themselves and can therefore be evaluated or analysed more easily than is the case for many types of data.

Regarding software development and IT, this implies that great care must be taken to protect metadata appropriately, because a large amount of metadata, for example, in the form of log files or the history of files or documents, is processed here.

2.3   Identifiability, Pseudonymisation and Anonymisation

The characterising property of personal data is that it relates to an identified or identifiable individual. In practice, this identification can be associated with very different levels of difficulty and effort. As a result, the demarcation between identifiable and non-identifiable data in practical terms often is not as clear as it is from a legal point of view, where identification of the person either is possible or not possible.[4] Figure 2.2 graphically represents this situation.

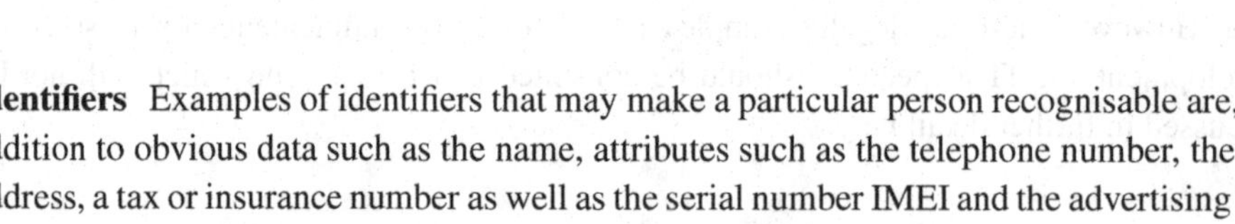

implementation view:	identified	identifiable e.g. pseudonymous	anonymous
legal view:	referring to individual		anonymous

Fig. 2.2 Levels of identifiability

Identifiers Examples of identifiers that may make a particular person recognisable are, in addition to obvious data such as the name, attributes such as the telephone number, the IP address, a tax or insurance number as well as the serial number IMEI and the advertising ID of smartphones and similar devices. However, there are different interpretations in different countries and regions. In the case of IP addresses, it was controversial in the EU whether

---

[4] While this section gives an overview of identifiability, pseudonymisation and anonymisation in general, Sect. 6.3 will discuss these topics in more (technical) detail.

this is considered as an identifying property until a corresponding ECJ ruling,[5] but this is now clearly the case in the EU. In the USA, on the other hand, an IP address is considered an identifier only with limitations (depending, e.g. on the relevant legal basis used.).

At least under EU law, you can use the following rule of thumb: if you can relate different sets of data to the same person, then these data are personal data and no longer anonymous data. For example, a persistent cookie that is retained between sessions can be used to identify a person and is thus usually considered an identifier, even if the person's name remains unknown in the process.

Logically, a personal data record consists of an identifier and information about the identified person. This can be an explicit identifier (identified person) or an implicit identifier (identifiable person). A dataset consisting of only an identifier does not describe personal data, because it lacks the data that could relate to an individual. Depending on the individual case, these data may however be present in the context, for example, if the identifier is contained in a list of customers.

The attributes of a dataset are therefore often grouped into identifiers, pseudo-identifiers (data that are not intended for identification, but nevertheless enable it), sensitive data (data that require protection) and other data.

Anonymous and Anonymised Information The opposite of personal data are anonymous data, defined as data that do *not* relate to an identified or identifiable person. This includes information about non-identifiable persons (such as "a buyer of product X, who is not identified any more precisely, is very satisfied with it") or about groups of persons (e.g. "20% of buyers of product X are very satisfied with it"). Whether data completely without reference to a person (e.g. "the product X costs € 42") are considered anonymous data depends on the exact definition used but for practical purposes does not really make a difference.

Depending on the degree of difficulty of identification, one also speaks of *absolute* anonymity, where an assignment to the person concerned is not possible at all, and *relative* anonymity, where this assignment is more or less difficult, but basically possible. However, it is questionable to what extent absolute anonymity is actually achievable, because with the appropriate additional knowledge, for example, because one knows the person concerned, re-identification is almost always possible.

A special case of anonymous information is anonymised information, i.e. information that was originally personal but became anonymous by removing information.

However, it would be too easy to assume that by simply omitting the identifier from a dataset, for example, the name, one would always obtain anonymous information. Depending on context, this may be sufficient in some cases, but there are also many counterexamples. On the other hand, completely removing all identifying information may

---

[5] See https://curia.europa.eu/juris/document/document.jsf?text=&docid=184668&pageIndex=0&doclang=EN&mode=lst&dir=&occ=first&part=1&cid=5125592.

also prevent the use for evaluations in which the exact person is not relevant, but different persons are to be distinguished, for example, in the evaluation of a log file of the visits to a Web site (Web analytics). Shortening the data can sometimes help here, for example, by deleting a certain number of digits from an IP address. This approach will be discussed in more detail in Sect. 6.3.2.

A simple example calculation shows why anonymisation by omitting the name is often not sufficient: If one keeps the birthday (without the year) and the postcode in a data record, there are about $30{,}000 * 365 \approx 11$ million instances of these data in Germany, so with about 83 million inhabitants, just providing these two attributes reduces the number of people to about 7–8 persons. Due to statistical fluctuations alone, it can be expected that in a number of cases, the person concerned can be clearly identified by these details, and in the other cases, only little additional information is needed for identification, for example, the (approximate) year of birth. Although this calculation of course depends a lot on the way postcodes are defined, the result is far from unusual. In the UK, with about 67 million inhabitants, there are about 1.7 million different postcodes, so the instances of birthday and postcode will actually be unique in many cases. A study in the USA showed that 87% of the population there can be unambiguously identified by the information of postcode, date of birth and additionally gender [Swe02, p. 558].

> **Example 2.2 (Anonymisation of a Log File)** Information systems often write log files that record essential activities and changes in the system. In order to analyse these log files with process mining techniques, it was planned to replace the names of the respective users logged in the log file with a randomly generated pseudonym. This was to ensure that different activities of the same person could be related without the data analysts being able to assign the individual data records to the person.
>
> During the piloting of the approach, however, it quickly became apparent that this was not sufficient, as the logged changes themselves sometimes contained information about the respective person, for example, if they had changed their email address stated some personal information in the free text fields whose changes were logged.

In addition to easily overlooked identifying characteristics as in the example, the second major danger for anonymised data is that the data are matched with other available data containing, for example, name, address and date of birth. Together, the two collections of data may then enable a re-identification of the persons belonging to the data. That this is not just a theoretical possibility but a real risk is shown by many examples, including the case where anonymised medical data (diagnosis, medication, etc.) of some 135,000 state employees in Massachusetts were published for research purposes. By matching the data against a voter registry, it was possible in many cases to match the data using the common attributes of postcode, date of birth and gender and thus re-identify the persons involved, including the governor of Massachusetts [Swe02]. In another well-known case, Netflix published anonymised data of its users and their movie consumption. By comparing this with publicly available data in the film database IMDB, in particular film ratings published there, it was possible to remove the anonymity in many cases [NS08].

From a legal point of view, in the EU, re-identification[6] of anonymised data is not explicitly forbidden, in contrast, for example, to the UK and to Japan.[7] However, since re-identification can also lead to unauthorised processing of personal data, even in the EU, such re-identification is usually not allowed.

Pseudonymisation One approach to make the identification of data subjects more difficult for unauthorised parties, but at the same time still possible for authorised persons if necessary, is the pseudonymisation of data. This term describes the processing of personal data in such a way that identification is not possible without additional, separately stored and secured information, for example, by mapping identities to random values and keeping the mapping table confidential. Put differently, the challenges for effective pseudonymisation are similar to those for effective anonymisation, since pseudonymous data should be just as difficult (for third parties who do not have access to the additional information) to assign to a person as anonymous data.

Pseudonymised data are still considered personal data, but pseudonymisation can help protect the data as required. This protection can, for example, be relevant when balancing interests to assess whether the data may be processed based on the legitimate interest of the processor (see Sect. 2.5.1). Depending on context, the protective effect achieved through pseudonymisation may be further increased if the information needed to map pseudonyms back to identities is stored externally with a separate entity such as a trustee.

Common forms of pseudonymisation include:

- Arbitrary (random) pseudonym with a mapping table
- IP address, possibly in combination with date and time,
- Identifier in a cookie,
- Cryptographic identity as represented by a public key (as in most variants of blockchain (see Sect. 3.5.3))

---

[6] Also called de-anonymisation. In detail, however, there is a difference, because re-identification presupposes that the data were already personal at one time and were then anonymised. De-anonymisation can also start from data that were anonymous from the beginning, but this anonymity is then nevertheless removed.

[7] According to Section 171 of the UK *Data Protection Act* (DPA), re-identification without the consent of the controller or the data subject is punishable by law. Similarly, Art. 38 of the Japanese *Act on the Protection of Personal Information* (APPI) explicitly forbids re-identification of anonymised data.

- Cryptographic hash value of an identifier or other properties such as place of residence and/or date of birth (discussed in more detail below)

A variant of pseudonymisation is the use of *tokens* to replace account numbers as done in the Payment Card Industry Data Security Standard (PCI-DSS) [PCI11, PCI15].

Case Study 2.1 (Anonymisation in Online Retail Company) The online retail company examined the extent to which it is possible to anonymise or pseudonymise the data generated when tracking customer activity on its Web site. It turned out that several cases have to be distinguished:

- As far as only Web analytics was concerned, i.e. the analysis of which pages are visited how often and in which order, it is necessary to recognise which different steps on the Web site can be assigned to the same visitor, but limited to one visit. If the visitor visits the Web site again the following day, then assignment is no longer necessary. Technically, this is usually implemented by recording the IP address, possibly also by using session cookies, which are automatically deleted once the browser is closed.
  - To ensure that the IP address provides genuine anonymisation and cannot serve as a pseudonym, the Web analytics tool was configured so that the IP address is only recorded in an abbreviated form, with a number of bits removed. In addition, it was decided to use the open-source software Matomo and install it on the company's own server, so that no agreement with a service provider on data protection (commissioned processing; see Sect. 2.7.4) is required.
  - Session cookies are somewhat more cumbersome to use and have the disadvantage that visitors to the Web site may delete them during the visit. Therefore, the company decided against the use of cookies for its Web analytics activities.
- When the shop analysed the use of persistent cookies in order to enable the tracking of customers for advertising purposes, this became far more challenging from a data protection point of view. Persistent cookies allow to identify multiple visits of the same person to the Web site, and thus, at least according to the GDPR, this is a case of identifying the visitors, i.e. it leads to the collection of personal data that must be treated accordingly. After some analysis and discussion, the retail company came to the conclusion that this kind of tracking does not actually provide sufficient benefit to make up for the difficulties and limitations involved and eventually decided against the use of persistent cookies for tracking.

(continued)

> • Clearly all data that arise from orders placed by customers in the online retail
>   shop are personal data. To place an order, customers must register in the
>   store and, in addition to the ordered products, at least provide their delivery
>   address and payment data. Since these data are needed for handling the order,
>   processing them for this purpose is allowed (see Sect. 2.5.1).

Use of Cryptographic Hash Functions Cryptographic hash functions are a specific type
of hash functions[8] that are practically impossible to invert ("one-way functions"), and it
is practically impossible to find two values which are mapped to the same hash value
or, given any value and its hash value, to find a second value mapped to the same hash
value (see Sect. 7.4.4 or [Art14] for more detail). The use of cryptographic hash functions
as pseudonyms helps, for example, to assign different datasets to a common identifier
without precisely identifying the person concerned. A use case of this approach concerns
patient data from different hospitals, where hash functions can be used to generate uniform
pseudonyms without a central directory.

However, this is only really secure if the number of possible identifiers is sufficiently
large and it is not possible to create a table of *all* identifiers with their associated hash
values,[9] as shown, for example, by [Pan14] for an anonymised listing of cab rides in
New York. This type of attack is also referred to as an *enumeration attack*, since in this
case the pseudonymisation can be removed by enumerating all records with the associated
pseudonyms. Similarly, [AE19] uses the example of Spanish telephone numbers to show
that while the number of possible 11-digit telephone numbers is huge (10^{11}), just knowing
that it is a Spanish mobile phone number reduces the number of possibilities considerably
because the first three digits become known. Out of this still large number, only about 20
million ($2 * 10^7$) are actually in use, so that compiling a table containing all telephone
numbers with their associated hash value becomes feasible.

As can be seen, the use of hash functions for pseudonymisation is only adequate if
the number of possible different identifiers is sufficiently large so that pseudonymisation

---

[8] In the context of cryptography and data protection, one often talks about hash functions when
actually referring to cryptographic hash functions. However, a hash function is a more general
concept used in computer science and refers to a function that maps arbitrary values to values of
a fixed length.

[9] Such a table is usually referred to as a rainbow table, although strictly speaking this term describes
the data structure most commonly used for this purpose and not its application to invert a hash
function.

cannot be broken by a table of all values. Even for IPv4 addresses, it is feasible to create such a table without much effort.[10]

Cryptographic Hash Function: Anonymisation or Pseudonymisation? The use of cryptographic hash functions still allows the linkage of data in certain use cases. It is possible to identify that two sets of data refer to the same person if they contain the same hashed identifier, and it is possible to check whether a given identifier maps to a known hash value. Therefore, using cryptographic hash functions is considered pseudonymisation but not anonymisation [Art14, p. 20].

Encrypted Data Encrypted data have a certain similarity to pseudonymised data, since here too the reference to a person is only possible using additional data, in this case the relevant key. However, there is a difference since in order to process data, they must usually be decrypted,[11] while the processing of pseudonymised data is generally possible without breaking the pseudonymisation.

2.4   Roles in Data Protection

There are different roles involved in the processing of personal data. These are illustrated in Fig. 2.3 and comprise the *controller* who takes the main responsibility for the processing, the *data subject* whose data are processed and in many cases a *processor* who performs the processing data on behalf of the controller. In addition, in the current context, there is software development and IT, which provide and operate software for the controller and/or the processor.

Controller The controller is defined as the entity that alone or jointly with others decides on the purposes and means of the processing of data. Thus, the controller is typically an entire organisation, not an individual. Internally, of course, in order to take those decisions, the organisation must also designate individuals who are responsible for specific subtasks.

The definition allows that several entities can jointly assume the role of the controller, for example, if several companies operate a joint Internet platform or jointly carry out a project. But even if one company acts on behalf of another, but in doing so decides itself about the purposes and means of the processing, both parties are data controllers. In this

---

[10] The author himself created such a table for IPv4 addresses on an ordinary, somewhat older laptop using a PHP library program without any additional optimisation. The program needed about 5 hours to complete this task.

[11] An exception to this statement is homomorphic encryption, which however is not yet usable on a large scale (see Sect. 7.4.3).

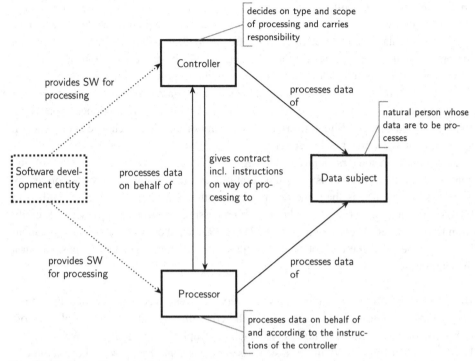

Fig. 2.3 Roles in data protection

case, one speaks of a *joint controllership* for the processing as defined in Art. 26 GDPR, where both parties are also jointly responsible for compliant processing.

Processor   As the name suggests, the processor processes data, which he does on behalf of the controller. The processor does not decide on the purposes and means of the processing but is bound by the controller's instructions. The responsibility of the processor regarding compliant processing is therefore limited to compliance with the controller's requirements. This is sometimes referred to as the *processor's privilege*, since the processor in general is *not* responsible for the lawfulness of the processing (see Sect. 2.5.1), but this responsibility remains with the controller. In order for the processor to be able to work in accordance with the specifications of the controller, these specifications must be clearly described and communicated. Therefore, according to Art. 28 GDPR, a prerequisite for commissioned processing is a contract between the parties involved that defines the essential context, in particular the processing to be carried out as well as specifications for the protection of the data at the processor. The responsibility for concluding such a contract lies with both parties: without a processing contract, the client usually has no legal basis for transferring personal data to the contractor, and the contractor has no legal basis for receiving and processing the data.

Distinction Between Controller and Processor In practice, the necessary distinction between controllers and processors often is not as clear as the definitions described above suggest. Particularly in the area of IT, it is often difficult to delineate the extent to which the processor itself co-decides on the type and manner of processing (joint controllers) or whether only the controller does so (commissioned processing).[12] However, due to the processor's privilege, this distinction is legally important, and most contractors, such as cloud service providers, try to frame the collaboration as commissioned processing. Chap. 5 deals with these different variants of cooperation and data exchange in more detail, specifically in the context of IT services.

A common misunderstanding regarding the distinction between the roles of the controller and the processor is to assume that processing of data is always performed by a processor, even if it is the same organisation as the controller. However, according to GDPR, the role of the processor only exists if processing is performed by a separate entity from the controller. According to Art. 28 (3) GDPR, a legal contract or similar agreement is required between the controller and the processor, which is not legally possible in a meaningful way if both are the same entity.[13]

Data Subjects The data subject may be very different types of persons, including, for example, (employees of) customers of the controller, possibly even (employees of) customers of customers, (employees of) suppliers, employees, visitors to a Web site, etc. Unlike the other roles listed, the data subjects are always *natural persons*. For example, a company, even if it is itself a customer of some other company, cannot be a data subject, while its employees can. In the case of a partnership or an independent trader, however, this is difficult to distinguish, so that a list of companies, for example, also contains personal data of data subjects.

Case Study 2.2 (Data Processing Roles in Online Retail Company) The controller for the processing of personal data at the online retail company is the company itself as the operator of the store, represented by its management.

Since many external services are used for the store, there are also various processors with whom corresponding agreements must be made, for example, the service provider who operates warehousing and shipping and the (third-party) IT company that operates the store's servers.

The data subjects are mainly customers and visitors to the Web site, as well as employees of the online retail company.

---

[12] For more information about these roles, see the EDPB guidelines published as [EDP21].

[13] An entity might still be both a controller and a processor, but not for the same processing.

2.5   Data Protection Principles According to GDPR

This section provides a summary of the principles of data protection as defined in Art. 5 GDPR. A more detailed discussion of these principles and their implementation in the area of software development and IT follows in Sect. 3. The wording of the relevant excerpts of Art. 5 and 6 of the GDPR is reproduced in Appendix A.2.

2.5.1   Lawfulness, Fairness and Transparency

The principles of lawfulness, fairness and transparency are contained in Art. 5 (1)(a) GDPR.

Lawfulness The principle of "prohibition with reservation of permission" applies to the processing of personal data and states that processing is in principle prohibited unless it is expressly permitted by a corresponding legal regulation. The conditions or legal bases under which processing is permitted are set out in Art. 6 (1) GDPR:[14]

- *Consent*: the first legal basis for processing consists of consent by the data subject in the processing of their data. There are a number of important requirements for such consent to be valid: it must be *voluntary*; the data subject must be *informed* about the meaning and consequences of the consent; the consent must relate to a specific *purpose*; it must be *unambiguous* (and thus usually explicit); and finally, it must be *revocable*, i.e. the data subject must have the possibility to withdraw it at any time (at least for future processing). These limitations make consent as a legal basis for processing rather difficult to handle in practice and—contrary to what one might expect at first glance— the use of another legal basis is often much easier to implement. Consent should only be used if it is truly voluntary and can also be withdrawn.
- *Performance of contract*: processing is necessary for the performance of a contract or for the preparation thereof (pre-contractual measures). Of course, only contracts in which the data subject itself is a party are considered; two parties cannot conclude a contract in which they agree to process the data of a third party and use this contract as the starting point to allow the processing.
  Note that the processing must be *necessary* for the performance of the contract, and this legal basis thus cannot be used to circumvent the requirements on consent.[15]

---

[14] See Appendix A.2 for the full legal text.

[15] For example, Facebook and Instagram at one time claimed that behavioural advertising was part of performing the contract with the data subjects, which was however rejected by the EDPB; see https://www.edpb.europa.eu/news/news/2023/facebook-and-instagram-decisions-important-impact-use-personal-data-behavioural_en.

- *Legal obligation*: the controller is under a legal obligation to process the data. This applies, for example, to the disclosure of employee data to the tax office and social security agencies.
- *Vital interests*: the processing is necessary to protect vital interests. It primarily relates to dealing with emergencies and is of little practical significance in the context of this book.
- *Public interest*: the processing is carried out in the public interest or in the exercise of official authority and must be based on a suitable law (Art. 6 (3) GDPR). This essentially concerns work by or on behalf of public authorities.
- *Legitimate interest*: processing is necessary to further the legitimate interests of the controller or of a third party, such as the controller's client. Circumstances that may give rise to such a legitimate interest include, for example, direct marketing (see Recital 47 GDPR), data exchange within a group of companies (see Recital 48 GDPR), the protection of network and information security (see Recital 49 GDPR) and also profit making. What is important when using this legal basis for a processing operation is that there must be an (explicit) balancing of interests between the legitimate interests of the controller or the third party against the "interests or fundamental rights and freedoms of the data subject". This balancing of interests should include consideration of how well the relevant data are protected, for example, by pseudonymisation, because appropriate protection reduces the risks to the data subject and can therefore contribute to a balancing of interests in favour of the controller and its interests.

Example 2.3 (Evaluation of Student Papers Using AI) A university considered the use of an AI system for evaluating and possibly marking student papers. To achieve this, the original idea was to use marked student papers as training material to train a machine learning-based system for this purpose.

An initial legal analysis of this situation showed that there are several different areas of law that had to be considered:

First, the students who had written the graded papers own the copyright for these papers. Therefore, using these papers for a different purpose requires an agreement with the student authors.

Second, the graded papers are personal data, and their processing therefore requires a legal basis according to Art. 6 (1) GDPR. Such a legal basis existed for the grading of the papers, but using the papers for training of an AI system constitutes a change of purpose of these data and requires a new legal basis. Consent would be an applicable legal basis, but if such consent is withdrawn, it would be technically very difficult to remove a single paper once a model has been trained. (Arguably, the resulting model does not actually include

(continued)

any training data any more, but there is a risk that training data unexpectedly reappear in the results of applying the model.)

Processing on the base of legitimate interest was considered infeasible since it would be susceptible in the event of a student complaint according to Art. 21 GDPR, leading to the same difficulties as withdrawn consent. (Even if legitimate interest was sufficient as a legal basis, the students would at least have to be informed about this processing of their data.)

Eventually, it was decided that the best solution would be to pay the students for allowing their papers to be used as training material. This would strongly move the balance of interests to the university, and it would also prevent students from objecting to this processing based on their specific situation (as generally possible according to Art. 21 GDPR).

Special Categories of Personal Data The legal bases described so far are sufficient for ordinary personal data, but not for special categories of personal data, for which Art. 9 GDPR defines an additional and more restrictive list of legal bases.[16] In particular, contract performance (without explicit consent) and legitimate interest are not considered sufficient legal bases in this case, and in most practical examples, consent turns out to be the only applicable legal base.

Specific Regulations Regarding Children A particular case of consent concerns the legal validity of consent of children (legally defined as people under age). Article 8 GDPR specifies that for an "offer of information society services made directly to a child", the minimum age for consent is 16 years.[17] For younger children, consent must be given by the holder of parental responsibility. The significance and implementation of these requirements are considered in more detail in Sect. 3.1.2.

Another special feature concerns the required balancing of interests when using legitimate interest as a legal basis for processing. Although there is no clear additional requirement here, there is a requirement that the balancing of interests must be carried out in particular and thus especially thoroughly in the case of children (Art. 6 (1)(f) GDPR).

---

[16] In the past, there was some discussion whether Art. 9 GDPR defines an additional or an alternative list of legal bases for the processing of special categories of personal data. With its 2023 judgement on case C-667/21, the European Court of Justice (ECJ) made it clear that the two requirements are cumulative, and both one condition out of Art. 6 (1) and one condition out of Art. 9 (2) GDPR must be satisfied for processing data of special categories.

[17] The said minimum age may be reduced by the member states. Austria, for example, has made use of this possibility and reduced the minimum age for consents to 14 years (§ 4 (4) Data Protection Law), and Norway (§ 5 Personal Data Act) and Estonia (§ 8 (1) Personal Data Protection Act) even reduced it to 13 years.

Necessity of Processing With the exception of consent, all of these conditions for lawful processing contain the requirement that the processing is necessary for the purpose under consideration and that it cannot be achieved with a lesser intrusion.

> **Example 2.4 (Necessity of Processing in a Game App)** Consider a game app where different players can play against each other and which is financed by advertising. For the game app to function, it is not necessary for the provider to have personal data about the players. However, the provider will probably want to collect such data, since the app is financed by advertising. The only possible legal basis for this is the consent of the players. The question still arises whether this consent can be considered voluntary if it is used as a prerequisite for using the game. However, this can probably be assumed as long as the game is not a particularly sought-after game with the character of a monopoly.

Multiple Legal Bases for Processing A doubtful practice is to argue for several different permissions for a particular processing operation, although only one really applies. This primarily concerns the case where consent is first obtained or at least requested in a situation where it is not really voluntary. If consent is not granted or is later withdrawn, then another element of permission is subsequently used as an argument, usually the legitimate interest.

This approach is first and foremost a case of misleading the data subjects, who are led to believe that they have a choice as to whether their data are processed in a certain way or not. This is likely to contravene the principle of fairness discussed below. Irrespective of possible legal consequences, moving from consent to a different legal basis at the very least leads to dissatisfaction on the part of the data subject concerned. In addition, in the event of a dispute, this approach is an indicator that insufficient thought has been given to the legal basis of the processing, and in particular that no sufficient weighing of interests has been carried out. If one's own legitimate interests do not clearly outweigh the interests of the data subjects, a supervisory authority or a court will be more likely to rule against the organisation than would have been the case if one had argued with the correct legal basis from the outset.

Except in special cases, only one legal basis should therefore be used for a given processing operation, and in particular, one should not move from consent to a different legal basis.

Case Study 2.3 (Lawfulness of Processing in Online Retail Company)
Different forms of processing at the online retail company need different legal bases:

- The processing of customers' orders is necessary for the performance of a contract to which the data subject is a party, and thus all processing necessary for this task is lawful. It should be noted that this only refers to the steps necessary for the performance of the contract. This includes, for example, the storage of shopping cart data in a cookie, but not the subsequent sending of advertising material.
- The processing steps necessary for the operation of the store's Web site, for example, the storage of the language selection of the data subject or the limited logging for security reasons, can be based on the legitimate interest of the company. In these cases, balancing these interests against the "interests or fundamental rights and freedoms" of the data subjects does not result in any restrictions, so these processing steps are lawful.
- In the case of tracking of visitors to the Web site, the balancing of interests shows that the interests of the person concerned in an unobserved visit to the Web site prevail, and such tracking therefore is only permitted with the consent of the data subject.

Case Study 2.4 (Supporting the Exchange Among Customers of the Software Company) The software company sent out newsletters to its customers by email. In line with an internal company policy, recipients were not entered as blind carbon copy (BCC) but as recipients, and thus all email addresses were visible to all other recipients, leading to customer complaints to the company DPO.

To ensure compliance, the internal policy was adjusted and now only applies to internal emails. For emails that go to multiple external recipients, the default is set that the recipients may only be entered in the blind copy field.

Furthermore, contact data of persons at customer companies had in the past occasionally been passed on if different customers had the same problem or a comparable complex task. In most cases, the customers were happy about this support, but in the context of the implementation of the GDPR, the company realised that there was no legal basis for such data sharing. Therefore, a new

(continued)

internal requirement was introduced that such sharing of contact data is only permitted with the express consent of the data subject.

Fairness The principle of fairness is rather vague and indeterminate, and its meaning is largely determined by case law. To some extent, it can be understood as a catch-all provision, intended to prevent a controller from taking unfair advantage of the frequently existing imbalance of power between the entities processing personal data and the data subject, even if the entity does not thereby violate one of the concrete legal requirements. In the context of processing personal data, such processing is usually considered unfair if it is surprising or unexpected for the data subject, in particular if the processing changes compared to what the data subject was told in the past.

Though not related to GDPR, a good example is described in a blog post by the US Federal Trade Commission FTC, which describes that quietly changing a company's terms of service or its privacy notice to allow processing of personal data, e.g. in the context of using the data for training of machine learning systems, can be unfair or deceptive and therefore illegal.[18]

Transparency The principle of transparency requires that the processing of personal data must be transparent for the data subjects, i.e. the data subjects must be able to see which of their data are being processed how and for what purpose. For example, personal data must not be collected or processed secretly. This requirement is defined in more detail in Art. 12–15 GDPR as corresponding rights of the data subjects (see Sect. 2.6).

2.5.2 Purpose Limitation

The principle of purpose limitation states that personal data may only be used for the purpose for which they were originally (and lawfully) collected and for compatible purposes. To judge when purposes are compatible, Art. 6 (4) GDPR contains a list of criteria when this is the case, but this still remains rather vague. A clear decision based on these criteria therefore is rarely possible, and each case must be judged individually.

There are some exceptions defined in GDPR describing when evaluating purpose compatibility is not required, which will be discussed in Sect. 3.2.2.

---

[18] https://www.ftc.gov/policy/advocacy-research/tech-at-ftc/2024/02/ai-other-companies-quietly-changing-your-terms-service-could-be-unfair-or-deceptive

In order to be able to limit purpose changes, the purpose of a processing operation must be clearly defined in advance. In the case of consent, this is implicit in the definition of consent, but it also applies if the processing uses some other legal basis.

2.5.3 Data Minimisation

The principle of data minimisation requires that the amount of data collected and stored must be limited to what is necessary for the defined purpose. Storing data because they might be useful in the future, even though one does not yet know how it will be evaluated, is thus not permitted. Even with the widespread collection of customer data in a CRM system, one must therefore be very cautious. For example, storing the customer's date of birth is usually not necessary and thus not allowed, even if you want to congratulate the customer on his birthday. Even more critical are rather private data about customers, as often collected by a sales department, such as "likes to drink wine", etc., and the collection of such data is in general not allowed without consent.

To the extent compatible with the purpose of the processing, the principle of data minimisation also implies the requirement to anonymise the data processed as soon as possible, as described in more detail in Sect. 2.3.

2.5.4 Accuracy

When it comes to the accuracy of personal data, it is not immediately obvious why this is important from the point of view of the data subject and therefore forms a principle of data protection. However, when one considers the damage that false information can potentially cause to the data subject, the need for accuracy becomes apparent. A particularly obvious example is the credit agency that has false information about an applicant's payment record for a loan and passes this incorrect information on to a bank.

Conversely, it follows that erroneous personal data also fall under data protection, and it is easy to see that in addition to the requirement for accuracy of the data, confidential treatment can be of particular importance.

2.5.5 Storage Limitation

The principle of storage limitation is closely related to the principle of data minimisation and supplements it with a temporal view, i.e. it demands that data are not kept longer than necessary. Of course, this immediately raises the question of how long retention is necessary. In most cases, it can be assumed that personal data are needed as long as the corresponding business process is running, but no longer after that. For example, as soon as a purchase is completed, the product is handed over and the purchase price is paid, the data are no longer needed for the processing of this purpose. However, legal retention periods may now start according to the relevant regulations on bookkeeping, tax law and similar. As far as such regulations apply, they typically require that records of relevant transactions are kept for 5 to 10 years.[19] As a result, storage is not only permitted for the relevant period of time but legally required, leading to a new legal basis. However, since the data are now no longer needed for current access, it should be archived and no longer accessible without special permission. As soon as the retention period has expired, the data must be deleted unless there is another important reason, or more precisely another legal basis, for the continued retention.

As a result, companies usually need a retention and erasure policy in which the storage and, above all, the subsequent erasure of the data is determined as described in Sect. 3.5.2.

> **Example 2.5 (Storing Job Application Documents)** The storage limit requirement naturally also applies to documents regarding job applications, including the associated internal records such as assessments or correspondence relating to the application. If applicants are subsequently hired, their application documents will be included in their personnel data. However, what happens if an applicant is not hired?
>
> In principle, job application documentation is no longer needed once the application procedure has been completed. However, it may still happen that a rejected applicant appeals against this rejection, and in this case, the company must still be able to justify the rejection.
>
> Therefore, it is usually assumed that application documents may be kept for another 3 to 6 months after the end of an application procedure. Retention of documents beyond this period, for example, in order to be able to consider an applicant in future procedures, is possible to a certain extent, but only with the consent of the applicant.

2.5.6 Integrity and Confidentiality

The principle of integrity and confidentiality requires that personal data be protected by appropriate security measures. It is true that information security has a fundamentally different orientation and considers the protection of data and infrastructures primarily

---

[19] In certain cases, data must be retained for longer periods. For example, different types of medical records have retention periods of up to 20 years and more in the UK. Adoption records may even have retention periods of 100 years.

from the point of view of the operator, not the person affected by the data. Nevertheless, data protection can only be successfully implemented if the relevant data are protected by suitable measures that implement the three *security objectives* of information security, namely, confidentiality, integrity and availability (sometimes called the *CIA triad*). Although availability is not named in the title of this principle, it is included in its description (as well as in Art. 32 (1)(b) GDPR) and thus also required by GDPR.

As a basis for the protection of data subjects, the GDPR requires an appropriate implementation of information security, taking into account, among other issues, the state of the art, the implementation costs and the risk for data subjects. These requirements are further specified in Art. 32 GDPR, and in Chap. 7 of this book, this topic is also considered in more detail.

2.5.7 Accountability

Accountability was newly introduced with the GDPR and was not previously common in other data protection laws. It requires that an organisation not only complies with the data protection principles as well as the other requirements but can also prove this through appropriate documentation (Art. 5 (2) GDPR) (e.g. in the *Records of Processing Activities* (RoPA); see Sect. 2.7.5).

2.6 Rights of the Data Subjects

In addition to the principles described, the GDPR defines a number of rights of data subjects. The most important of these rights are summarised in Chap. 3 (Art. 12–23) of the GDPR, although some of the rights of data subjects defined there are actually obligations of the controller. The following list provides an overview of these data subjects' rights, and Chap. 4 of this book will discuss the rights and in particular their implementation in more detail.

Transparent Information Transparency of the processing of personal data is one of the core requirements of GDPR, with the goal to make sure that data subjects know which data about them are processed where, when and how. The principle of transparency as stated in Art. 5 (1) GDPR is explained in more detail by the data subject's rights to transparent information and to access, as stated in Art. 12–15 GDPR.

Strictly speaking, the right to transparent information (Art. 12 GDPR) does not describe an independent right of data subjects but rather defines important requirements on how to implement the rights of data subjects described in subsequent articles. These include, in particular, that information to be provided or made available about the processing must be "in a concise, transparent, intelligible and easily accessible form, using clear and plain language ...". This requirement is very difficult to implement in practice because, as the data protection policies on many Web sites show, it is hardly possible to formulate the relevant information in a legally precise and complete manner and at the same time in an understandable, clear and simple manner. Most operators therefore opt for legally precise wording, even if this is sometimes at the expense of comprehensibility.

Time Limit for Answering Data Subject's Requests For all data subjects' rights as defined in the GDPR, Art. 12 (3) GDPR states that the relevant information must be provided without undue delay, normally within 1 month. In the case of particularly complex requests, this time limit may be extended to three months, but in this case, the controller must inform the data subject and give reasons for this.

Information to Be Provided to Data Subjects In Art. 13 and 14, GDPR defines a set of information obligations that controllers have to comply to, informing the data subjects about the processing. In the case of Web sites, this is usually implemented via a data protection policy on the Web site.

It is important to clearly distinguish this *information* of the data subjects from the *consent* described in Sect. 2.5.1. Here, the data subjects are informed about which of their data are being processed, how and why, and is required for *each* of the possible legal bases, including situations where consent is not required. This difference should also be clearly reflected in the wording of the information in order to avoid misunderstandings.

Right of Access According to Art. 15 GDPR, data subjects have the right to information about which data concerning them are processed and how, as well as the data themselves. There are no formal requirements as to how such information must be requested, so that it can be requested informally, such as by email or in person, provided that it is ensured that the data are provided to the correct person. When providing such data as requested, it is important to ensure that it contains the complete data on the person concerned, but does not contain any data on third parties or internal, confidential data.

Authentication When implementing the right of access, it is important to authenticate the respective data subjects appropriately to ensure that the information is not passed to another person. (The same applies for most other rights of the data subjects—for example, one does not want to rectify data because of a request by an unauthorised person.) In this case, instead of fulfilling a data subject right as intended, one would have caused a data breach. The challenge here is to make authentication sufficiently secure, but not so complex to make it unreasonably difficult for data subjects to claim their rights.

Example 2.6 (Authentication for Exercising the Right of Access at a Credit Agency) A credit agency collects information about the creditworthiness of persons and makes it available to credit institutions. In this case, it is particularly important that the data collected are correct, and therefore the data subjects have an increased interest in knowing what data are available about them. On its Web site, the credit agency offers to request a copy of the data in accordance with Art. 15 GDPR, but does not make it available directly on the Web site, but sends it by post to the data subject's known postal address. This way, the credit agency ensures that although it is difficult to authenticate data subjects in this context and an unauthorised third party can request such information, the unauthorised party will not receive it. Instead, the information will always be sent to the data subject.

Right to Rectification One step to implement the principle of integrity is the right to rectification under Art. 16 GDPR, according to which data subjects have the right to require the controller to correct without delay inaccurate personal data concerning them. Of course, there may be significantly different opinions as to which data are considered inaccurate and therefore needs to be corrected. In some cases, this right also leads to conflicts with the right to freedom of expression, especially in countries like the USA where this right is given a very high priority. (Of course, the GDPR does not apply directly in the USA, but indirectly such conflicts still occur.)

Right to Erasure This right under Art. 17 GDPR, also known as the "right to be forgotten", gives data subjects, under certain conditions, the right to request the erasure or deletion of certain data concerning them, for example, if consent is withdrawn or if the data are no longer necessary for the original purpose.

The right to erasure has a very different starting point but in effect is very similar to the principle of storage limitation, since both regulations make statements about when personal data must be deleted. The main difference is that the principle of storage limitation is a generally applicable principle, whereas the right to erasure is the right of data subjects to demand the deletion of data only in certain cases.

Right to Restriction of Processing Article 18 GDPR gives data subjects the right to request the restriction of the processing of their data under certain conditions. In this case, the data may be retained but may only be further processed in special cases, for example, if the data subject consents to the processing or if the processing serves to assert legal claims. To achieve this, restriction of processing is defined as a marking of the data with the aim of limiting future processing (Art. 4 (3) GDPR).

The right to restriction of processing exists on the one hand in cases of legal action, for example, when the accuracy of the data is disputed and has not yet been clarified, or as long as an objection to processing is being clarified. While in these cases, it is not quite obvious why this is a *right* of the data subjects, this becomes clearer in the other cases when the data subject rejects the deletion of the data that is actually pending and instead demands the restriction of processing, for example, because he needs it to assert certain legal claims.

Notification Obligation Regarding Rectification or Erasure of Personal Data or Restriction of Processing According to this obligation,[20] if a controller has disclosed personal data to third parties, for example, to a processor, then in the event of rectification, erasure or restriction of processing, the controller is obliged to inform these third parties so that they might also address this request. In addition, the data subject may also request to be informed about these third parties.

This obligation to notify seems relatively unproblematic at first glance, but on closer inspection, it is relatively complex. In particular, the question of who was given which personal data, and how to reach these third parties sometime later, can be difficult to answer.

Right to Data Portability This right was newly introduced with Art. 20 GDPR and goes beyond data protection in the strict sense. It gives data subjects the right to transfer their data from one controller to another, typically when moving to another service provider or at least using an additional service provider. However, this right is limited to data that the data subject has provided to the controller himself, while data that the controller has collected by other means (possibly at great expense) are not covered.

Right to Object In the case of processing on the legal basis of legitimate interest (Art. 6 (1)(f) GDPR) or public interest (Art. 6 (1)(e) GDPR), data subjects have the right to object to the processing of their data "on grounds relating to his or her particular situation". In this case, processing is only permitted under Art. 21 GDPR in the event of "compelling legitimate grounds" worthy of protection or in order to assert legal claims. Put differently, in these cases that are both based on a balancing of interests, this balancing has to be renewed, taking into account the particular situation of the data subject.

If a given consent is withdrawn, this right does not apply, but the withdrawal of the consent itself has almost the same effect. For the other three possible legal grounds (performance of contract, legal obligation, vital interests), there is no such right of objection, as this would not be appropriate in these cases.

---

[20] Again, although contained in the chapter on the *rights* of data subjects, this is not really a right but an obligation on the controller.

Automated Individual Decision-Making   This right is about limiting the possibilities of assessing the situation of individuals by algorithms or artificial intelligence. To this end, data subjects have the right under Art. 22 GDPR that decisions with legal effect on them shall not be taken solely by automated processing, i.e. there must be at least a substantial possibility of human intervention in the decision. This right primarily relates to so-called profiling, deciding, for example, whether a credit, employment, rental or insurance contract should be concluded with the data subject.

This restriction does not apply if the decision is *necessary* (not just useful) for the conclusion or performance of a contract or if the data subject has consented to automated decision-making. Even in these cases, however, the data subjects must at least have the possibility to request an intervention by a person, to present their own point of view and to challenge a decision. In these cases, an automated decision is therefore possible in the first place, but the data subject can then still demand manual intervention (despite prior consent).

Whether this right involves the right of data subjects to get an explanation of the decision or whether such an explanation is just strongly recommended is under discussion [SL20, Sect. 3.6.5]. In either case, controllers should be able to explain automatic decisions taken, at least on a generic level, if not on the level of each individual decision. At least in the case of high-risk AI systems, such an explanation is required according to Art. 86 AI Act.[21]

2.7   Further Requirements for Data Protection According to GDPR

The following section provides an overview of the most important further requirements of the GDPR that have a more or less direct impact on software development and IT.

2.7.1   Technical and Organisational Measures (TOM)

In order to implement the data protection requirements and to be able to prove this, Art. 24 GDPR requires the implementation of "appropriate technical and organisational measures" (TOM). The GDPR explicitly mentions measures such as pseudonymisation and encryption to be implemented as appropriate (Art. 32 GDPR). The decision of which measures are appropriate and suitable is left up to the controller. There are a variety of further TOMs that should be considered, for example, password protection as technical measure and training of employees or definition of relevant processes as organisational measures.

---

[21] See Sect. 2.9 for more information about the AI Act.

Closely related is the requirement in Art. 32 GDPR for security of processing through appropriate technical and organisational measures, i.e. this article provides more detail about the requirements on TOMs regarding security.

A detailed discussion of the various TOMs can be found in Sect. 6.1, and Chap. 7 covers the appropriate information security measures.

2.7.2 Data Protection by Design

Data protection by design, also known as *privacy by design*, has been discussed as a concept for several years but was required by law for the first time in the GDPR (Art. 25 GDPR). The precise meaning of this legal requirement is quite elusive, especially since the GDPR does not explain the term in any detail. The central requirement of data protection by design is that data protection must be taken into account from the outset, especially in the design of an information system, and one should not try to incorporate data protection retrospectively on the basis of a review of the finished system, which in most cases would only be possible to a very limited extent.

This requirement therefore affects software development very directly, with considerable influence on the design of (IT and other) systems, and is therefore considered in more detail in Sect. 6.5.

2.7.3 Data Protection by Default

The concept of data protection by default (also known as privacy by default)) is closely related to data protection by design and relates to the configuration of information systems. This too is a topic that must be implemented largely by software development and IT operations and consists of two requirements: first, the standard configuration of systems must be data protection-friendly in the sense that as little personal data as possible are collected or otherwise processed. Second, the use of additional data for personalisation or similar optional purpose must be explicitly selected by the data subjects, i.e. it is not selected by default. Data minimisation must be the default, and more extensive processing and personalisation can be additionally selected by the data subjects through appropriate configuration, i.e. consent, if the data subject considers this useful.

It may be argued that the requirement of data protection by default is not a new requirement but "only" provides more detail to a specific aspect of the principle of data minimisation. However, experience has shown that such detail is at least helpful, if not necessary, to ensure the concept is implemented.

2.7.4   Cooperation of Multiple Parties

With the strong specialisation and division of labour in business in general and in IT in particular, data are often processed jointly by several parties, for example, when a company uses cloud services or a Web hoster, or when a software development project is carried out jointly by multiple parties. Even within a group of companies, data are often exchanged between different companies, for example, when a central internal service provider is responsible for payroll accounting for all group companies.

The GDPR describes two basic constellations for the exchange of data between different companies:

- *Commissioned processing* considers the case where one company processes data on behalf of another. In this situation, Art. 28 GDPR requires a written contract between the controller and the processor, which specifies that the processor will work according to the specifications of the controller, will adequately protect the data, etc.

  The main advantage of commissioned processing is that it gives the controller the right to transfer the data to the processor while retaining the responsibility for the lawfulness of the processing. The processor, on the other hand, does not need its own legal basis but can "share" the controller's. The responsibility for fulfilling the data subject's rights and information obligations also remains with the controller. Typical examples include the use of cloud services or of Web hosting.
- *Joint controllership*, on the other hand, assumes that several controllers jointly process data or at least jointly "determine the purposes and means of processing" (Art. 26 GDPR) and therefore also jointly assume responsibility for it. In this case, each controller needs its own legal basis, both for the processing in the strict sense and for the transfer of the data to the other controller.

  Again, an agreement between the parties involved in the processing is required, specifying, for example, how data protection obligations will be shared and who will inform the data subjects. However, this is an internal agreement between the joint controllers, and the data subjects can assert their rights against either of the controllers.

The demarcation between the different forms of cooperation is sometimes difficult or even controversial and is dealt with in more detail in Chap. 5. There, the additional question of what must be considered when data are transferred to a company outside the EU as part of the cooperation is also addressed, because in this case additional safeguards are required to ensure the protection of the data and thus of the data subjects.

2.7.5   Records of Processing Activities (RoPA)

In order to clarify what an organisation must do with regard to the protection of personal data, as well as for proving conformance to the principle of accountability (as introduced in Sect. 2.5.7), it is necessary to have an overview of which personal data are processed in the organisation and how. For this reason, the GDPR requires in Art. 30 that controllers and processors must create "records of processing activities" (RoPA) that compile and document this information. These records comprise, after an introductory section with the names and contact details of the parties involved, more detailed information on the processing, such as the purpose, the categories of data subjects and their data and the categories of recipients of the data if they are passed on. As far as possible, the records also contain the retention and deletion periods and a description of the technical and organisational measures used to protect the data. Since slightly different information is relevant for controllers and for processors, Art. 30 defines two similar but not identical lists.

A quick search of the Internet will find many templates and tools for preparing a RoPA, including templates provided by different supervisory authorities. Alternatively, it is easy to set up one's own template based on the list of information to be included in a RoPA defined in Art. 30 GDPR. The legal basis for the processing of the personal data is not legally required to be included in the RoPA, but for practical purposes, it is strongly recommended to include this information.

For small enterprises, defined in this case as enterprises with less than 250 employees, the obligation to keep a RoPA does not apply. However, this exemption rarely applies, as there is also an exemption to the exemption for the case of processing of special categories of personal data, which applies to almost all companies with employees. It is currently disputed whether in this case only the processing activities in which special categories of personal data must be processed must be described in the RoPA or whether the RoPA must include all processing activities.

The responsibility for maintaining the RoPA lies with the controller. This typically needs support from the data protection officer (for the correct interpretation of the data protection terms and requirements) as well as from software development and IT operations (for a detailed understanding of which data are processed and how).

Integration with Other Records The information to be recorded in the RoPA overlaps substantially with other information collections, for example, with a configuration management database (CMDB) in ITIL-based service management, or with the documentation of the IT infrastructure as used for setting up information security activities. It therefore makes sense to integrate these documentations and the associated processes, for example, by incorporating the RoPA into an existing CMDB.

Publicity of the RoPA According to GDPR, the RoPA is required as an internal document but does not need to be published. It must only be made available to the competent supervisory authority upon request, for example, after a complaint or a personal data breach, when the supervisory authority wants to clarify these issues.

Although this leads some organisations to ignore this requirement since they consider it unlikely that such a request will ever come, this is a considerably risk since such a request may come quite suddenly and unexpected. Furthermore, as described above, the RoPA forms a basis for identifying which data protection measures are needed.

The RoPA in Switzerland In Switzerland, there is a publicly accessible "Register of Data Collections" where federal agencies need to document their processing of personal data. In the past, private organisations were also required to register their processing, but this was changed with the revised data protection law that came into force in 2023.

Case Study 2.5 (RoPA in Software Company) The software company did not have a RoPA when the GDPR was introduced and therefore had to create one from scratch. For this purpose, a template was first developed, consisting of a cover sheet with administrative information on the controller and the DPO, as well as a form used for describing the processing performed.

The template was supplemented by a section for each type of processing to check whether a data protection impact assessment (DPIA) is required (see Sect. 2.7.7), based on the criteria from [Art17], and a first analysis of the need for data protection measures.

In the next step, a representative of the software company and the DPO jointly documented the following processing operations according to the template:

- Personnel management
- Handling of job applications
- Business travel
- Time recording of employees
- Consultant's profiles
- Customer projects
- Web site
- Social networks
- CRM system

A corresponding RoPA was created for the legally independent branch in Austria, which was identical to the RoPA of the German parent company except for minor adjustments. In addition, it became clear that the parent company carried out some administrative processes for the branch within the framework of commissioned processing, so that in addition to a commissioned processing contract, documentation in the parent company's RoPA was also required.

2.7.6   Reporting of Personal Data Breaches

A personal data breach is a "breach of security leading to the accidental or unlawful destruction, loss, alteration, unauthorised disclosure of, or access to, personal data transmitted, stored or otherwise processed" (Art. 4 (12) GDPR). This is the case, for example, if personal data have been stolen, a device containing (in particular unencrypted) personal data has been lost or if, as in Case Study 2.4, mails were sent to external parties and the recipients are able to see the mail addresses of other recipients.

In such a case, Art. 33 GDPR requires to inform the competent supervisory authority within 72 hours, including a description of the data breach and its likely consequences, as well as the countermeasures taken or proposed. The only exceptions are cases which are "not likely to result in a risk to the rights and freedoms of natural persons" (Art. 33 GDPR (1)). In addition, in the event of a high risk for the data subjects, these data subjects must be informed (Art. 34 GDPR), which can also involve a great deal of effort if there the number of data subjects is large. Although this information of the data subjects is not required in the case of disproportionate effort, initial court rulings have set the limit for this very high.

This concept of requiring incidents to be reported to a supervisory authority is not specific to data protection. Many countries have defined similar reporting obligations for other types of security breaches, for example, in the case of disruptions to systems in critical infrastructures such as energy supply, transport or banks. There may well be overlaps here if, for example, data are stolen from a large bank, in which case it may be a security incident to be reported to the banking supervisory authority as well as a data protection breach to be reported to the competent data protection supervisory authority.

Recently, some ransomware attackers have started to make use of this requirement: if a controller refuses to pay the required ransom, the attackers not only threaten that the controller's data are encrypted and thus no longer available but also to report their attack to the competent data protection authority, in the assumption that the controller may not have reported the attack adequately and on time.

2.7.7   Data Protection Impact Assessment (DPIA)

A *data protection impact assessment* (also known as privacy impact assessment (PIA)) is required pursuant to Art. 35 GDPR if a planned processing operation "is likely to result in a high risk to the rights and freedoms of natural persons". This applies, for example, if the processing involves extensive evaluation of personal data for automated profiling and decisions or if special categories of data are processed on a large scale. In particular, if processing uses new technology such as AI, it becomes likely that this processing is considered high risk and therefore requires performing a DPIA. Even though this may make the use of new technology more difficult, one has to admit that new technology often does involve higher risks, and it therefore seems quite adequate that GDPR requires a closer look at these risks before using such technology.[22] A working group of the EU data protection authorities has published a list of nine criteria which should be used to judge whether a certain type of processing requires a DPIA [Art17]. Additionally, various supervisory authorities within the EU have published *white lists* for which type of processing a DPIA is required in any case.

The responsibility for performing a DPIA lies with the controller, but the DPO—if a DPO has been nominated—must be involved. However, in many cases, the DPO better knows how to perform a DPIA and therefore takes a leading role in the DPIA.

From the software development and IT point of view, it is important to make sure that the DPIA is performed early since the DPIA is likely to lead to requirements on the software and its use. For example, the DPIA may come to the conclusion that certain data are not necessary for the purpose of the system or they need to be protected by anonymisation, pseudonymisation or encryption, and it is much easier to address these protection measures early on in development. Even if the DPIA is performed at a later stage, support by software development and IT will usually be required since they typically know best the details of the processing performed or intended and which data are needed for which purpose.

To help with performing a DPIA, the French supervisory authority CNIL provides a *PIA tool*[23] which is recommended by many other supervisory authorities and has been translated into many European languages, sometimes by the supervisory authorities themselves.

There are various descriptions of how to perform a DPIA, for example, the norm ISO/IEC 29134[24] defines the following steps:

- *Determine whether a DPIA is necessary*: this determination is supposed be based on the relevant legislation, such as Art. 35 GDPR. However, since in practice it is rather difficult to interpret that legislation adequately, using the list in [Art17] is usually recommended. Additionally, the relevant list of applications for which a DPIA is required, as published by the respective supervisory authority, needs to be checked.
- *Preparation of the DPIA* including setup of the team, planning and provision of necessary resources.
- *Performing the DPIA* including the identification of the context and an assessment of the data protection risks involved. This step can be performed based on the abovementioned CNIL tool.

---

[22] The AI Act as passed by the EU in 2024 goes beyond the data protection risks and requires that other types of risks are considered as well for AI systems.

[23] Available from the CNIL Web site

[24] ISO/IEC 29134:2017 Information technology—Security techniques—Guidelines for privacy impact assessment.

- *Follow up* starting with the preparation of the report (e.g. using the tool). Further activities in this step include the implementation of suitable measures and a review that the identified risks have been addressed adequately by these measures.

Case Study 2.6　(Performing a DPIA in the Software Company)　As part of the preparation of the RoPA (see Case Study 2.5), the criteria from [Art17] were used to check whether the different processing operations pose a high risk. In the case of the client projects, this review concluded that this was the case, at least in some projects, and it was therefore decided to perform a DPIA, addressing the entire class of client projects within one DPIA. The DPIA was planned and facilitated by the DPO; other participants were the managing director, a project manager and an experienced project staff member.

The DPIA was conducted in the form of a one-day workshop with the following steps:

- Analysis of the processing context: here, the roles involved were identified from a data protection perspective, in this case the software company itself, the respective client and the data subjects. In particular, it had to be clarified which personal data were processed in the different client projects.
- Legal assessment: this step was primarily concerned with clarifying whether it was a case of processing on behalf of the controller or of joint controllership. Eventually, the conclusion was reached that although in the case of pure software development, the software house largely decides on the processing itself, in the case of the data analysis based on that software, the respective client decides on the "purposes and means of the processing", and these client projects are therefore a case of processing on behalf of the controller. As a first measure, it was derived from this that in future, a processing contract must be agreed for all customer projects concerned and that an internal guideline for handling personal data in customer projects was required.
- Identification and assessment of risks: here, the protection goals defined in (a previous version of) the German Standard Data Protection Model [AK22], i.e. an extended list of information security protection objectives, were used as a basis. The need for protection for the objectives "data minimisation" and "confidentiality" was assessed as high (at least for some projects) and as low or normal for the other objectives. This risk assessment also resulted in initial content for the policy to be developed.

(continued)

- Target-actual comparison: For the two protection targets rated as high, the existing threats and the measures already implemented were analysed in detail, and new measures were defined for the remaining threats.
- Feedback: In this last step, the results were summarised, the responsibility of the management for the implementation of the measures was emphasised again and subsequently the results were documented in a report.

2.7.8 Data Protection Officer

Many organisations are required to designate a data protection officer (DPO) who has the task to assist in the implementation of data protection as well as to monitor this implementation (see Art. 37, 38 GDPR). This role thus involves a combination of advisory and supervisory functions, while implementing data protection is explicitly *not* part of the DPO's tasks. On the contrary, a DPO's implementation responsibility would in many cases lead to a conflict of interest and is therefore not allowed. Persons with a management function in the organisation, such as managing directors or IT managers, are not allowed to assume the role of DPO. This distinguishes the DPO from a *data protection manager*, also called a data protection coordinator or privacy manager, whose role is not legally defined and whose tasks and area of responsibility an organisation is therefore free to define. A DPO, on the other hand, has certain legally defined tasks and works independently and free of instructions, i.e. management is not allowed to give him instructions on how to fill this role. The DPO is therefore also described as an "advocate of the data subjects", as he is supposed to represent the interests of those affected by the data processing.

In order to be able to perform the tasks set, a DPO must be appropriately qualified, i.e. he or she needs basic legal and technical expertise, where the extent of this knowledge depends on the specific company and its context. For example, the DPO of a large credit agency needs considerable expertise regarding data protection law as well as financial regulation, while the DPO of a small company that does little work with personal data will get away with far less expertise. As a minimum qualification requirement for DPOs of small companies, one usually assumes a training of several days with a final certification exam.

Duty to Name a DPO Controllers are obliged to appoint a DPO, when certain conditions are satisfied, where these conditions differ significantly in different countries, despite the GDPR. According to the GDPR, a DPO must be appointed primarily if the core activity requires extensive, regular and systematic monitoring of data subjects or consists of the extensive processing of special categories of personal data. These are relatively high requirements that do not apply to most companies, even though the wording of the provision in the GDPR is vague and leaves much room for interpretation.

In many countries, for example, Austria, this provision has not been supplemented in the national data protection law, so that the aforementioned conditions of the GDPR apply. Similarly, the UK incorporated the provision into its UK GDPR, without any major changes.

DPOs in Germany In Germany, on the other hand, an opening clause was used in order to retain the pre-GDPR regulation, according to which organisations must appoint a DPO if they usually have at least 20 persons working with personal data.[25] The term "working with personal data" is to be interpreted rather widely, so that most companies in Germany, with the exception of really small companies, fall under this regulation and are therefore obliged to appoint a DPO.

DPOs in Switzerland Switzerland did take a different approach, stating no obligation for controllers to appoint a DPO (except for federal bodies). Instead, it introduced the optional role of the data protection consultant (Art. 10 Swiss DSG), who has similar tasks and qualification requirements to those of a DPO according to GDPR, for example, regarding independence and qualification. The main legal advantage of designating a data protection consultant concerns the follow-up of DPIAs: if the controller has identified a high risk when performing the DPIA, he usually must consult the supervisory authority about the handling of this high risk (Art. 22 Swiss DSG). If, however, he has designated a data protection consultant, it is sufficient to consult with this consultant instead.

DPOs in Brazil In contrast to GDPR, the Brazilian LGPD in Art. 41 requires *all* controllers to appoint a data protection officer (DPO), not only in case of extensive processing with considerable risk involved. On the other hand, processors who only process data as a service under the responsibility of a controller do not have to appoint a DPO according to LGPD. Nevertheless, when the LGPD came into force, Brazil needed up a large number of DPOs, which is quite a challenge even considering that the LGPD describes tasks to be performed by a DPO but does not explicitly state any requirements on the qualification or the independence of a DPO as done in Art. 37 (5) GDPR.

Voluntary Designation of DPO Irrespective of the possibly existing obligation to appoint a DPO, it is advisable for many companies to voluntarily appoint a DPO, even if this is not required by law. The reason is that the implementation of all other regulations is of course necessary irrespective of whether a DPO was appointed, and it helps have a competent and independent professional, similar to how most companies have a tax advisor, even if this would not be required by law.

---

[25] Originally, this limit was set at 10, but it was increased to 20 in July 2019.

Case Study 2.7 (DPO in Software House) Since the software company in question has more than 10 (actually, more than 20, so the revised regulation does not make any difference) developers who regularly deal with personal data, the software company is obliged to appoint a DPO. However, the subsidiary in Austria, which also has more than ten developers, is not subject to the provisions of the German data protection law, but to the much more open provisions of the GDPR, and is therefore not obliged to appoint a DPO.

As there was no in-depth know-how on data protection internally, the software company decided to appoint an external DPO to take over this task. This person was then also appointed as DPO of the subsidiary in Austria, even though appointing a DPO there was not legally required. However, it was considered helpful as there was little data protection know-how available at the subsidiary, and this step also facilitated the clarification of data exchange between the parent company and the subsidiary.

In addition to the legal tasks of a DPO defined by law in Art. 39 DPA, the DPO took on the following tasks:

- Annual training of the employees on relevant data protection topics
- Maintenance of the RoPA in cooperation with the software house
- Preparation of an annual data protection report
- Support by responding to requests for information from data subjects in accordance with Art. 15 GDPR
- Support in the implementation of data protection impact assessments, as needed

2.7.9   Certification

The GDPR provides for voluntary certifications as proof that the relevant legal requirements for data protection have been met (Art. 42, 43 GDPR). Currently, there are preliminary certifications offered by some providers, but so far, no such certification is confirmed as conformant to Art. 42.

2.7.10 Supervisory Authorities

The GDPR has also strengthened the role of data protection supervisory authorities. Each EU member state has a designated national supervisory authority,[26] which must be independent, i.e. they are not themselves subject to supervision by government or any other body. Additionally, there is a supervisory authority that is responsible for supervising the EU organisations called the *European Data Protection Supervisor* (EDPS). To varying extents, all these authorities go beyond supervising and, if necessary, fining non-compliance and publish guidelines as well as tools and templates that help organisations implement data protection. To name one of the most active ones, the French CNIL publishes many information documents (in French as well as English) and also a tool for privacy impact assessments (PIA) (see Sect. 2.7.7).

In order for these different and independent supervisory authorities to arrive at similar results throughout Europe, there is a coordination body called the *European Data Protection Board* (EDPB), which is the successor to the so-called Article 29 Working Party. The EDPB regularly publishes opinions on the interpretation of the GDPR requirements.[27]

Many non-EU states have set up similar supervisory bodies, for example, the *Federal Data Protection and Publicity Authority (FDPIC)* in Switzerland, the *Information Commissioner's Office* (ICO) in the UK (which is quite active providing guiding documents on their Web site) and the *Autoridade Nacional de Proteção de Dados* (ANPD) in Brazil. Due to its different approach to data protection and privacy, the USA does not have a federal data protection supervisory authority.

The EU supervisory authorities have a great influence on the interpretation and implementation of the GDPR, but in case of doubt, it is not they but the respective competent courts that decide on the interpretation of the GDPR and any fines due. Nevertheless, it is usually highly advisable to pay attention to the statements of the supervisory authorities.

Supervisory Authority in Ireland   The Irish *Data Protection Commissioner* (DPC) has been under particular scrutiny since the introduction of the GDPR for several reasons. First, many large Internet companies (in particular Alphabet/Google and Meta/Facebook) have their EU base in Ireland and therefore fall under the jurisdiction of the DPC. As a result, the DPC was one of the direct participants in the Schrems I and II cases (see Sect. 5.4). Additionally, the DPC has been criticised for allegedly not enforcing the GDPR

---

[26] A special case to this rule is Germany, which currently has a total of 18 supervisory authorities: one authority for each of the 16 federal states, with the exception of Bavaria, where there are separate supervisory authorities for the private sector and for public authorities; additionally, there is a national supervisory authority for federal organisations.

[27] Information from and about the EDPB can be found at https://www.edpb.europa.eu/edpb_en.

adequately. This has resulted in several of its decisions being overruled by the EDPB and in one case has been the subject of a censorious EU parliament resolution.[28]

2.8   Consequences of Non-conformance

A set of rules such as the GDPR naturally needs to define consequences if these rules are not observed. One of the main reasons why GDPR is taken far more seriously than its predecessors is that these consequences, in particular the fines, are considerably higher. Possible consequences include:

- Right to compensation and liability (Art. 82 GDPR)
- Fines set by the supervisory authority (Art. 83 GDPR)
- Loss of market trust, in particular by customers
- Penalties under criminal law

Right to Compensation and Liability   As with other areas of law, an organisation that breaches data protection regulations and thereby causes damage is liable for that damage, as explicitly provided for in Art. 82 GDPR.

This does not only concern immaterial damage when, for example, information about a person becomes public, which is more or less harmful for that person. Such information can also be used, among other things, for identity fraud,[29] which can lead to direct financial loss.

Fines Imposed by the Supervisory Authority   The possible maximum fines for non-compliance with data protection requirements have been greatly increased in GDPR compared to the predecessor laws, and some consultants use this as an argument for the necessity of implementing data protection (and the commissioning of these consultants) ("If you do not have a correct data protection statement on your Web site you must expect a fine of millions of Euros . . . "). In principle, fines of up to 20 million Euros or 4% of the worldwide annual turnover, whichever is higher, are possible. However, in practice, the fined applied are proportional. Thus, for example, very high fines do not apply to a missing data protection statement on the Web site of a small software company, but to massive and/or repeated data protection violations by large companies. According to Art. 83 (1) GDPR, the fines imposed shall be "effective, proportionate and dissuasive"

---

[28] See https://www.europarl.europa.eu/doceo/document/TA-9-2021-0256_EN.pdf.

[29] Identity fraud is also mistakenly called "identity theft". However, a person's identity cannot actually be "stolen" because the person naturally still retains his or her identity. However, identity in the sense of relevant data about a person can, for example, be used for various types of fraud, such as the purchase of goods at someone else's expense.

in each individual case. In this respect, it is indeed true that fines for infringements are much higher than in the past, but apart from exceptional cases, they are far from the huge amounts sometimes claimed.

Fines show that the supervisory authorities take into account the size of the companies to set *appropriate* fines. As the overview of published fines[30] shows, fines for small companies are mostly in the three- to four- or occasionally five-digit range, with several fines in the range of hundreds of millions of Euros for large breaches caused by large Internet platforms.

Loss of Market Trust Not directly a legal consequence, but also of great practical importance, is the possible loss of trust in the market. Customers provide their data to a company, trusting that these data will be protected and processed appropriately. If it turns out that this is not the case, there is a serious risk that customers will lose trust and move to other providers. Although there is considerable difference between what customers say about the importance of the security of their data and their subsequent actions, the risk for providers is nevertheless serious, especially if they are not monopolists but have competitors.

Some providers therefore try to conceal data protection problems. If the problems do become generally known, however, the loss of customer confidence is all the greater, and the fines for neglecting the obligations to inform the supervisory authority and the data subjects according to Art. 33, 34 GDPR are correspondingly greater.

Penalties Under Criminal Law In particularly serious cases, going beyond simple non-compliance to data protection regulations, criminal sanctions (including custodial sentences) may become applicable, as, for example, defined in the German BDSG (§ 42). This applies, for example, if data are made accessible on a commercial basis to a large number of people or if data are processed without authorisation in return for payment or with the intention of enriching oneself or harming another person. Strictly speaking, most processing is performed in business for payment or with the intention of enriching oneself. This condition refers to organisations that deliberately and knowingly seek profit through non-compliance.

2.9   Data Protection, AI and the EU AI Act

There is a certain overlap between the topics of AI and data protection, in particular regarding the training of AI systems using (personal) data and the effect that decisions taken by AI systems may have on the individuals concerned. The AI Act is concerned with product safety, and one of its main goals is to protect individuals against harmful effects

---

[30] Available at https://www.enforcementtracker.com/?insights.

of AI systems while at the same time supporting innovation. Where the two regulations overlap, the AI Act points to the GDPR, but it does not set up any specific regulations concerning data protection in the context of AI.

One of the first challenges in regulating AI systems is to define what exactly is meant by such a system. In Art. 3 (1) AI Act, this is defined as follows:

> "AI system" means a machine-based system that is designed to operate with varying levels of autonomy and that may exhibit adaptiveness after deployment, and that, for explicit or implicit objectives, infers, from the input it receives, how to generate outputs such as predictions, content, recommendations, or decisions that can influence physical or virtual environments.

This is a rather complex definition, but for all practical purposes, it means that if a system looks like AI or is sold as AI, it probably is AI in the sense of the AI Act.

To achieve the stated goals, the AI Act distinguishes different types of AI systems.

- AI systems that are deceptive, implement social scoring or other unacceptable risks are prohibited (Art. 5 AI Act).
- AI systems that are considered to cause a high risk are heavily regulated to ensure that these risks are under control. The same applies to *General Purpose AI* which includes systems that are not developed for a specific purpose but can be adapted to many different purposes, such as a large-language model.
- AI systems that cause limited or acceptable risk are regulated very little. The main requirement in this case concerns transparency, for example, stating that users must be informed when interacting with an AI system such as a chatbot (Art. 50 AI Act).
- Finally, certain AI systems are exempt from the application of the AI Act, which is the case for most open-source AI systems (unless they are high-risk systems and put into service) and for systems in research and development before they are put into productive use. Additionally, AI systems for defence or national security may involve very high risks but are exempt as well.

Example 2.7 (Evaluation of Student Papers Using AI) This example continues the discussion of Example 2.3.

With the AI Act, a number of additional legal requirements need to be addressed. The first step concerns the classification of the system: Annex III of the AI Act lists a number of applications of AI systems that are considered high-risk systems, and one of these applications concerns AI systems used in the context of education to evaluate learning outcomes. However, AI systems that only perform a narrow procedural task or a preparatory task for an assessment are excluded and not considered high risk (Art. 6 (3) AI Act).

(continued)

If the desired system is considered high risk, then this leads to a number of challenging requirements on the use of the system, including the need to set up a risk management system, human supervision of the system and its use and ensuring by appropriate technical and organisational measures that the system works as intended. A fundamental rights impact assessment of the system needs to be performed, which is similar to a data protection impact assessment but with a somewhat larger scope.

It was therefore agreed to start with a limited scope of the desired system, ensuring that it does not actually perform any marking of student papers but is restricted to an evaluation of certain limited aspects such as formal aspects (correct formatting of citations, checking that all referenced sources exist, etc.).

As long as the system is only developed as a research project, additional functions such as marking papers are possible as long as they are not put into productive use. To prepare for a possible later extension, it was agreed that already the training, validation and testing of the system would have to use high-quality data, satisfying the requirements stated in Art. 10 AI Act such as "appropriate measures to detect, prevent and mitigate possible biases". This was considered necessary anyway to eventually get a system of adequate quality, independent of any legal requirements. Similar, suitable functions to keep records (Art. 12 AI Act) were to be included and a technical documentation to be created in parallel with the development.

Defined Roles According to the AI Act   The AI Act defines two main roles which are however different to those defined in GDPR. These main roles are the *provider*, who develops an AI system or commissions its development, and the *deployer*, who is responsible for the operation and use of the system.

The provider of an AI system is roughly comparable to software development which does not have a direct legal responsibility that their developed software systems actually satisfy any data protection requirements. However, if they do not do this, the software developed can hardly be deployed in production if it is not GDPR-conformant, and there is a legal responsibility towards the controller and the processor (if it exists) rather than towards the data subject. In contrast to GDPR, the AI Act defines explicit responsibilities for the provider of an AI system that is put on the market or put into service.

However, during the training of an AI system, providers may often process personal data themselves and therefore act as controllers as well.

Once an AI system has been developed, the deployer takes responsibility for the adequate use of the system and thus becomes the controller according to GDPR.

References

AE19. Agencia española de protección de datos (AEPD) and European Data Protection Supervisor (EDPS): *Introduction to the hash function as a personal data pseudonymisation technique.* Technical report, EDPS, 2019. https://www.edps.europa.eu/sites/default/files/publication/19-10-30_aepd-edps_paper_hash_final_en.pdf.

AK22. AK Technik of the Independent Data Protection Supervisory Authorities of the Federation and the Länder: *SDM. The Standard Data Protection Model. V3.0a (English version)*, November 2022. https://www.datenschutz-mv.de/static/DS/Dateien/Datenschutzmodell/SDM_V3_en.pdf.

Art14. Article 29 Data Protection Working Party: *Opinion 05/2014 on Anonymisation Techniques*, April 2014. https://ec.europa.eu/justice/article-29/documentation/opinion-recommendation/files/2014/wp216_en.pdf.

Art17. Article 29 Data Protection Working Party: *Guidelines on Data Protection Impact Assessment (DPIA) and determining whether processing is "likely to result in a high risk" for the purposes of Regulation 2016/679.* Technical Report WP 248 rev. 01, European Commission, 2017. https://ec.europa.eu/newsroom/article29/items/611236/en.

EDP21. European Data Protection Board (EDPB): *Guidelines 07/2020 on the concepts of controller and processor in the GDPR – Version 2.1*, 2021. https://www.edpb.europa.eu/our-work-tools/our-documents/guidelines/guidelines-072020-concepts-controller-and-processor-gdpr_en.

NS08. Narayanan, Arvind and Shmatikov, Vitaly: *Robust de-anonymization of large sparse datasets. In 2008 IEEE Symposium on Security and Privacy, pages* 111–125, 2008.

Pan14. Pandurangan, Vijay: *On taxis and rainbows*, June 2014. https://tech.vijayp.ca/of-taxis-and-rainbows-f6bc289679a1.

PCI11. PCI Security Standards Council: *PCI DSS Tokenization Guidelines*, 2011. https://www.pcisecuritystandards.org/documents/Tokenization_Guidelines_Info_Supplement.pdf.

PCI15. PCI Security Standards Council: *Tokenization Product Security Guidelines*, 2015. *https://www.pcisecuritystandards.org/documents/Tokenization_Product_Security_Guidelines.pdf*.

SL20. Sartor, Giovanni and Lagioia, Francesca: *The impact of the General Data Protection Regulation (GDPR) on artificial intelligence.* EPRS – European Parliamentary Research Service, 2020. https://www.europarl.europa.eu/RegData/etudes/STUD/2020/641530/EPRS_STU(2020)641530_EN.pdf.

Swe02. Sweeney, Latanya: *k-Anonymity: a model for protecting privacy.* International Journal on Uncertainty, Fuzzyness and Knowledge-based Systems, 10(5):557–570, 2002.

Data Protection Principles and Their Implementation

3

Abstract

The GDPR defines a number of data protection principles in Article 5, for example, lawfulness or data minimisation as introduced in the previous chapter. Requirements for software development, and in particular for the software to be developed, follow from these principles. The current chapter provides an overview of the interpretation of the principles of data protection in the context of software development and IT and of the resulting requirements on software and its development. For example, in order to implement the principle of memory limitation, an erasure concept and the appropriate erasure functionality are required, both for structured and unstructured data.

3.1 Lawfulness, Fairness and Transparency

In the following, the various principles of data protection according to GDPR will be explained and expressed as software requirements, as was described in Sect. 1.5.[1]

Article 5(1)(a) GDPR defines the principle of lawfulness, fair processing and transparency, with lawfulness being specified in more detail in Art. 6 (1) of the GDPR. As a rule, the responsibility for implementing this principle lies with the respective controller. However, in order for the controller to be able to fulfil this responsibility adequately, support from software development is required. Conversely, the software development group should know in advance which processing is to be based on which legal basis in order to take it into account and not to go beyond it.

---

[1] Most of these SW requirements were originally published in [Kne20].

© The Author(s), under exclusive license to Springer-Verlag GmbH, DE, part of Springer Nature 2025
R. Kneuper, *Data Protection for Software Development and IT*,
https://doi.org/10.1007/978-3-662-70639-8_3

3.1.1 Lawfulness of Processing

In Art. 6 (1) GDPR, six conditions are listed, at least one of which must be met for the processing of personal data to be lawful. If personal data of special categories are also to be processed, for example, biometric data, additionally one of the more restrictive conditions from Art. 9 GDPR must be met (see Sect. 2.5.1).

Requirement (C-01-v2: Identify legal basis)

(a) *Before performing any processing of personal data, the relevant legal basis according to Art. 6 GDPR and—if applicable—Art. 9 GDPR shall be identified and documented.*
(b) *Before starting the development of any software for processing of personal data, the relevant legal basis according to Art. 6 GDPR and—if applicable—Art. 9 GDPR should be identified and documented.*

The most appropriate place for this documentation is usually in the records of processing activities (RoPA, cf. Sect. 2.7.5). The second part is only a "should" requirement, but it is at least very helpful if the planned legal basis for the processing is known in advance, during development, and can be taken into account accordingly.

3.1.2 Consent

If processing of personal data is to be based on consent, the system under consideration must satisfy some additional requirements, following from the properties of valid consent as described in Sect. 2.5.1.

An initial challenge concerns the question of when consent is truly voluntary. For example, if access to a service depends on consent, although this is not technically necessary, then the so-called prohibition of tying introduced in Art. 7 (4) GDPR applies, which states that it is in general prohibited to tie the performance of a contract or the provision of a service to some processing of personal data that is not necessary for performing the contract or providing the service. The assessment of whether some processing is a case of non-permitted tying depends primarily on what alternatives the user has. Thus, consent is generally not considered freely given in the case of an important monopoly-type service where the data subject has little chance to refuse. Similarly in the case of employee consent, this is not normally considered freely given because of the power imbalance between employer and employee that usually exists. On the other hand, if there are equivalent alternatives, then this speaks for genuine consent. For example, a case was decided where information was available on the portal of a magazine in return for consent to use tracking cookies or alternatively as a printed edition or electronically in return for a (small) fee.[2]

Requirement (F-01-v2: Freely Given Consent) *The system shall provide users with access to data and functionality even if they did not provide consent, unless this consent is factually necessary for such access or functionality.*

An example of factually required consent is the storage of user preferences for a system. If users do not consent to such storage, then they must still be given access to the system, but of course without storage of the preferences, so that these may have to be re-entered each time the system is used.

Requirement (F-02-v2: Collecting Consent)

1. *If the processing of personal data is based on consent, the system shall collect consent before the start of processing.*
2. *Before collecting consent, the system shall inform data subjects about the purpose of the processing and the implications of giving or refusing consent.*
3. *When the consent refers to personal data of special categories, the system shall inform the users about this fact explicitly and in advance.*
4. *The system shall collect consent on an adequate level of granularity (detail).*
5. *The system shall only collect consent that is given actively and unambiguously, for example, by clicking on a check box.*

Simply continuing to surf after a corresponding cookie message is not considered as an explicit and thus valid consent, even though this has long been controversial, especially in the area of advertising. The same applies to the double function of an action, for example, the completion of a registration together with a consent in one step.

An important prerequisite of consent is that it actually comes from the relevant person, i.e. that this person is authenticated accordingly:

Requirement (F-02a: Authentication of the Person Giving Consent) *When consent for processing of personal data is collected, the system shall ensure that the person consenting is indeed the data subject whose data are to be processed.*

---

[2] Whether and under what conditions such a "Pay or OK" concept is acceptable, in particular what size of a fee is considered acceptable, is still under discussion. The approach has been heavily criticised by the privacy rights group noyb ("none of your business") which was initiated by the Austrian lawyer and privacy activist Max Schrems, well-known for the "Schrems I" and "Schrems II" judgements by the European Court of Justice ECJ discussed in Sect. 5.4.

As long as consent is given in the context of the collection of personal data, for example, when visiting a Web site, it can usually be assumed that the consent was given by the same person who entered the personal data. In such a case, identification of the person giving consent by name, etc. is usually not necessary, as long as the consent can clearly be assigned to the data, for example, via a cookie.

Some organisations try to make refusing consent on Web sites considerably more difficult than giving consent, for example, by making the "refuse" button difficult to see while the "accept" button is placed prominently and much larger or by requiring to deselect each cookie that is refused. However, the EU national data protection authorities consistently confirmed that this is not allowed, and they set several fines on controllers.[3] The following requirement summarises the adequate handling of consent and its refusal:

Requirement (F-02b: Refusal of Consent No More Difficult Than Giving Consent) *When a system asks for consent to processing of personal data, giving and refusing such consent shall be equally easy or difficult. In particular:*

- *The number of clicks needed to refuse consent shall be no larger than the number of clicks needed to give consent.*
- *The visual representation of the button (or similar mechanism) for refusing consent shall be comparable to that of the button for giving consent.*

When the processing addresses children, the following additional requirement regarding consent applies:

Requirement (F-03: Consent for Children) *If consent is to be given for a child and refers to an "offer of information society services directly to a child", the system shall ensure that consent is given by the holder of parental responsibility. (Art. 8 GDPR)*

So what is an "information society service", and when is it offered directly to children? An information society service is understood to be a service provided against payment and electronically on demand. The recipient of the service does not necessarily have to pay for the service directly, but financing via online marketing is also included here. This term primarily includes social networks. A service is offered directly to children not only if it addresses only children but also if it addresses both children and adults.[4] The only services that are excluded are those that are clearly aimed at adults only.

---

[3] Just one example from the Belgian authority: https://gdprhub.eu/index.php?title=APD/GBA_(Belgium)_-_113/2024.

[4] Additionally, there may be other relevant regulations for the protection of minors which however will not be considered any further here.

For the providers of online services, this leads to the challenge to even recognise whether certain subscribers to their services have reached the minimum age to give valid consent or whether consent actually comes from a parent or guardian if needed. The providers do not need a 100% solution, but they are expected to undertake reasonable efforts, taking into account the available technology as well as the type of data and of processing and the risk involved.

Requirement (F-04-v2: Withdrawal of Consent) *The system shall provide the data subject with the ability to withdraw consent previously given and to give consent previously refused.*

Withdrawal of consent must always be possible and shall not involve more effort than giving consent.

In order to be able to work with the consents given or refused, the relevant information must be stored in a traceable way in order to be able to answer questions such as "Who gave consent when and for what purpose? What information did the person receive beforehand?"

Requirement (F-05: Traceability of Consent) *The system shall provide the controller with the ability to trace consent given, refused or withdrawn, including information about when and in what form this was done.*

On the other hand, the data subjects need to be able to track which processing they consented to and to store these permanently in their own systems.

Requirement (F-06: Storage of Consent by Data Subject) *The system should provide the data subject with the ability to store consent given or refused beyond the individual session.*

For example, this gives visitors of a Web site the option to store consent beyond the individual session.

A challenge regarding the traceability and storage of consent is how to fulfil the principle of data minimisation, i.e. how to manage with as little additional processed information as possible. In Web applications, a common approach is to ask users for their consent when they visit a Web site, for example, to set cookies, and then to document the consent given in a cookie. Depending on context, this cookie can usually be defined as technically necessary, so that there is a legitimate interest for processing it, and no consent is required for this specific cookie.

The following requirement sounds like a matter of course but can become very complex, especially if consent is defined granularly as required and has been partially granted, partially denied, and these decisions have even changed over time. Depending on the individual case, a relatively simple cookie may be required. Again depending on context, a relatively simple solution may be to document the consents granted in a cookie and to read this cookie whenever consent is required.

Requirement (F-07-v2: Compliance to Consent) *The system shall comply to the consent given, refused or withdrawn, always based on the current status of consent.*

In order to implement this requirement, especially if the use of cookies is not possible or desired, the use of a consent management tool may be helpful. This can help track and, if necessary, prove consent and—especially if consent is defined in granular terms— also to correctly take into account the consent given or refused, for example, as an intermediate layer in a system that checks access requests for legitimacy, similar to how this is sometimes implemented to check authorisations from an information security perspective. Alternatively, ISO/IEC TS 27560 *Privacy technologies – Consent record information structure* defines a data structure that can be used to store consent as a basis for complying with it.

Conclusion: The use of consent looks simple and helpful at first glance but can become very complex in practice. As a result, consent that has been obtained has repeatedly been deemed invalid by the competent supervisory authorities.

Example 3.1 (Handling of Consent at an Insurance Company) An insurance company initially had considerable problems with the correct handling of consent, which was later uncovered by an internal data protection audit:

When the GDPR became applicable law, the company began to obtain all necessary consents when concluding an insurance contract. However, the company went too far and also asked for consent for the processing of data that were required for the performance of the contract, i.e. data that were actually processed in accordance with Art. 6 (1)(b) GDPR. As a result, personal data was sometimes collected on the basis of consent with the statement that it would not be possible to conclude a contract if consent was refused. As a result, the voluntary nature and therefore the legal validity of this consent was at least doubtful.

In addition, the audit found that although the consents were collected in a formally correct way, there was no systematic procedure for dealing with amended or withdrawn consent; instead, this was processed manually and on an ad hoc basis. Such handling of consent was not only time-consuming but also error-prone, although this was hardly visible to the outside world and was therefore had not been noticed previously.

Personal Information Management Systems (PIMS)   While asking for consent to the use of cookies gives users the choice to accept or reject such use, it also makes surfing the Web cumbersome due to many cookie banners and other pop-ups asking for consent. A technology that aims to make this easier and allow users to manage and control which (types of) cookies to accept or refuse is the personal information management system (PIMS)[5] that was extensively discussed, e.g. in [EDP16] but so far is rarely used. There are plans to include a requirement for Web sites to support PIMS in the ePrivacy Regulation, but currently, it seems completely open whether this will indeed be the case—apart from the question when the ePrivacy Regulation will actually be enacted.

Germany has included the idea of "services for consent management" in § 26 TDDDG since 2021[6] but even there, many details are left open, and this requirement has not brought any practical effects yet.

3.1.3   Other Legal Bases

The other legal bases for the processing of personal data mentioned in Art. 6 (1) GDPR (or in Art. 9 for special categories of personal data) usually lead to organisational requirements, but not to requirements on the software that go beyond C-01-v2 "Identify legal basis". The main responsibility therefore lies with the controller and not with software development or IT. For all legal bases, however, it is necessary to check and document that this legal basis actually is applicable.

In particular, in the case of legitimate interest, a comprehensive check in accordance with Art. 6 (1)(f) GDPR is needed that addresses the following questions [Art14, Sect. III.3.4]:

1. Is there a genuine legitimate interest of the controller or a third party? This includes ensuring that the intended purpose is lawful and that the planned processing is necessary to satisfy the interest.
2. What impact would the processing have on the data subjects? To what extent would it affect their rights and interests? This will, for example, depend on the kind of data processed and the way this is done.
3. Does this legitimate interest weigh higher than the interests, fundamental rights and freedoms of the data subject in the specific case?
4. What can the controller do to reduce the impact on the data subjects?

Once these questions have been answered, the result must be documented in order to show that the balancing of interests has indeed been performed adequately.

---

[5] Not to be confused with the privacy information management system (PIMS) as defined by ISO/IEC 27701; see Sect. 1.4.

[6] This law was originally called the "Telekommunikation-Telemedien-Datenschutzgesetz" (TTDSG) but was renamed as "Telekommunikation-Digitale-Dienste-Datenschutz-Gesetz" (TDDDG) in 2024.

3.1.4 Lawfulness of Processing Personal Data in Machine Learning

Machine Learning The branch of artificial intelligence based on systems "learning" from—often large collections of—data is called machine learning. The learning process extracts relevant information from the data which is turned into a model that can, for example, be used to take decisions about specific situations or to generate new results such as texts or images (generative AI). The resulting model can either be stable until a new learning process is initiated, for example, using new or additional data or applying improved learning algorithms. Alternatively, the model may be adapted continuously using data collected from running the system, such as the prompts entered to generate new results.

From a data protection point of view, the learning process usually involves processing of personal data, and data protection applies. As a result, controllers need a legal basis for machine learning (see below), as well as a legal basis for the change of purpose that is typically involved (see Sect. 3.2.5). Additionally, operating the system may process personal data, for example, when analysing data about individuals or when entering prompts to generate new results ("generate an offer for customer X ..."). The latter can be particularly problematic if the model is operated by some external provider but used by the controller who possibly transfers personal data to the external provider via the prompts used (see Sect. 5.3).

Lawfulness of Training a Machine Learning System Since in general training a machine learning system is a form of processing of personal data, a legal basis is required to do so. In practice, only the following legal bases are relevant:[7]

- *Consent*: when collecting consent, it is necessary to state the purpose of the processing to be performed, in this case machine learning. This is difficult to implement in practice since in many cases, the controller does not yet know the exact purpose pursued by machine learning at the time he collects consent for the initial processing (which in most cases has nothing to do with machine learning but serves some operational purposes). As a result, the controller will have to go back to the data subject and ask for consent to using the data for machine learning in addition to the original operational purpose. Even if the analysis has been planned in advance and can be described in concrete terms, only a few data subjects will generally give their consent to such a data analysis, and the analysis results are like to become heavily biased as a result.

  In the case of special categories of data, consent is usually the only legal basis that is applicable.

---

[7] For an extensive discussion of the effects of data protection on AI and machine learning, see [SL20].

An additional challenge is the possible withdrawal of consent at a later stage. If the data of a particular data subject have been used for training some AI model, it is often technically very difficult or even impossible to take the data out again without completely re-training the model—which would often lead to a huge effort and thus be unfeasible.

- *Contract*: in some cases, using the data for machine learning may be part of performing a contract. For this to apply, that use of personal data must be *necessary* for performing the contract, and it must be a genuine bilateral contract with adequate benefits for the data subject as well as the controller.
- *Legitimate interest*: in many cases, the controller has a legitimate interest in using the data for training a system. This, however, might conflict with the interests of the data subjects, and the controller must identify and balance the interests of both parties and document the result.

Additionally, the controller must be prepared to handle objections (according to Art. 21 GDPR) by the data subjects, which may lead to a similar situation as data subjects withdrawing their consent.

Overall, this discussion shows that setting up a legal basis for the use of personal data for machine learning is not easy, and it is important to clarify which legal basis a machine learning system is going to use before starting to train the system.

Safeguards in Machine Learning Depending on context, it is sometimes possible to reduce the processing of personal data or even perform machine learning without using personal data. Possible technologies for doing so include the anonymisation of training data (see Sect. 6.3), federated learning (see Sect. 6.4.4), generation and use of synthetic data or confidential computing (see Sect. 6.4.1). While these techniques are in many cases in conflict with the purposes of the processing, they should be used wherever possible.

3.1.5 Fair Processing

The principle of fairness is rather vague and therefore results in the following, also vague, software requirement:

Requirement (F-08 No Surprising and Unexpected Processing) *The system shall not perform any processing of personal data that is surprising or unexpected to the data subject. It shall not perform any processing that unfairly exploits the imbalance of power between controller and data subject.*

3.1.6   Transparency

The main purpose of transparency is to ensure that data subjects know which data about them are processed and how this is done. This principle is supported by various rights of data subjects regarding information and access (which will be discussed in Sect. 4.1) that help turn it into specific (software) requirements.

Transparency of AI Applications   The need for transparency is a particular challenge for the use of artificial intelligence since in many AI applications, it is difficult to understand why a certain result was provided. When the AI system is used to take decisions regarding individuals (including profiling), an explanation of the logic used is however explicitly required.[8] Even if the processing is not about making decisions concerning individuals, it must be for a certain purpose, and the controller must be able to argue that the processing does indeed support that purpose. If one is not able to even explain how the used algorithms work, this seems hardly possible.

Apart from data protection which is of course the main area of law considered here, there are a number of other areas of law that also can require that decisions made with AI must be explained. For example, laws on equality require that decisions are taken without bias due to age, sex, race, etc. To ensure this and to be able to prove it in court, one must be able to explain how the AI system came to a certain decision. The main reason for such requirements is that AI systems generally learn from previous decisions and behaviours. If these contain any bias or discrimination, there is a high risk that the AI system will "learn" this bias and discrimination and perpetuate and strengthen it. Even worse, adversaries sometimes manage to "teach" bias to AI systems if these systems "learn" from user input in addition to the initial training.

Requirements like these, both from a legal and an ethical point of view, are currently addressed by research on *explainable AI (XAI)*, which tries to adapt AI methods such that they provide an explanation with the decisions and recommendations they make. Although this is an area under development and XAI methods are (at least currently) less powerful than general AI methods, it is important to ensure that one is able to explain one's decisions and recommendations that have an impact on individuals (or, going beyond data protection, elsewhere).

3.1.7   Lawfulness and Transparency in the Case of Web Sites and Online Marketing

Online marketing is an economically important topic that is very challenging from a data protection perspective. There are major differences of opinion between the parties involved as to the extent to which the various tracking mechanisms are permitted or

---

[8] Art. 13 (2)(f), Art. 14 (2)(g), Art. 15 (1)(h) GDPR. See [ICO22b] for an extensive discussion of the need for explaining decisions made with AI.

not, to what extent they should be permitted and how much transparency or information for the data subjects is appropriate. As described in Sect. 1.2.2, these differences of opinion have also led to the situation that the ePrivacy Regulation, originally intended to become applicable in parallel with the GDPR in 2018, is still under discussion in 2024. The following description is primarily based on the ePrivacy Directive and the current published opinions of supervisory authorities, largely supported by the legal literature, but in the knowledge that online marketing as currently practised is quite different in many respects without any resulting consequences. However, decisions by high courts can lead to a reassessment at any time. The following description focuses on the underlying concepts and distinctions while briefly summarising the current legal assessment. When applying tracking mechanisms in practice, one should analyse the current legal situation thoroughly and seek legal advice.

When looking at Web sites and their processing of personal data, three groups of functions can be distinguished:

- Visitor data may be processed for *technical reasons* or for reasons of *information security*.
- *Web analytics* has a certain overlap with online marketing but has a fundamentally different focus, as it is primarily concerned with the question of how visitors move around a Web site, where they come from, which links they click on, etc. The main aim is usually to optimise the Web site so that visitors stay there for as long as possible and visit many individual pages, so that a lot of online advertising can be shown to them.
- *Online marketing* is normally based on a comprehensive collection of data about the data subjects, primarily through various forms of tracking, in order to be able to target advertising as precisely as possible. This leads to an inherent conflict of interests with data protection, which can hardly be resolved, but where a compromise must be found at a political and legal level.

In the following, these three groups of functions as well as their legality and transparency will be discussed in more detail. As a basis for this, however, some basic concept about http(s) and cookies need to be introduced.

http The http protocol (and its encrypted variant https) generally used on the Web is stateless, which means that no information about previous interactions is remembered in the state of a session. This implies that, without additional tools, a Web server that processes a request from a client cannot relate this to any previous requests from the same client. While this is not necessary for simple informational Web sites, more complex functionalities, such as a shopping basket at an online retail site, need information about what happened in previous steps. There are several common techniques for "remembering" such data and combining different interactions that belong together: the http referer[9]

---

[9] This is actually a typo in the standard document—the correct spelling is "referrer".

field is optional but usually filled and contains the URL of the previous page the user came from. This can be used to establish the connection between several consecutive requests and is mainly useful for Web analytics. A second technique is to include corresponding information in the query part of the URL to get a call in the format `https://www.example.com/directory?session=123`.

Cookies The third and probably most widely used technique is the use of cookies, i.e. small texts that are stored in the browser and whose content can then be sent along with further interactions. A distinction is made between two types of cookies according to their lifespan: *session cookies* are valid for one session and are deleted when the browser is closed. The lifespan of *persistent cookies*, on the other hand, is defined by the server, often as unlimited. Unless the users delete these persistent cookies themselves, they remain in the browser permanently and allow the server to recognise users every time they visit the server.

While in the past, there was discussion is whether the use of persistent cookies involves *pseudonymous* or *anonymous* data, there is now widespread agreement that persistent cookies are used to recognise visitors to a Web site and thus identify them, implying that the cookies are pseudonyms and therefore the stored data are still personal data. The situation is different with session cookies, which are deleted after each session and therefore preserve the anonymity of visitors.

Based on the type of use, the following types of cookies can be distinguished, even though this distinction is not clear-cut:

- Necessary cookies are session cookies that are required for technical reasons for the Web site, for example, to save the selected language or a shopping basket.
- Functional cookies support the functionality of the Web site, for example, personalisation or login.
- Performance cookies are used to track the behaviour of users on the Web site in order to improve the information and services provided (Web analytics).
- Advertising or tracking cookies are also used to track user behaviour, but in this case with the purpose of collecting information about the user and displaying advertising that is targeted at the user.
- Third-party cookies are set by a third party, i.e. not by the operator of the Web site itself. These are usually also tracking cookies, but they can track the behaviour of users across different Web sites. However, today, many browsers disallow third-party cookies, at least by default.

User Tracking for Technical Reasons or to Support Information Security From a data protection perspective, this is the simplest case. For example, a Web server requires the IP address as well as information about the hardware used and the visitor's browser in order to be able to deliver its content correctly. After the content has been delivered to the server, these data are no longer required (for this purpose) and must be deleted unless they are used for another legitimate purpose.

Similarly, a cookie may be needed to store information about the consent given or refused by the data subject.

Another possible purpose is the detection of attacks on the provider's IT. For this purpose, data may be collected, stored and analysed to a limited extent, but as long as there is no attack, these data may only be stored for a short period of time.

In all these cases, the legitimate interest of the provider can usually serve as an adequate legal basis for processing, and this is usually largely unproblematic as long as the data are deleted again quickly. For the sake of transparency, it is important that the relevant information on processing and the data retention period is stated in the privacy policy of the Web site.

Web Analytics In the simplest case, processing for technical reasons or to support information security is based on logging the page views including the IP address of the user device. All requests from the same IP address within a short period of time are likely to originate from the same person and therefore belong together. (There may be exceptions when using proxies.) This way, it is possible to track the path visitors take on the Web site, how long they stay, etc. This information can be very helpful for the design of the Web site, but it contains personal data that are not actually needed for the purpose and therefore should not be collected in the first place.

Anonymisation of IP Addresses Fortunately, there is a middle way by shortening (anonymising) the IP addresses, i.e. by storing only part of the IP address. This way, there is still enough information to track the path of visitors on the Web site, but not enough to identify the visitors. Chapter 6.3.2 takes a closer look at this approach to anonymising data, in particular the question of how much the IP addresses need to be shortened.

A technical difficulty when anonymising IP addresses is that you usually cannot adapt the relevant HTML code for IP anonymisation yourself if you work with a content management system such as WordPress. In this case, you need an additional plugin (or a similar tool), and there are various such plugins available on the market.

Online Marketing Including User Tracking Online marketing tries to generate precise profiles of potential customers in order to be able to place the most targeted advertising possible. This is often used to finance "free" services (messenger or email services, search engines, storage space, information and news, etc.), which are not paid for in money but in personal data. With a strict interpretation of data protection, there is a serious risk that such business models based on online marketing will no longer remain viable. Of course, no provider can provide information or other services to the general public on a permanent basis if the costs incurred are not offset by some kind of revenue, be it through direct payments from the customer, online marketing or possibly some other model.

This situation, with conflicting interests of the parties involved, is sometimes summarised as "either you pay for the product, or you are the product". This is also referred to as the *privacy paradox*, because many data subjects—when asked—attach great importance to the privacy of their data. On the other hand, they are very generous with their data in order to use apparently free services, receive discounts or personalise services for their own convenience.

This use of tracking to place targeted advertising is usually based on third-party cookies set by an advertising platform, which collects and collates data about visitors across different Web sites, leading to detailed profiles of the visitors to the Web sites over time.

Tracking visitors for usage-based marketing is an intrusion into the privacy of those affected, as a transfer of the concept to the analogue world shows. Just imagine that when you visit a shopping centre, the centre's employees constantly follow you and note down which products you look at or buy and, based on this, make recommendations as to which products to buy next [Dat15, p. 8].

Lawfulness of User Tracking for Online Marketing The only possible legal bases for tracking Web site visitors using cookies are consent and legitimate interest, in special cases also the performance of a contract, although opinions differ as to when legitimate interest may be applicable and when consent is required. In a decision that gained a lot of publicity,[10] the ECJ stated that only cookies necessary for the operation of the Web site may be set without consent on the basis of a legitimate interest, which means that the discussion has now shifted to the question of which cookies fall under this definition.

Consent to User Tracking The planet49 judgement also made clear that consent must be *active* (opt-in) and an opt-out solution is not sufficient since it is not a sufficiently clear statement of the user's intent.

One approach to introducing a globally standardised and simple opt-out rule is the *do-not-track* mechanism, a parameter set by the user, which was intended as a W3C standard and is supported in many browsers. However, since many online marketing companies refused to honour this parameter, standardisation efforts were discontinued in 2018.

There are a few more important points to consider when using cookies, even though you will always find Web sites that do not fulfil these obvious requirements:

- If consent is used as the legal basis, cookies may only be set *after* the corresponding consent has been given.
- A cookie banner *without the option to (de-)select* cookies may serve to inform visitors, but certainly does not constitute valid consent.
- It is also important that a cookie banner does not cover the links to the privacy policy or to the legal notice—these must always be accessible with one click.

---

[10] This judgement is known as the planet49 judgement.

Transparency in Online Marketing The technical environment makes transparency diffi-cult if not impossible to achieve in usage-based online marketing, even with the goodwill of all involved. Due to the complexity and changing nature of advertising networks, even most of those involved are unable to understand and describe the network structure in detail. Informing Web site visitors about the data collected and their disclosure to third parties, in this case the participants in the advertising network, is primarily the responsibility of the operator of the Web site who however does not usually possess this information. Only rather abstract information about the cookies and other tracking mechanisms used by advertisers is possible, so that the visitor can at least roughly estimate what is happening.

Another important limitation of transparency: if visitors to a Web site try to obtain information from the participants in the advertising network about the data stored about them, it is difficult to assign the data collected to the person concerned, as the data usually do not include the name. The Web site visitor however does not usually know the ID actually used and can only occasionally read it from a cookie if this has not already been deleted.

The IAB, an international advertising industry association, has developed an *IAB Transparency & Consent Framework* as a tool for implementing the requirements of the GDPR in online marketing.[11] This framework is also supported by Google but contains some questionable decisions from a data protection perspective (see, e.g. [MSB20]).

Embedding Third-Party Services The embedding or use of information from other services (e.g. videos, fonts, social media buttons) also usually leads to a transfer of the IP address of the visitor to the Web site and thus to a transfer of personal data, for which a legal basis, usually consent, and appropriate information of the visitor are required. There are various tools available in the Internet that help ensure that such embedded services are only called if the user has consented to this.[12]

Tools for User Tracking in Online Marketing Several tools are available for user tracking that are widely used, in particular *Google Analytics*. Over time, there have been a number of complaints about Google Analytics, in particular from the organisation noyb, and several decisions by different supervisory authorities. The main problems addressed were:

- Data transfer to US: when users visit a Web site that uses Google Analytics, then this information is transferred to Google and their US base. This was a major problem while there was no adequacy decision for the USA (cf. Sect. 5.4) but currently is not.

---

[11] See https://iabeurope.eu/transparency-consent-framework/.

[12] For example, the *c't Shariff*; see https://github.com/heiseonline/shariff.

- Commissioned processing: since Google processes the personal data of Web site visitors, it acts as a commissioned processor on behalf of the Web site provider. The controller of the Web site must therefore set up a processing agreement or contract with Google beforehand. Even then, it is often argued that Google also uses these data for its own purposes and therefore needs its own legal basis for the processing.
- Inadequate information and access for visitors to Web sites: providing such information is the responsibility of the providers of the Web sites but is difficult to perform adequately since they have little knowledge about what Google does with these data, even though this is supposed to be described in detail in the processing agreement.
- Legal basis: as explained above, only consent (which will often be refused) is acceptable as a legal basis for the use of Google Analytics.

Compliant Usage of Matomo In principle, the same statements apply to the Matomo tool, but as the data protection requirements have already been taken more into account in the design of the tool, implementation is simpler. For example, Matomo offers the option of installing the tool on one's own server instead of that of the software provider, so that in this case, there is no commissioned processing. In addition, Matomo can also be operated without the use of tracking cookies, and in this case, the consent of visitors to the Web site is not required, but the legitimate interest is sufficient as a legal basis.

Alternative Tracking Technologies Since users can easily delete cookies set in their browser, other tracking mechanisms have been developed, such as *super cookies*, where the identifying information is stored or hidden elsewhere in the system. Other mechanisms are based on tracking pixels (one-pixel graphics that are not visible to users and whose retrieval from the server indicates that the corresponding page has been read) or on browser or device fingerprinting.

Browser Fingerprinting A form of user tracking that, for a user, is almost impossible to recognise or prevent is (browser) fingerprinting. When sending a request to a Web server, a browser includes various information about itself and the device it runs on, such as screen size and resolution, browser software and version, operating system, etc. In combination, this information in many cases uniquely identifies the browser and thus the user [Eck10].[13]

Obviously, transparency is required independent of the technology used, and providers of Web sites that use fingerprinting are required, as controllers, to inform the visitors of the Web site about this fact, even though non-compliance in such a case is almost impossible to recognise.

---

[13] There are some Internet services that allow users to check whether their "fingerprint" is indeed unique, e.g. https://amiunique.org/ and https://coveryourtracks.eff.org/.

It is clear that browser fingerprinting, where the data subjects cannot even recognise that their data are being collected, is only permitted with consent. However, since the main purpose of these mechanisms is precisely to recognise data subjects who do not want to be recognised, it is practically useless if the requirements of the GDPR are met.

3.2   Purpose Limitation

Software and software development have only limited influence with regard to the definition of the purposes and to purpose limitation. However, IT operations must ensure that the relevant documentation is available. In the context of software development and IT, the principle of purpose limitation leads to some particular challenges, such as the use of original data for software testing, which will therefore be considered in more detail below.

3.2.1   Requirements

The principle of purpose limitation in Art. 5 (1)(b) requires that personal data are only collected for specified, explicit and legitimate purposes. Further processing of the data for a new purpose is only allowed if this new purpose is compatible with the original purpose.[14] Compatibility is assumed to hold if the further processing is performed "for archiving purposes in the public interest, scientific or historical research purposes or statistical purposes", provided that appropriate safeguards are in place to protect the data subjects. If the further processing is based on consent or on a relevant law, then evaluating purpose compatibility is not required. For all other cases, Art. 6 (4) defines a set of criteria to evaluate whether the new purpose is compatible with the original purpose. These criteria actually go beyond an assessment of compatibility and put the focus on the expectations of the data subjects and the risks involved for these data subjects.

The resulting software requirements can be expressed as follows, once again noting that they do not actually refer to the software as such but to the conditions under which the software may be operated later on. Nevertheless, this defined purpose should be available to the development organisation during the development of the system so that it can be taken into account accordingly in development. If necessary, the development organisation should also draw attention to this if a change in the purpose arises during development, which must then be dealt with accordingly by the controller.

---

[14] To be exact, the GDPR actually states that the purpose of further processing may *not be incompatible* with the original purpose.

Requirement (C-02-v2: Document Purpose) *Before any personal data are collected or otherwise processed by the system, the controller shall define and document the purposes to be achieved.*

Requirement (C-03-v2: Purpose Limitation) *If the system processes any data for a different purpose than the one initially defined, the controller shall ensure that this processing is analysed and justified, and it is documented why the new purpose is considered consistent with the old one.*

An open issue concerns the question whether any processing for a new but compatible purpose needs a legal basis of its own or whether it can be based on the legal basis of the original processing. Put differently, the question is whether a positive assessment of purpose compatibility only confirms that the principle of purpose limitation is satisfied or whether this also confirms that the principle of lawfulness is satisfied. Currently, this is an open question, with many authors arguing for (e.g. [Alb19, Rn. 12f], [ICO22a]) and against (e.g. [FHS18, p. 37], [Sha20, p. 149]) the need for an additional legal basis in this case. However, the arguments for that need seem more convincing, and such need will therefore be assumed in the following discussion. A final decision will only be available once this question has been decided by the European Court of Justice.

Coming back to the case of an online retailer, a common objective is to perform various analyses on the customer data collected. To a very limited extent, this may be done based on the condition of legitimate interest, but beyond that, consent by the customer is usually needed. In many cases, it will be easier and more efficient to work with anonymised data instead.

3.2.2   Checklist for Purpose Changes

Since the different conditions that (dis-)allow purpose changes are rather complex, Table 3.1 provides an overview of the relevant conditions and the consequences if they are satisfied or not satisfied. The use of this checklist is explained below, with the example of using production data in software test.

3.2.3   Legal Basis for Further Processing After Purpose Change

It is important to note that the checklist above only concerns the question whether a purpose change is legitimate and the principle of purpose limitation is satisfied. Assuming that this is the case, it is an open question whether this is sufficient to allow the further processing of personal data for a new purpose or whether additionally the further processing needs its own legal basis. Both views can be found in the relevant literature, but the arguments in favour of the need of a new legal basis seem stronger and are also

Table 3.1 Checklist for purpose changes

	Condition	Condition satisfied	Condition not satisfied
1.	Genuine change of purpose?	Continue with 2.	Purpose limitation not relevant
2.	Original processing based on consent?	Further processing only based on consent (continue with 5.) or vital interests (continue with 7.)	Continue with 3.
3.	Further processing for privileged purposes as defined in Art. 5 (1)(b) (archiving etc.)?	Safeguards according to Art. 89 (1) required; continue with 4.	continue with 5.
4.	Safeguards according to Art. 89 (1) available?	Purpose compatibility assumed; legal basis required	Continue with 5.
5.	Further processing based on consent?	Purpose compatibility not required according to Art. 6 (4); legal basis consent available	Continue with 6.; *special case*: original processing based on consent → further processing not allowed
6.	Further processing based on a qualified law according to Art. 6 (4)?	Purpose compatibility not required according to Art. 6 (4); legal basis required for further processing	Continue with 7.
7.	Purpose compatibility according to the criteria in Art. 6 (4)?	Purposes compatible; legal basis for further processing required	Further processing not allowed (except starting with new collection of data)

confirmed by the leader of the negotiations between the European Parliament and the Council of Ministers on the adoption of the GDPR, Jan Philipp Albrecht [Alb19, para. 12–14].

In this book, it will therefore be assumed that further processing of personal data for a changed purpose requires that both the principle of purpose limitation is satisfied, as presented in Table 3.1 *and* a new legal basis according to Art. 6 (1) GDPR.

3.2.4 Software Test Using Production Data

The use of production data for software testing is a frequent point of conflict that arises in software development with regard to purpose limitation. The challenge consists in the fact that the production data were usually collected for the relevant business processes, but not for the test, and the information of the data subjects about the processing and, if applicable, their consent does not include the use of the data for testing software. In addition, the development organisation that wants to carry out the test may be legally separate from the controller organisation so that the following questions must be clarified if a software test with production data is desired:

- Is the use of personal data from productive use for software testing permitted? On what legal basis?
- To what extent must the data subjects be informed about the use of their data for software testing?
- Is this a case of commissioned processing on behalf of a controller?

The following discussion will address the first of these questions.

Is the Use of Personal Data from Productive Use for Software Testing Permitted?
The prerequisite for such use being considered at all is that the production data are only used for tests that are not possible or at least not meaningful without the production data. The early test phases must have been completed, and the problems identified must have been largely resolved. A test with production data may only be necessary as part of the system test, for example, to ensure that all special cases that occur in practice have been taken into account during a data migration or in the case of complex bug fixes. Even then, it must be ensured that access to the personal used in the test is handled restrictively and that only those developers or testers who really need this access for their work have access to it for as long as they need it.

If these basic requirements are met, the checklist introduced in Table 3.1 can be used to decide whether the test is allowed.

1. Genuine Change of Purpose? Before going into the details of deciding whether there is a legal basis for a change of purpose, one should check that indeed a change of purpose is involved. This will usually be the case, but occasionally, the use for testing may already have been included in the original definition and communication of the processing purpose or the original consent.

2. Original Processing Based on Consent? If the original processing was based on consent, it would be unfair to the data subject (and thus not satisfy the principle of fairness) to further process the data for a different purpose without new consent. The only exception is if the processing is necessary in order to protect the vital interests of the data subject (or some other natural person), but this can hardly apply in the case of software testing.

In summary: if the original processing was based on consent, using the personal data for testing is only possible with new consent of the data subjects.

3. Further Processing for Privileged Purposes as Defined in Art. 5 (1)(b)? The privileged purpose as defined in Art. 5 (1)(b) are archiving purposes in the public interest, scientific or historical research purposes or statistical purposes. None of these are applicable in the case of software testing.

4. Safeguards According to Art. 89 (1) Available? This check item is not relevant since it only applies in the case of privileged purposes as discussed in check item 3. If processing is performed to one of those privileged purposes, there is the additional requirement that adequate safeguards must be available to ensure the data are not misused.

5. Further Processing Based on Consent? Independent of the legal basis for the original processing, software testing using production data is allowed if the data subjects consent to it.

The difficulty with this solution is that asking the data subjects for consent to using their data for software testing involves a lot of effort, while it is unlikely to be successful on a large scale. Typically, many data subjects will not reply, for whatever reason, or they will refuse consenting to this use of their data. Additionally, as usual with consent, such consent may be revoked at any time, in which case the relevant test data would have to be removed from the set of test data.

6. Further Processing Based on a Qualified Law According to Art. 6 (4)? Art. 6 (4) GDPR defines that further processing for a new purpose is allowed if it is based on a law (which must satisfy certain additional conditions, therefore a "qualified" law).

While in general software testing is not required by law, there are certain contexts where this is the case, for example, in finance were banks and insurance companies must prove to the supervisory authorities that their systems have been adequately tested (cf. Example 3.2).

In such cases, the use of production data for software testing may be based on a (qualified) law and therefore be legally allowed. Nevertheless, in order to satisfy the transparency principle, the data subjects must be informed about this use of their data, which may still involve considerable effort for the controller.

In many situations, the law on which the further processing is based will also provide a legal basis. However, this is not necessarily the case since it may allow the purpose change without requiring it, in which case Art. 6 (1)(c) does not apply.

7. Purpose Compatibility According to the Criteria in Art. 6 (4)? If the lawfulness of processing the personal data for the new purpose has not been decided according to any of the previous check items, then the compatibility of the new purpose with the original purpose needs to be ascertained.[15] Although purpose compatibility is just one out of the seven check items listed, this compatibility check is actually the most important and most challenging one.

For that check, Art. 6 (4) defines a set of five criteria to be considered. These address the relationship between the original and the new purpose, the context in which the data were collected, the kind of data, possible consequences for the data subjects and the existence of appropriate safeguards. Although GDPR here talks about "purpose compatibility", a

---

[15] The purpose limitation principle in Art. 5 (1)(b) actually only requires that the purposes are *not incompatible*, while Art. 6 (4) defines criteria for *ascertaining compatibility*.

closer look shows that this check is mainly concerned with a balancing of interest, and only the first two actually refer to the purposes and their compatibility at all.

Applying these criteria to the use of production data for software testing, the first two criteria emphasise that there must be a clear relationship between the system to be tested and the system which is used for the initial processing of the data. If the system to be tested is a new version or the successor of the current system, then this is an indicator of purpose compatibility. If, on the other hand, the tested system is something completely new or independent, then purpose compatibility is probably not given. As the third criterion shows, a change of purpose may also concern personal data that are particularly sensitive, such as health data, but this is an indicator that processing the data for a new purpose should not be done unless really necessary. The consequences of using the data for testing are likely to be very low provided that adequate security measures (safeguards) are taken to ensure that the data do not leave the testing environment and are only accessible to those developers and testers who really need that access for testing.

If, on the other hand, the evaluation comes to the conclusion that the purposes are not compatible, then the further processing for software testing is not allowed. The only way to get around that would be to collect the same data again from scratch. In this case, the principle of purpose limitation does not apply, but the effort involved will make this solution infeasible in most practical cases.

Overall, depending on context purpose compatibility may or may not be given when planning to use the data for software testing. Again, it is important to note that even if the purposes are considered compatible and the principle of purpose limitation satisfied, it is still required to inform the data subjects about this further processing. Additionally, a legal basis for the further processing is still required, but since the criteria require a similar balancing of interests as the legal basis of legitimate interest, this will often be a suitable legal basis when the purposes are considered compatible.

In addition to the possible use of production data, there are of course other data protection issues that need to be considered during software tests (see Sect. 6.6.4).

Example 3.2 (Migration Testing Using Customer Data at an Insurance Company) An insurance company had updated its core IT system, which now required the migration of customer data to the new system. Of course, it was important that all data were transferred correctly, and the insurance company had to be able to prove this to the supervisory authority (in this case the financial services authority, not the data protection authority).

While artificial test data were used for the functional test of the new system, the migration testing was to be carried out on the basis of original production data. The only possible legal basis under these circumstances was the legitimate interest of the insurance company. The required balancing of interests resulted in the conclusion

(continued)

that the insurance company had considerable interest in a thorough migration test and that a test with anonymised or even pseudonymised data would lead to considerable risks with regard to the quality of the test. At the same time, the risk for those affected was minimised by handling access to the data very restrictively— only those employees who also have access to the production environment were allowed access to the production data in the migration test environment.

3.2.5 Changing Purpose: Data Analysis, Big Data and Machine Learning

Analysing personal data or using them for machine learning in general involves a change of purpose, as the data were initially collected for some operational purpose, and this was communicated to the data subjects. As a result, processing of personal data for these purposes needs a legal basis for the change of purpose (according to Table 3.1) in addition to the legal basis for the processing as discussed in Sect. 3.1.4.

Starting from a different legal background, the US FTC has come to a similar conclusion, warning that companies have to comply to their commitments about (not) processing personal data and may not quietly change their terms of service to allow processing for purposes such as data analysis and machine learning.[16]

Similarly, the Brazilian data protection agency decided in 2024 that posts from social networks may not be used to train AI models.[17]

Legal Basis for Change of Purpose Assuming that there is a legal basis for processing the personal data for purposes of data analysis, big data or machine learning, a legal basis for the change of purpose is needed, using the check items in Table 3.1:

- When using personal data for data analysis, etc, there is usually a genuine change of purpose involved.
- If the original processing was based on consent, then using these personal data for data analysis, etc. must also be based on consent, while performance of a contract or legitimate interest (see Sect. 3.1.4) is not applicable.

---

[16] See https://www.ftc.gov/policy/advocacy-research/tech-at-ftc/2024/01/ai-companies-uphold-your-privacy-confidentiality-commitments and https://www.ftc.gov/policy/advocacy-research/tech-at-ftc/2024/02/ai-other-companies-quietly-changing-your-terms-service-could-be-unfair-or-deceptive.

[17] See https://www.gov.br/anpd/pt-br/assuntos/noticias/anpd-determina-suspensao-cautelar-do-tratamento-de-dados-pessoais-para-treinamento-da-ia-da-meta (in Portuguese).

- Data analysis, etc. is often performed for privileged purposes such as scientific research or statistics. In this case, adequate safeguards are needed to protect "the rights and freedoms of the data subject". For example, access to personal data should be restricted, only those data that are genuinely necessary for data analysis should be stored and where possible, data should be pseudonymised. (Of course, anonymising the data would be even better since in this case, they are no longer personal data.)

  If these safeguards are available, then purpose compatibility is assumed. There is still the need for a legal basis for data analysis, which is likely to be given by legitimate interest.
- Alternatively, the data subject may consent to the analysis of the data or their use for machine learning, or such further processing may be required by law. In either case, this would form a legal basis for both the purpose change and the further processing.
- If none of the above applies, then purpose compatibility must be checked according to the criteria given in Art. 6 (4) GDPR. Depending on the specific situation, this may or may not lead to allowing the change of purpose.

This applies to the personal data used for the initial training but also to the training data collected during operating the system such as prompts entered by users.

3.3   Data Minimisation

According to the principle of data minimisation, personal data must be "adequate, relevant and limited to what is necessary in relation to the purposes for which they are processed" (Art. 5 (1)(c) GDPR). Therefore, only those data may be collected and processed that are necessary for the defined purpose of processing, while storing data "just in case" is not allowed. This can be quite a challenge in the context of big data and data science where one often collects data to find out later what information may be gained from them.

As a result, the task of software development is to limit the amount of personal data collected to the minimum and not to collect data because it might be used later. For example, no data on individual persons should be collected if you actually only need aggregated information such as average or maximum values. Instead, you should check in advance which data are really needed for the planned functionality and limit yourself to these. Apart from these associated restrictions, this principle has the benefit of saving effort for the collection and processing of data that is not actually required.

The principle of data minimisation leads to the following software requirement:

Requirement (C-04 Data Minimisation) *The system may only collect and process data that are necessary for the defined and documented purpose. This includes each individual data attribute as well as the overall data set.*

Depending on context, it may be useful to convert personal data into anonymous or at least pseudonymous data in order to protect them against unauthorised usage:

Requirement (C-05 Data Anonymisation and Pseudonymisation) *The system should store data in anonymised or at least pseudonymised format where this is possible without limitation for the intended purpose.*

Pseudonymous data are still personal data and need to be protected accordingly, but pseudonymisation forms part of this protection since access to the data is restricted considerably. As for anonymous data, these are no longer considered as personal data, but protecting the data against unauthorised access still is recommended where possible since experience shows that anonymisation often can be broken.

Case Study 3.1 (Data Minimisation at the Online Retailer) There are several topics regarding data minimisation that need to be considered by the online retailer. Three of them will be discussed here:

Processing of payments via a service provider: Customer payments are processed via various service providers. To ensure that each party involved only receives the personal data it needs, the following procedure is used: The seller only sends information about the amount to be paid to the service provider, without any information about what the payment is for. The service provider, in turn, only confirms whether this payment will be made, regardless of what kind of account is used and whether it is well filled or the payment requires an overdraft facility.

Customer requests via a contact page on the Web site: The online retailer offers to answer customer questions via a contact page. To answer any such questions, it is usually sufficient to know either the email address or the telephone number, and collecting any personal data beyond that, such as name or postal address, must therefore at least be optional, stating clearly what these data are used for, or better not done at all.

Web analytics: In order to analyse the movement of visitors to the Web site of the online retailer (Web analytics, as opposed to user tracking), the IP addresses of visitors are usually anonymised by deleting part of them. This is still sufficient to identify subsequent movements by the same visitor, but does not allow the identification of visitors.

3.4   Accuracy

The principle of accuracy (Art. 5 (1)(d) GDPR) may be summarised as follows:

Requirement (Q-01 Accuracy) *Data processed and stored shall be accurate and, where relevant, kept up to date.*

This implies the following additional requirements:

Requirement (F-09 Rectifying Data) *The system shall provide the controller with the ability to rectify or update data.*

Requirement (F-10 Consistency Check) *The system should check input data for consistency to recognise and prevent invalid input.*

The latter requirement is not legally required but helps implement requirement Q-01. An approach to implement F-10 is the use of drop-down lists where possible rather than allowing free text.

In most cases, it is in the controller's own interest to ensure the accuracy of the data. The definition as a legal requirement is intended to ensure that the controller takes care of the accuracy and timeliness of the data even if they themselves have little or no interest in it.

> **Case Study 3.2 (Correctness of Customer Data at the Online Retailer)** Customer data, for which accuracy is particularly important from a customer and therefore data protection perspective, include information such as interests and preferences, but especially information about the payment of invoices. Incorrect information can lead to inappropriate regulations on payment methods offered, which may even be passed on to a credit agency and thus also lead to restrictions for other providers.

Accuracy and Machine Learning The principle of accuracy is independent of the technology and applies to information systems based on machine learning. However, since machine learning is based on probabilistic reasoning, it cannot ensure accuracy of the processing results.

The problems involved become very obvious in a complaint by the *noyb* group about OpenAI and its tool ChatGPT:[18] when asked about the birthdate of Max Schrems, ChatGPT gives an incorrect answer. noyb asked OpenAI to correct this, but OpenAI refused, arguing that this is not technically possible, and factual accuracy cannot currently be ensured in *large language models* such as those used in ChatGPT. Even if OpenAI were able to correct or delete this incorrect statement from their large language model now, there could be no guarantee that the system would not re-invent the data when asked again.

This is an aspect of machine learning that is important both from the viewpoint of data protection law and from the viewpoint of users of such systems: systems based on machine learning try to derive new information from their training data, and there is no way to prevent them inventing incorrect information, including incorrect personal data, in this process. There are various approaches to reduce this problem, including post-processing and filtering of generated results, techniques for bias detection and prevention and explainable AI (XAI), but none of them is able to guarantee accuracy of the learned model or the contents generated.

3.5 Storage Limitation

The principle of storage limitation (Art. 5 (1)(e) GDPR) extends data minimisation by a temporal view and states that personal data may only be stored as long as they are needed for their defined purpose. After that, they must be deleted or at least turned into anonymous data.

The following description first looks at the implementation of this principle in software development and IT, in particular its translation into software requirements. Storage limitation implies that data must be deleted after a certain period of time. In order to tackle this systematically, it usually makes sense to create a corresponding erasure concept, and this task will therefore be considered in Sect. 3.5.2. In Sect. 3.5.3, we look at particular challenge for storage limitation, namely, the blockchain.

3.5.1 Implementation of Storage Limitation

To implement storage limitation when developing a software system, it must be clarified how long the data must be stored and when they must or may no longer be stored. Furthermore, in many cases, there is the intermediate step of archiving, which applies when

---

[18] See https://noyb.eu/sites/default/files/2024-04/OpenAI%20Complaint_EN_redacted.pdf for more information about that complaint which was filed with the Austrian Data Protection Commission. As of October 2024, this complaint is still in discussion, and no decision was taken so far.

the data must still be stored to comply with retention periods but may only be accessed to a very limited extent because it is no longer required for the usual business processes.

To be able to implement storage limitation, the following requirements must be satisfied by relevant software systems:

Requirement (F-11 Identify Data No Longer Required) *The system shall provide the controller with the ability to identify any personal data no longer required.*

For example, this includes identifying the data whose required legal retention period has passed.

Once data are no longer needed, the controller may choose between anonymising and deleting them. Even if the data are anonymised, the controller must be able to delete the original data and only keep the anonymised version. Additionally, to implement the right to erasure as introduced in Sect. 4.3, the controller must also be able to delete personal data. Therefore, the deletion requirement F-13 is expressed as a shall-requirement, while the anonymisation requirement F-12 is expressed as a should-requirement.

Requirement (F-12 Anonymisation of Personal Data) *The system should provide the controller with the ability to transform stored personal data no longer required into anonymous data. The anonymous data shall be in a format that prevents de-anonymisation with realistic effort. When data are anonymised, the system shall replace all copies of the original data by the anonymised data, unless they are deleted.*

This requirement is similar to C-05, except that C-05 refers to the anonymisation of entire collections of data, while F-12 refers to selected parts, for example, individual data records.

Anonymisation Instead of Erasure of Data Until now, we have assumed that anonymisation of data is a legitimate substitute for deletion. However, whether this really always applies is controversial for two reasons: first, when data are anonymised, there remains an appreciable risk that the data subjects can be re-identified, meaning that the anonymisation is reversed. The second reason relates to the possibility that the (anonymised) data are evaluated for a different purpose than originally stated and the data subject does not agree to this different purpose. For example, it may be a medical or sociological study for a purpose that is questionable from the data subjects' point of view and for which they do not consent to their data being used.

If an organisation still wants to anonymise data instead of deleting them, it should therefore be very careful to implement anonymisation thoroughly, e.g. using the methods described in Sect. 6.3, and not just superficially. This applies in particular if the data are supposed to be deleted because of an erasure request according to Art. 17 GDPR and not just to implement storage limitation.

Requirement (F-13-v2 Deletion of Data) *The system shall provide the controller with the ability to delete personal data identified as no longer required, including all instances of the data such as backups.*

When deleting data in accordance with this requirement, it must be taken into account that deletion must be permanent, i.e. it cannot be undone (or at least only with considerable effort). Deletion at the operating system level is therefore not normally sufficient; instead, a secure form of deletion is required, for example, by repeatedly overwriting the data carrier or, in case of high confidentiality requirements, by physically destroying the data carrier.

Both requirements F-12 and F-13 explicitly require that the erasure or deletion must relate to *all* copies or instances of the respective data. This is to ensure, for example, that data that are stored in a data backup or an archive are also deleted.

> **Case Study 3.3 (Storage Limitation at the Software House)** Storage limitation is of particular importance in the software house as in some projects, data are provided by the customer, either as test data (see Sect. 3.2.4) or to enable the software house to carry out the required analyses. In both cases, the legal basis for storing the data ceases to apply at the end of the project, and it must be deleted at this point at the latest.

The storage limitation principle also applies to IT operation's own data, for example, error reports and support tickets as well as log data. For example, it may be important for maintenance to know which problems have been reported for a system in order to improve the system, but since it is not normally important to know who originally reported them, this information should be deleted as soon as possible.

In addition to the principle of storage limitation, the data subject's right to erasure also defines a requirement according to which data must be deleted under certain conditions. While the principle of storage limitation still leaves some leeway as to how quickly erasure must take place, this is very limited in the case of the right to erasure, which must generally take place within one month.

What may be surprising at first glance is the fact that the erasure of data is also data processing and requires its own legal basis. However, the fulfilment of legal requirements or otherwise a legitimate interest in most cases provides an adequate legal basis. Only in exceptional cases will the data subjects have an interest in their data not being erased while the controller wishes to erase it. Such an exceptional case exists primarily if the data subject has requested the restriction of processing in accordance with Art. 18 GDPR, and in this case, the data may of course not be deleted.

What Is "Erasure"? The term erasure is not explicitly defined in the GDPR. It is understood to mean that the data in question are rendered unrecognisable, i.e. the information represented by the data can no longer be read out. Deleting the data at the operating system level is in general not sufficient (depending on the storage medium used), as this usually only deletes the entry in the corresponding file allocation table, but the data itself is still present. If data are stored on a hard drive or comparable medium, secure erasure is required in which the data on the drive are overwritten repeatedly. In the case of very sensitive data, of data carriers to be disposed of (e.g. a defective PC) or of data on paper, physical destruction of the data carrier is usually appropriate.

3.5.2   Retention Periods and Erasure Concepts

The need to delete data that are no longer needed raises several questions regarding its practical implementation:

- How long must data be stored in order to fulfil legal requirements?
- Under what conditions and for how long may data also be retained in the company's own legitimate interest?
- How can you ensure that data to be deleted is actually deleted but at the same time data to be retained is not deleted? This is particular challenging if there are retention obligations for some data records or even individual attributes of the data in question, but others must be deleted at the same time.
- How can you ensure that all copies of data to be deleted are deleted, including, for example, backup copies?
- How quickly must such data be deleted?

Some of these questions will be answered below.

Retention Period and Regular Deletion Period   With regard to the first question, there are a number of different legal requirements, particularly under commercial and tax law, to retain data. For example, in Germany, trading books, inventories, accounting documents, etc. must be kept for 10 years, while received and sent commercial letters, including many emails, and other documents relevant for taxation must be kept for 6 years. Similarly, in Austria, trading books, accounting vouchers and business letters must be kept for 7 years, and in Switzerland, all these documents must be kept for 10 years. There are many more regulations on the retention of special data that differ from country to country, for example, for medical records, time sheets, property documents and many more, but these cannot all be listed here.

These retention periods set by law at the same time define the deletion periods, as they determine when data are no longer required and must therefore be deleted. In individual cases, there may still be a legitimate interest of the controller to continue to store the data, for example, to combine multiple deletion processes or to defend against liability claims, but to do so, you will have to prove specific reasons and not just the general and abstract risk of liability claims so that your own interest prevails when balancing interests.

Deletion Policies and Procedures According to ISO/IEC 27555 The international standard ISO/IEC 27555[19] defines how to set up policies and procedures for the deletion of personal data and will be summarised in the following. Note that this standard talks about "deletion" of data, while GDPR uses the term "erasure". However, this is only a difference in terminology used and does not refer to any difference in contents. To systematically define personal data when they are due to be deleted, ISO/IEC 27555 recommends the following steps:

Define Clusters of Data A cluster of data serves to group data objects that are processed for a common purpose and are therefore subject to retention periods that are at least almost the same length. Examples of data types are invoice data or customer master data or log files of visits to a Web site. The difficulty is that these data are often not stored separately according to retention periods, so that different attributes in the same table may contain different types of data. A decision must then be taken on a case-by-case basis as to whether it is justifiable to store all data according to the longest retention period or whether another solution must be found.

Specify Deletion Periods In the next step, the deletion periods are defined for each cluster of data. Starting point for this definition are the required retention periods, which may then be combined in standard deletion periods in order to keep the number of different periods used manageable. Of course, these standard deletion periods must not deviate too much from the retention periods, as the legal requirement as legal basis no longer applies after the end of the retention period.

Define Deletion Classes In addition to the duration of a retention period, it must of course also be specified when this period begins. There are three typical starting points, namely, the time of collection of the data, the end of a process or, as a special case, the end of the relationship with the data subject. This third start time is difficult to define unambiguously—for example, when does the relationship with customers end if they have not ordered anything for some time? The answer depends on factors such as whether the customer has created an account or only placed a single order and what type of products is involved. In addition, the relevant legal regulations sometimes specify a start time, for example, for book-keeping documents, the end of the calendar year in which the booking took place.

---

[19] ISO/IEC 27555:2021 Information security, cybersecurity and privacy protection—Guidelines on personally identifiable information deletion.

The deletion periods together with a start date then define the deletion classes, and each kind of data is assigned to the relevant deletion class. In practical implementation, this assignment will often be an iterative process in which the kinds of data are broken down further in order to assign them to the adequate deletion class.

Implementation Once it has been clarified at the functional level when data should be deleted, this must be translated into a design that technically and organisationally defines the measures to be taken to delete the correct data at the correct time. This design must, for example, take into account that the data are stored in different IT systems, often with multiple copies including backup systems, and that the data are stored on different storage media. Furthermore, depending on how sensitive the data are, deletion must be performed on different levels of thoroughness, ranging from simple deletion on the level of the file system to physical destruction of the storage medium.

Finally, this design must be implemented in a technical solution which is then continuously operated.

> **Example 3.3 (Storage Limitation at a Training Provider)** A training provider offers training courses that conclude with an external exam. The company's management attaches great importance to data protection, including data minimisation, which posed two major challenges. The first related to the fact that very different data were required for different trainings offered; for example, for certain exams, the attendance rate was stored because it was a prerequisite for participation in the examination, but after the exam was taken, this information was no longer needed. In other cases, the stored data had to be kept for many years (e.g. invoice data). The second challenge was that data on training participants that was no longer required should be deleted as soon as possible, but it should also be possible to confirm that a particular participant has passed an examination even after a long period of time.
>
> Although the company did not apply ISO/IEC 27555, it did use similar basic ideas as follows: The first challenge was solved by checking and recording how long the individual attributes of the participant in the database are required. This is a very fine-grained formation of data types at the level of attributes to which the respective deletion rule was assigned. The definition of data types, deletion periods and deletion classes was therefore not really separated.
>
> Based on these definitions, scripts were created that run daily to delete data that are no longer required. Running these scripts on a daily basis would not really be necessary, but management decided to implement these data protection requirements thoroughly. Additionally, this reduced the risk if anything went wrong since there is only a very small number of records deleted each day. Initially, however, it took many weeks from the completion of the scripts, including a thorough test, until

(continued)

the courage was summoned up to use these scripts to irrevocably delete the data (including backups) that are no longer required.

The second challenge was solved by an approach based on "data protection by design" (Art. 25 GDPR). The training participants each receive a certificate for passing the exam, which also contains a URL with the exam data. The information about the passed exam itself can then be deleted by the company, and only hash values of the data are stored. If the participants now enter the URL, the training company's system checks that the hash value of the entered exam data is contained in the hash value table and confirms the passed exam in this case. Participants are free to pass this URL on to third parties, such as their employer, but the training company treats this URL confidentially and deletes it after it has been sent to the participants with the examination data.

At first, it was considered whether this approach was really an anonymisation or just a pseudonymisation, but the conclusion was reached that the stored hash values themselves can no longer be assigned to an individual person but only serve to verify the data stored on the data subject himself.

Deviations from the Standard Storage Periods In addition to the standard procedure described above, there are also special cases in which certain data are required for longer (e.g. due to legal disputes) or need to be deleted more quickly (e.g. because they turn out to be incorrect). The defined internal processes must therefore also be able to cover such exceptional cases.

Data Backups and Archiving In this context, it is important to distinguish between data backups and archives. The purpose of a data backup is to ensure that the backed-up data remains available even in the event of technical problems. Their lifespan is usually no more than several months. An archive, on the other hand, is used to make the archived data available on a long-term and cost-effective basis. This primarily involves the fulfilment of retention obligations but also other cases such as proof of liability for long-life products.

Both approaches have great potential for conflicts with the principle of storage limitation. In the case of data backups with their limited lifespan, it is usually justifiable on the basis of a legitimate interest not to delete the data from the backups but to wait until the end of the backup's life. (The case is more difficult if data subjects assert their right to erasure in accordance with Art. 17 GDPR; see Sect. 4.3.) However, it must be ensured that data that have been deleted from the production system for data protection reasons cannot subsequently be restored from a data backup.

Secure Archiving Archives, on the other hand, are designed for a long data lifespan, where there is a conflict between the accounting and auditing standards which require that relevant data are kept for a long time (typically 5 to 10 years, depending on the exact type of data and the applicable legislation) and the data protection requirement of storage limitation.

Even in audit-proof archiving systems, it is therefore necessary that data can be deleted—naturally only according to certain defined rules. The first major fine in Germany under the GDPR related to precisely such a case, as it essentially concerned the fact that (contrary to a corresponding request from the supervisory authority) an archiving system was used in which no data could be deleted. Archiving systems must therefore allow data to be classified according to their required retention period, and they must delete the data once this period has expired. Guaranteed and unalterable storage of accounting data must therefore be limited to the legal retention period, combined with the deletion of the data after its expiry. Depending on how sensitive the data are and depending on the technical environment, it may be justifiable that the data are not deleted in the strict sense but made inaccessible without major effort, for example, when they are stored on a WORM[20] storage medium and deleted from the index.

The deletion of data from a secure long-term archive must be logged, but of course, the deleted data are not allowed to appear in the deletion log. Instead, such a log entry must take an anonymous form such as "all data of customers who did not buy anything since data X were deleted".

Archiving in the Public Interest A special case is the processing and, in particular, archiving of data for archiving purposes in the public interest, scientific or historical research purposes, or for statistical purposes. However, for reasons of space, this special case dealt with in Art. 89 GDPR cannot be discussed here any further.

Expiry of a Retention Period Before data may be deleted after expiry of a retention period, the following conditions need to be verified:

- Did the data subject request the restriction of processing pursuant to Art. 18 GDPR? In this case, the data may of course not be deleted but may only be accessible within the organisation to a very limited extent.
- Are the data still required for other legitimate purposes of your own, for example, to process warranty claims or for scientific analyses? In this case, it must be clarified in detail whether these other purposes constitute a sufficient legal basis for continuing to store and process the data.

---

[20] WORM memory: "Write Once, Read Many".

Case Study 3.4 (Online-Shop: Handling of Order Data and Customer Data No Longer Needed) Naturally, the online retailer has some customers who have not purchased anything for several years. In accordance with the principle of storage limitation, these customer's data may no longer be stored, as far as they are not subject to some statutory retention periods from accounting or tax regulations:

- Data that are subject to statutory retention periods, both master data and transaction data, are first copied from the ordering system to the accounting system. They remain there until the annual financial statements for the year in question and are then moved to an archiving system and stored there until the end of the retention period. They are then deleted. Access to the accounting and, above all, the archiving system is handled restrictively and is limited to the purposes of accounting and tax law.
- In the operative systems, the following cases are distinguished:
  - The online retailer offers customers the option of ordering without creating a customer account. Customers who have not created an account for their order thereby make it clear that their data should not be stored any longer than necessary and should not be used for marketing purposes. These data are therefore deleted from the ordering system at the end of each year after processing has been completed and is only stored in the accounting or archive system.
  - If the customers themselves have created an account with the online retailer, it can be assumed that they will normally delete it themselves if they no longer need or want it. The option of deleting such an account with little effort has therefore been created. Special care has been taken to ensure that the effort involved is no greater than that required to set up the account.

    However, it is not always possible for customers to delete their account themselves if they no longer need it (loss of access, forgetting, death, etc.). After 2 years of inactivity, customers are therefore asked to confirm that they wish to keep their customer account. At the same time, this is combined with a discount campaign for new orders in order to reactivate customers where possible.

    Accounts of customers who do not respond within a few months are then cancelled. This is usually not only necessary from a data protection perspective but also in the company's own interest in order to clean up inactive records.

3.5.3 Example: Blockchain

Blockchain is a technology that has been much discussed in recent years. Apart from Bitcoin and other cryptocurrencies, which are certainly the most widespread applications, there are a number of other pilot applications, and it is to be expected that the importance of blockchain will grow, at least for certain types of applications.

Technically speaking, a blockchain is a data structure which consists of a chain of blocks (hence the name), where each new block contains the hash value of the previous block in addition to user data such as transactions. This structure ensures that blocks cannot be subsequently changed—or at least any change will not go unnoticed.

In functional terms, a blockchain is a distributed and immutable register ("Distributed Ledger"), with which a group of participants, who generally do not know each other and therefore do not trust each other, can agree on a common, unchangeable history of transactions, the so-called consensus, without the involvement of a central authority such as the state, a bank or a notary. The extent to which these objectives can actually be realised in practice will not be discussed further here, but we will assume below that the finished blocks of a blockchain are actually immutable as intended.

While this property can be very useful, it also can be problematic from a data protection perspective as it contradicts the principle of storage limitation and makes it impossible to delete personal data that are no longer needed. Similarly, the rights to erasure and to restriction of processing cannot be implemented in a blockchain. The right to rectification can only be realised to a very limited extent, as the relevant data record itself cannot be rectified, but at best, a correction can be defined in a later block.

In order to use blockchain technology in a data protection-compliant manner, personal data may therefore only be included in the blocks to a very limited extent, if at all. Depending on the specific application, the following approaches should be considered, possibly in a combination:

- Personal data can be recorded in pseudonymised form, as is the case in Bitcoin. Here, a user can use a pseudonym (or several) in the form of a "cryptographic identity", i.e. a key pair (see Sect. 7.4), where ideally only the users themselves can establish the link between the pseudonym and the appropriate user identity. Depending on the quality of the pseudonyms and the entire context, a certain degree of confidentiality can be achieved this way. However, at least at the interfaces between the blockchain world and the real world, for example, when exchanging real currency for cryptocurrency and vice versa, this only applies to a limited extent. Anyway, the extent to which complete confidentiality would be desirable is questionable, as it would also enable illegal transaction such as money laundering.
- Confidentiality can be increased by encrypting transaction data, although all parties involved in a transaction must of course be able to decrypt the data. If a suitable encryption method and long keys are selected, a high level of confidentiality can be achieved, at least in the short and medium term, but it must be expected that the

encrypted data can be decrypted at some point over a period of many years. Anyway, this approach of encrypting does not fit well with the overall concept of the blockchain which was designed to allow everyone to read all data on the chain and only limit writing to the chain.

- An even higher level of protection of data confidentiality, at the expense of a lower level of consensus, can be achieved by not storing the personal data themselves (or other confidential data) in the blockchain but only their hash value. Of course, this requires the use of a cryptographic hash function with correspondingly high collision resistance.[21] Since in this case, the personal data are not stored in the blockchain, the level of confidentiality of the data can be increased beyond that achieved by pseudonyms.

Another issue to be considered when using blockchain concerns *smart contracts*, i.e. automated contracts that can be included in a blockchain. As long as standard applications are involved, such as the provision of a service after payment, this is relatively straightforward, but a smart contract can also contain automated decisions on individual cases. According to Art. 22 GDPR, however, data subjects have the right to demand that such an individual decision is not made exclusively by automated means, which contradicts the basic idea of smart contracts. Therefore, to include such decisions in a smart contract, you should clarify to what extent this can be made compliant with Art. 22, for example, via one of the exceptions formulated there.

3.6 Integrity and Confidentiality

The principle of integrity and confidentiality requires an appropriate implementation of information security. Availability, the third protection goal of information security, is not explicitly included in the name of the principle (cf. Sect. 2.5.6), but nevertheless addressed in the statement of the principle. To a large extent, the implementation of this principle is usually the responsibility software development and IT who do so by standard mechanisms such as access restrictions based on a role and rights concept or encryption of data. When implementing access restrictions within a company, there is often a conflict between the "need-to-know" principle of information security and data protection on the one hand and open communication and collaboration on the other, so that a suitable and GDPR-compliant compromise must be found.

GDPR addresses this conflict in the principle of integrity and confidentiality (Art. 5(1)f) by requiring adequate security. Of course, this immediately leads to the question of what is considered adequate. Article 32 GDPR provides some more detail on this topic, but

---

[21] See Sect. 7.4.4 for a quick introduction to the concept of cryptographic hash functions and their collision resistance.

the answer obviously depends largely on the specific environment and the personal data involved. In many cases, the requirements on information security management systems as defined by ISO/IEC 27001 provide a good guideline. In Chap. 7, the requirements on information security will be discussed in more detail.

Taken almost literally from GDPR, the resulting software requirement states:

Requirement (Q-02 Integrity, Confidentiality and Availability) *The system shall provide adequate security of personal data, including protection against unauthorised or unlawful processing and against accidental loss, destruction or damage.*

Although the name of the legal principle only talks about integrity and confidentiality, it actually also addresses protection against accidental loss, destruction or damage, which concern the protection goal of availability.

Particularly important for data protection are measures such as the restrictive handling of access rights, the secure storage of access data (e.g. no storage of passwords in plain text) and encryption of data at least when transferring them between systems.

3.7 Accountability

Accountability is a fairly new principle of data protection that is not currently widespread in other data protection legislation. It states that it is not sufficient to *implement* data protection, but controllers need to be able to *show* that they do so by providing adequate documentation such as the "records of processing activities" introduced in Sect. 2.7.5.

A key purpose of accountability (Art. 5 (2), Art. 24 (1) GDPR) is to force companies to give serious thought to the implementation of data protection requirements. Of course, this could easily be claimed later, even if it was only done very superficially in reality. Accountability requires that the implementation can be proven, i.e. that at least the essential steps have been documented. In practice, you will rarely be required to actually do this. However, if there are (justified or unjustified) complaints about your organisation to the supervisory authority or something has gone wrong and you have to report a data breach, then the supervisory authority will probably ask for this evidence as one of the first steps in order to be able to assess the situation.

This requirement has a direct impact on software development, as the relevant software must be documented in such a way that it is possible to understand which personal data are processed and how. This results in the following software requirement:

Requirement (C-06 Documentation) *The system, in particular its processing of personal data, shall be documented and this documentation be versioned and kept up to date.*

Versioning is important in this context in order to show, in case of problems, what processing was performed at a certain point in time in the past.

Apart from satisfying the legal requirements, such documentation helps identify the personal data processed and the resulting needs for data protection measures.

The required documentation includes the records of processing activities (RoPA) introduced in Sect. 2.7.5, for which the software documentation provides some of the required information. Even if software development and IT are not directly responsible for satisfying this requirement, their support is of course required. The technical and organisational measures are optional in the RoPA but must be described as part of accountability. Depending on the scope of these descriptions, it makes sense to describe them in the RoPA itself or to refer from there to a more comprehensive description elsewhere, for example, to logs of a DPIA or of data protection audits that have been carried out.

Requirement (C-07 Records of Processing Activities) *The controller shall document the processing of personal data as performed by the system, including its purpose, the categories of data processed, the recipients of the data and the technical and organisational measures performed to protect these data.*

As can be seen, the requirements C-06 and C-07 are closely related. C-06 considers the documentation from the point of view of the software, while C-07 considers the documentation from the point of view of the processing (possibly supported by the software).

References

Alb19. Albrecht, Jan Philipp: *Einführung zu Art. 6 (in German)*. In Simitis, Spiros, Hornung, Gerrit, and Spiecker gen. Döhmann, Indra (editors): *Datenschutzrecht*. Nomos, 2019.

Art14. Article 29 Data Protection Working Party: *Opinion 06/2014 on the notion of legitimate interests of the data controller under Article 7 of Directive 95/46/EC*, April 2014. https://ec. europa.eu/justice/article-29/documentation/opinion-recommendation/files/2014/wp217_en.pdf

Dat15. Datatilsynet: *The great data race. How commercial utilisation of personal data challenges privacy*, November 2015. https://www.datatilsynet.no/globalassets/global/english/ engelsk-kommersialisering-endelig.pdf

Eck10. Eckersley, Peter: *How unique is your web browser?* In Atallah, Mikhail J. and Hopper, Nicholas J. (editors): *Privacy Enhancing Technologies*, pages 1–18, Berlin, Heidelberg, 2010. Springer Berlin Heidelberg, ISBN 978-3-642-14527-8. https://coveryourtracks.eff.org/static/ browser-uniqueness.pdf

EDP16. European Data Protection Supervisor (EDPS): *Opinion 9/2016 – EDPS Opinion on Personal Information Management Systems*, 2016. https://www.edps.europa.eu/sites/default/files/ publication/16-10-20_pims_opinion_en.pdf

FHS18. Forgó, Nikolaus, Hänold, Stefanie, and Schütze, Benjamin: *The principle of purpose limitation and big data*. In Corrales, Marcelo, Fenwick, Mark, and Forgó, Nikolaus (editors): *New Technology, Big Data and the Law*, pages 17–42. Springer, 2018.

ICO22a. ICO – Information Commissioner's Office: *A guide to lawful basis – what happens if we have a new purpose?*, 2022. https://ico.org.uk/for-organisations/uk-gdpr-guidance-and-resources/lawful-basis/a-guide-to-lawful-basis/#purpose

ICO22b. ICO – The Alan Turing Institute: *Explaining decisions made with AI, v.1.0.3*, 2022. https://ico.org.uk/for-organisations/uk-gdpr-guidance-and-resources/artificial-intelligence/explaining-decisions-made-with-artificial-intelligence/

Kne20. Kneuper, Ralf: *Translating data protection into software requirements*. In Furnell, Steven, Mori, Paolo, Weippl, Edgar, and Camp, Olivier (editors): *Proceedings of the 6th International Conference on Information Systems Security and Privacy (ICISSP), Valetta, Malta*, pages 257–264. Scitepress, 2020. http://www.scitepress.org/DigitalLibrary/Link.aspx?doi=10.5220/0008873902570264

MSB20. Matte, Célestin, Santos, Cristiana, and Bielova, Nataliia: *Purposes in IAB Europe's TCF: which legal basis and how are they used by advertisers?* In Antunes, Luís, Naldi, Maurizio, Italiano, Giuseppe F., Rannenberg, Kai, and Drogkaris, Prokopios (editors): *Privacy Technologies and Policy. APF 2020 - Annual Privacy Forum*, pages 163–185. Springer International Publishing, October 2020, ISBN 978-3-030-55196-4. https://hal.inria.fr/hal-02566891

Sha20. Sharma, Sanjay: *Data Privacy and GDPR Handbook*. Wiley, 2020.

SL20. Sartor, Giovanni and Lagioia, Francesca: *The impact of the General Data Protection Regulation (GDPR) on artificial intelligence*. EPRS – European Parliamentary Research Service, 2020. https://www.europarl.europa.eu/RegData/etudes/STUD/2020/641530/EPRS_STU(2020)641530_EN.pdf

Rights of Data Subjects and Their Implementation

4

Abstract

In addition to the data protection principles already considered, the GDPR defines a number of rights for data subjects, i.e. the persons whose data are processed. These rights include the right to information and the right to rectification or erasure of data. In order to implement these rights, a software system must provide certain functionalities. For example, it must be possible to find data about a specific person in unstructured data collections in order to provide information about the data processed, to correct it or to delete it. This chapter describes the importance of data subjects' rights for software development and IT, including the requirements for software to be developed resulting from these rights, taking into account that these partially overlap with the requirements resulting from the principles.

4.1 Transparency Rights and Obligations

The relatively abstract principle of transparency described in Sect. 2.5.1 is made more specific by the information obligations and rights to information defined in Art. 13–15 GDPR. These information obligations do not define any requirements on the software itself, but rather on the environment for its use and indirectly on its documentation. The situation is somewhat different with regard to the right of access, as in order to implement this right, the software must provide search functions that can be used to search for data relating to a specific person.

4.1.1 Information to Be Provided and Right of Access

There are two different cases of information obligations, namely, the collection of data directly from the data subject (Art. 13 GDPR) or elsewhere (Art. 14 GDPR). This results in the following software requirements:

Requirement (F-14 Information When Collecting Personal Data Directly from the Data Subject) *If the system collects or otherwise processes personal data collected directly from the data subjects, it shall provide the following information to the data subjects in a simple and easily understandable form:*

- *Name and contact details of the controller and the contact details of the data protection officer, if available*
- *Purposes and legal basis of the processing*
- *Legitimate interests of the processor if these form the legal basis for processing*
- *Recipients of the data, if relevant*
- *The intention of the controller to transfer the data to a third country (a country outside the EEA), if applicable*

Example 4.1 (Visiting Cards) Visiting cards are often exchanged between visitors at trade fairs and other events. As long as the recipient of a business card only keeps the printed card, the data are not collected or processed in the sense of GDPR. However, if the data are transferred to a customer relationship system (CRM) in order to be used for marketing purposes, the data subject must be informed accordingly, typically by means of a corresponding email.

It is certainly debatable whether this is appropriate, as the purpose of handing over a visiting card is precisely to provide the other person with one's contact details so that they can get in touch. On the other hand, this provides the data subject with more precise information about what happens to their data and who they may need to contact if the data are to be deleted or corrected at a later date.

Requirement (F-15 Information When Not Collecting Personal Data Directly from the Data Subject) *If the system collects or otherwise processes personal data that are not collected directly from the data subject, it shall provide the following information to the data subjects in a simple and easily understandable form:*

- *Name and contact details of the controller and the contact details of the data protection officer, if available*
- *Purposes and legal basis of the processing*

- *Categories of personal data to be processed*
- *Recipients of the data, if relevant*
- *The intention of the controller to transfer the data to a third country (a country outside the EEA), if applicable*

A further set of information does not have to be provided to the data subjects but shall be made available. This is usually implemented by providing this information in a data protection policy on the controller's Web site.

Requirement (F-16 Information That Must Be Made Available) *If the system collects or otherwise processes personal data, it shall provide the data subjects with the following information in an easily accessible and easily understandable form:*

- *The planned duration of storage or the criteria for determining this duration*
- *The legitimate interests of the controller, if these form the legal basis for the processing (this information is only to be made available if the data are not collected from the data subject directly)*
- *Information on the data subject's rights to information, right to lodge a complaint with the supervisory authority, etc.*
- *Information on the right to withdraw consent if the processing is based on consent*
- *Source of the data*
- *The existence of automated decision-making, if relevant*
- *The intention to further process the data for another purpose, if relevant*

It should be noted that this information must be easily accessible. In the case of a Web site, this means that there must be a clearly labelled link to the privacy policy containing this information on every page so that this information can be accessed with one click.

Case Study 4.1 (Information Obligations of the Online Retailer) In the online retailer shop, customer data are collected from the data subjects directly when they create an account or place an order. When creating an account or placing an order, a link to the privacy policy is therefore displayed, which contains all information on the requirements F-14, F-15 and F-16 (or Art. 13, 14 and 15 GDPR). Customers must confirm that they have read this privacy policy by clicking on a checkbox. There is also the option of printing out the privacy policy or saving it as a PDF file. The reference to the privacy policy (incl. link) is also included in the emails confirming the creation of an account or the order, and this link is additionally included on all pages of the Web site.

(continued)

In the past, the company used several different privacy policies for account creation, orders and Web site visitors, but it turned out that there were significant overlaps and sometimes inconsistencies between the policies. It was therefore decided to merge the various declarations and cover all topics within a single declaration, even if this made it somewhat more extensive than each of the individual declarations. This new policy starts with a block with the information that is applicable to all forms of processing (e.g. the contact data of the controller and the DPO and the explanation of the user rights) and then includes separate chapters for each of the individual forms of processing.

The right of access pursuant to Art. 15 GDPR goes well beyond these information obligations and gives data subjects the right to obtain information about the personal data stored about them, not just as a general statement that, for example, their contact details are stored but with the specific data stored. In order to be able to provide such information, the relevant data must first be found, which leads to the following software requirement:

Requirement (F-17-v2 Right of Access) *The system shall enable the controller to select and report personal data for a specified person, including the source of these data.*

Such selection and reporting shall include any log data that were collected in the system and refer to the specified person.

When doing so, the system may not report any further confidential content, in particular personal data of other persons or trade secrets.

The first part of this requirement is easy to satisfy as long as it concerns information systems based on structured data, such as a customer management system. It becomes much more difficult if the data contain little or no structure, for example, emails or text documents. The difficulties often already start with the question of which systems are relevant and need to be searched. A properly maintained record of processing activities helps, but you should also think in advance about which requests for information may be made and need to be answered. As decided in an ECJ judgement in 2023, collected log files are also considered as personal data if they refer to an identified person and must therefore be included in the information of a data subject if requested according to Art. 15 GDPR.

The restriction on the data to be reported contained in the second part of the requirement must already be taken into account when defining the data structures so that the data to be reported can be reliably separated from the data not to be reported. In the GDPR, this second aspect is only implicitly included, but in some other laws, for example, the *Austrian Data Protection Act*, it is even formulated as an explicit restriction of the right to information (§ 4 (5) and (6) DPA Austria).

Case Study 4.2 (Right of Access at Online Retailer) In order to gain a better overview of the various data available, it was agreed to manage all customer data in two connected systems, a customer relationship system (CRM) and an order processing system. All previously used small additional systems, spreadsheets, etc. were eliminated, and the functionality was transferred to the CRM or the order processing system. This helped improve the handling of access requests, but above all, it made day-to-day operation of the shop much more efficient and less error-prone.

Corresponding search and reporting functions were incorporated into these two systems in order to be able to process access requests from customers relatively easily. These are currently still processed manually, but due to the growing number of requests, this process is to be largely automated in future.

Example 4.2 (Right of Access in Car Rental Company) In the past, a car hire company manually generated the response to access requests using screenshots from the booking system. In addition to the data on any existing user account, this primarily involved information on the bookings made, plus any third-party bookings in which the person was entered as a driver. Several screenshots were required for each booking, resulting in a large number of screenshots for customers with many bookings. It was important to ensure that any data of other persons, e.g. the person making the booking if the enquirer was only entered as the driver, had to be deleted from a screenshot. This was obviously a time-consuming and error-prone task, and when such requests became more frequent after the GDPR came into force, it was decided to automate this task. This was also intended to reduce the amount of information sent as printouts by registered mail and thus save postage and paper costs. A new function was then developed to automate the information process, which prepares the information previously displayed as a screenshot as a table. This is then printed out and sent to the data subject. The table is stored together with the proof of dispatch for 6 months in order to be able to process any follow-up questions or complaints. In addition, the identity of the data subject is stored for 1 year so very frequent requests can be identified and possibly charged.

As part of the automation process, it was discovered that other systems in the company also contain relevant personal data, in particular the invoice data in the ERP system, which had not previously been taken into account when providing information. These were therefore now also included. In addition, the process for access requests in the call centre was refined, particularly with regard to

(continued)

the authentication of enquirers. However, as the information is then sent to the customer's known postal address, this is not as critical as initially assumed.

Further automation is being considered, at least for customers who have a customer account, so that customers can order a report via the corresponding Web site, which is then generated and sent without manual intervention. However, experience with the existing solution is to be gathered first, in particular whether the algorithms implemented for deleting third-party data in the report work sufficiently well.

In addition, the transmission of information by email is being considered. This would have to be encrypted, but the person concerned would have to have the appropriate infrastructure (PGP or S/MIME key, etc.), which is rarely the case. Alternatively, the data could first be encrypted and then be appended to a mail, for example, as an encrypted ZIP file, but it is expected that many customers would struggle to open such encrypted files. Additionally, this would require to send out the key used for encryption via some secure channel. As a third option, customers could be offered this dispatch method with explicit consent for unencrypted dispatch, but this would also place increased demands on the authentication of the enquirer. Sending information by email has therefore been postponed for the time being.

4.1.2 Authentication of Data Subjects

One challenge in the implementation of the right of access concerns the authentication of the data subject, as the information must of course only be provided to the data subject and not to unauthorised third parties. Authentication is the verification of the identity of an entity, in this case the data subject, as a prerequisite for authorisation to exercise certain rights, in this case the right of access. Such authentication is closely related to authentication as used in IT security as a prerequisite for authorisation to access ICT systems or data (see Sect. 7.3), and in some cases, the two variants overlap, for example, when requesting access via an IT portal.

Like for the right of access, authentication is also important for the exercise of other data subject rights, specifically the rights to rectification, erasure, restriction of processing, data portability and objection. There are a number of different approaches as to how such authentication can be ensured. Most of these lead to organisational requirements, but do not affect the software or IT [Pet19]. An exception to this is authentication via a user account, which leads to the following software requirement:

Requirement (F-18 Authentication of Data Subjects When Exercising Their Data Protection Rights) *If the system supports user accounts, then it shall provide users the*

opportunity to exercise their user rights directly from this account, without any additional
authentication.

In most cases, it will then make sense to show the data directly to the data subjects within
the system in question, so that no human intervention is required. In some cases, however,
it is easier to send it to them separately, possibly by post. This is particularly the case if
not all the relevant data are available in the system in question, i.e. the data have to be
collated from different systems. Linking the various systems so that the data subjects can
also view data from other systems within their user account may increase the security risk
of unauthorised persons gaining access to the data, so that a case-by-case assessment is
required.

Data subjects must thus be able to assert their right to access within the system, but
this does not necessarily mean that they should also receive the corresponding information
within the system.

4.1.3   Transparency and Data Protection Policies of Web Sites

Transparency of processing in case of Web sites, especially in online marketing, has
already been briefly considered in Sects. 3.1.7 and 4.1.1 and will be supplemented here
from the perspective of the rights of data subjects. The description assumes that a suitable
legal basis for the processing exists and only considers the necessary information for data
subjects.

Web sites collect data from their visitors because, for technical reasons alone, they need
at least their IP address so that the content of the Web pages can be delivered correctly.
Even if these data are deleted again immediately afterwards, it is a short-term collection
and storage of personal data. Cookies and possibly other tracking mechanisms are often
used as well, and in the case of Web sites with visitor registration, a lot more data are
usually added. Visitors must be appropriately informed about this collection and further
processing of the data, and since the data are collected from the data subjects themselves,
the information defined in Art. 13 GDPR must be provided.

Data Protection Policy   This information of Web site visitors is usually implemented by
means of a data protection policy on the Web site, also known as *privacy policy* or *privacy
notice*. This policy must be easily accessible, i.e. with just one click on a clearly marked
link, from anywhere on the Web site.

All of the required information must be provided in a simple and easily understandable
form. At the same time, however, there is a requirement for complete and legally correct
information. As a glance at the privacy policies of many Web sites shows, satisfying
both requirements at the same time is difficult, leading to many conflicts in practice. For
example, in France, Google has been fined a considerable amount because information
on the use of the data collected and the storage period was not accessible to users in

an appropriate form.[1] Many parties including supervisory authorities and consultancies provide templates for privacy policies that are available on the Internet and try to find a suitable compromise between the competing requirements.

Another approach to resolve the conflict is to split the descriptions into an easy-to-understand explanation containing only high-level, easy-to-understand description of the essential concepts and a second, legally accurate and complete description.

Cookies Web sites must inform their visitors about their use of cookies. This raises the question of how this should be done, especially if a large number of cookies are set. (For example, Web sites of newspapers and magazines often set dozens, sometimes even over 100, of different cookies.) A list of all these cookies is usually not helpful and therefore not necessary (see [BBM18, Question 52]). Instead, a list of the different categories of cookies, for example, technically necessary cookies, cookies for better usability or cookies for advertising tracking, should be provided. In the case of third-party cookies, however, it must be taken into account that although the cookies themselves do not all have to be listed, information must be provided about the associated transfer of data.

Authentication The implementation of requests for information pursuant to Art. 15 GDPR (as well as for rectification, etc.) is problematic when data subjects are identified via cookies, as the controller is generally unable to establish the link between the person requesting the information and the cookie. The only option here is for the data subject to prove their identity by presenting the cookie.

4.2   Right to Rectification

The right to rectification pursuant to Art. 16 GDPR serves to implement the principle of data accuracy. Accordingly, there are no new requirements for the software here, but the right to rectification can be implemented with requirement F-09 (see p. 92) defining the possibility to correct data.

Similar to the right of access, the technical implementation of this right is fairly simple for structured data but can be very complex for unstructured data. A further challenge is that the rectification must relate to *all* copies of the data concerned. In the case of archive systems or data backups, it must at least be ensured that it is not possible to continue working with the uncorrected data, for example, after a system failure and subsequent import of the backup.

From an organisational point of view, the right to rectification leads to a complex process, similar to the process for implementing the right to erasure described below and

---

[1] See https://www.edpb.europa.eu/news/national-news/2019/cnils-restricted-committee-imposes-financial-penalty-50-million-euros_en.

illustrated in Fig. 4.1. For example, both rights are subject to the notification obligation under Art. 19 GDPR, according to which other recipients of the rectified data must also be informed of the rectification or erasure (see Sect. 4.5).

As explained in the context of accuracy, the rectification of incorrect data is particularly difficult in data analysis and machine learning. First, once data are analysed or a model has been trained, correcting personal data that were included would imply that the analysis or training would have to be redone. Second, if the result of an analysis or a trained AI model contains or delivers inaccurate personal data, correcting this is technically very challenging (see Sect. 3.4).

4.3   Right to Erasure

According to GDPR, there are two constellations when erasure of data is required. On the one hand, this is the principle of storage limitation considered in Sect. 3.5, which states that data that are no longer needed must be erased, and on the other hand there is the right to erasure introduced in Art. 17 GDPR. The principle of storage limitation applies to *all* personal data and without a specific request, while the right to erasure only applies to data for which a data subject expressly requests erasure.

The right to erasure applies if (at least) one of the following conditions is met:

- The data are no longer needed for the original purpose.
- The data subject withdraws his consent.
- The data subject objects to the processing of his data according to Art. 21 GDPR.
- The data were processed without adequate legal basis.
- The erasure of the data is required by law.
- The data processed refer to a child and were collected with the permission of the parent or guardian. This primarily concerns the case that the data were collected when the data subject was still a child. In this case, data subjects can later request that the data be deleted (Recital 65 GDPR).

To some extent, these conditions overlap with other requirements, such as the principle of storage limitation. Nevertheless, these requirements are not completely identical, as the right to erasure is based on a stricter interpretation. In particular, this means that the more generous erasure periods are discussed in Sect. 3.5.2 do not apply when the data subject requests erasure of data but that the period of 1 month defined for the implementation of data subjects' rights normally applies (Art. 12 (3) GDPR). In addition, it is sometimes assumed that anonymisation of the data is not sufficient to fulfil the right to erasure, but this interpretation is controversial.

Erasure Process The erasure process is triggered by a request from a data subject to erase their data such as "delete all my data" or "delete my account". Unless retention periods are affected, this requires deletion in all relevant systems (customer account/access data, customer database, order processing and order management system, data warehouse, marketing system, tracking system, etc.).

The implementation of such an erasure request involves much more than the simple deletion of one or more data records, as the example process in Fig. 4.1 shows. A centralised system that sends erasure requests to the systems via interfaces can therefore be useful. The process does not lead to any new requirements on the system under consideration but can be implemented using the existing requirements, in particular F-13 (see p. 95).

Before the start of implementation an erasure request, it must be ensured that the request actually originates from the data subject (or another authorised person), whether one of the conditions for the right to erasure is fulfilled and whether the processing of the data is not restricted (see Sect. 4.4). If these conditions are met, the data must be erased, and this requirement then applies to all copies of the data, i.e. all own systems including archiving and data backup systems, as well as the systems of processors, if applicable. Special cases exist if there are still open processes, such as an unpaid invoice or if the data are at least partially subject to a retention obligation. Open processes must be completed before the data concerned are erased. The processing of data with a retention obligation must be restricted, but the data may not be erased (yet).[2] If the data have also been passed on to third parties or published, for example, in the context of joint controllership, the controller has no direct responsibility for deleting the data there but remains responsible for ensuring that the recipients of the data are at least informed where possible (Art. 19 GDPR).

> **Example 4.3 (Storing Hash Value to Prove Compliance to Erasure Request)**
> The following example is based on a case decided by the Irish DPA in 2024 (see https://www.dataprotection.ie/sites/default/files/uploads/2024-08/Inquiry-into-Apple-Distribution-International-Limited-Final-Decision-March-2024-EN.pdf).
>
> A challenge for the controller is how to log that data have been erased in order to demonstrate compliance and prevent inadequate reuse of accounts, without storing the erased data in the log file. Apple addressed this by storing a (cryptographic) hash (cf. Sect. 7.4.4) of the email address associated with an account once the account was deleted due to an erasure request. This way, Apple was able to prove, when needed, that a certain account had been erased and also to identify when a new request for creating an account referred to the same email address.
>
> This led to a complaint by a user who had requested erasure of his account but later tried to set up a new account using the same email address. When this
>
> (continued)

---

[2] This is very similar to the restriction of processing, which data subjects can request in accordance with Art. 18 GDPR (see Sect. 4.4) but is initiated by a different trigger.

was refused by Apple, he complained to the competent authority that his data had not been completely erased following his erasure request. However, the authority rejected this complaint, confirming that Apple had a legitimate interest in storing the hashed email address and that the approach used satisfied the principle of data minimisation.

The authority thus stated that such a hash value is still considered personal data, which refers to an identifiable person, and the resulting data are pseudonymous data, not anonymous data. The controller therefore needs to inform the data subject about this processing and set an adequate retention period, after which even the hashed email address must be deleted.

Partial Erasure   Depending on the wishes of the data subject, the request for erasure can also relate to only part of their data. This makes sense in terms of content but can be difficult to implement. Depending on the individual case, the controller may decide to delete all data, provided that this is still fair to the affected data subjects.

The same applies if the right to erasure only relates to parts of the data or if, for other reasons, only parts of the data may be erased, for example, due to retention periods or because processing of some of the data is still pending.

4.4   Right to Restriction of Processing

As explained in Sect. 2.6, the right to restriction of processing gives data subjects the right, under certain conditions, to demand that their data may only be processed to a very limited extent (Art. 18 GDPR). The aim is to eliminate temporary ambiguities, for example, if the accuracy of the data is disputed or if it is unclear whether there is a right to object under Art. 21 GDPR.

The procedure for handling requests for restriction of processing is similar to the procedure already described for handling requests for erasure of data (see Fig. 4.1). However, it is not normally permitted to erase the data instead of the requested restriction of processing, as the data subject may need the data to assert their rights and is therefore requesting the restriction of processing.

In order to implement this right in software, the data concerned must be marked accordingly so that it is easy to see which data may only be processed to a very limited extent, as formulated in the following requirements:

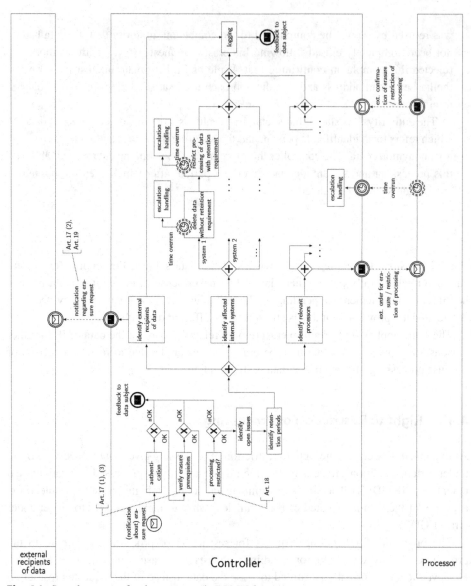

Fig. 4.1 Sample process for data erasure (in BPMN format)

Requirement (F-19 Marking of Data as Restricted) *The system shall allow the controller to mark data as restricted. In this case, the system shall mark all copies of these data as restricted, including backup copies.*

If data are marked as restricted, the system shall allow the controller to remove this mark. In this case, the system shall unmark all copies of these data.

Requirement (Q-03 Restriction of Processing) *If data are marked as restricted according to requirement F-19, then the system shall ensure that access to these data is only possible if there is explicitly confirmation by a designated person that this access conforms to the conditions stated in Art. 18 (2) GDPR.*

4.5   Notification Obligation in Case of Rectification, Erasure or Restriction of Processing

This notification obligation considers the case where personal data have been passed on to other recipients, for example, in the case of joint controllership, and the data subject then requests the rectification, erasure or restriction of processing of their data in accordance with Art. 16, 17 or 18 GDPR. Unless this is technically impossible or would involve disproportionate effort, the controller must pass on the information about the data subject's request to the other recipients of the data so that they can also rectify, erase or restrict the processing of the data. Figure 4.1 shows how this can be incorporated into the erasure process.

Conversely, this notification obligation shows that a request for rectification, erasure or restriction of processing does not necessarily come from the data subject. If you have received the data from another controller, the request can also come as a notification from this other controller.

The notification obligation does not place any direct requirements on the software in question but must primarily be implemented at an organisational level. Depending on context, this may result in indirect requirements on the software.

4.6   Right to Data Portability

The right to data portability (Art. 20 GDPR) above all leads to technical requirements on software development, even if the exact requirements are still under discussion. To implement this right, an export functionality is needed, which supports the selection and export of personal data provided by the data subjects. The main purpose of this right is to give customers of service providers the option of using another service provider in addition or as an alternative to the current service without having to re-enter all their data. This applies, for example, to clothing sizes and explicitly stated preferences at a clothing shop or profile data at a social network. Depending on the data subjects' wishes, these data must then be made available to the data subjects themselves or to the other service provider.

In order to implement this right, the software requires suitable selection and export functionalities for the relevant personal data. This results in the following software requirements:

Requirement (F-20 Data Export) *If personal data are processed on the legal basis of consent or to perform a contract, the system shall allow the controller to select and export the personal data provided by the data subject in a structured, commonly used and machine-readable format. When doing so, it must be ensured that the data export does not infringe the rights of third parties.*

Since this data export itself leads to personal data, these must be transferred via a secure channel.

Requirement (F-21 Secure Data Transfer) *If the system supports data export in accordance with requirement F-20, then the system shall transfer these data to the data subject (or another recipient as designated by the data subject) via a secure channel.*

If data can be exported, this implicitly implies that there must be the possibility to import such data as well.

Requirement (F-22 Data Import) *If it is likely that data subjects will request the transfer of their personal data from external sources to the system, the system should give data subjects the option of importing the data from a common or simple format.*

The GDPR does not require controllers to also provide a corresponding import. Therefore, this is a should-requirement, but failure to satisfy it may lead to customer dissatisfaction.

> **Case Study 4.3 (Data Portability at the Online Retailer)** The right to data portability is of little relevance to the order data of the online retailer. However, the retailer also offers the option of creating customer profiles with clothing sizes and similar information, and data portability is relevant for these data. Initially, it was difficult to estimate how often such requests would be received, and it was therefore decided to wait and process incoming requests manually. A simple CSV format was defined for this purpose. At the same time, contact was made with competitors to discuss a common XML format, but these efforts were unsuccessful.

Structured, Commonly Used and Machine-Readable Format A major challenge in implementing this right (and especially when later importing the data) is the requirement that the data must have a "structured, common and machine-readable format". In many cases, there is no format of this kind, so that you have to define your own format or have to cope with the format defined by another controller when importing data. In sectors where this right is used more frequently, it can therefore be expected that controllers will agree on a common format. As long as this is not the case, controllers have to define a suitable, simple format themselves, based on structures such as CSV, XML or JSON.

Portable Data The right to data portability applies to data processed on the basis of consent or for the performance of a contract, but not to data processed on any other legal basis. In addition, the right is limited to data provided by the data subject themselves, although it can be difficult to decide whether this is the case. These data include not only explicitly entered data such as profile data but also implicitly entered data such as metadata, recordings of a fitness tracker or a playlist on an audio streaming service [KB20, Art. 20, para. 11].

In some use cases, the data to be provided are also limited by the fact that the rights of third parties must be taken into account, for example, in the case of a list of contacts in a social network.

4.7   Right to Object

The right to object (Art. 21 GDPR) gives data subjects the right to object to the processing of their data under certain conditions. This is primarily a matter of addressing particular individual situations of the data subjects of which the controller may not be aware and which it has therefore not taken into account when weighing up interests. In this case, the data must be erased or at least its processing restricted, which leads to the same software requirements as already seen with the right to erasure (F-12, F-13) and the right to restriction of processing (F-19, Q-03), even if the legal trigger for these functionalities is different. Separate software requirements do not arise from the right to object.

The relevant conditions for this right to apply are organisational and not technical conditions and will therefore only be briefly summarised here: the right to object exists if the data are processed on the legal basis of a public interest or a legitimate interest (Art. 6 (1)(e), f) GDPR), in the case of direct marketing and in the case of processing for scientific or historical research purposes or for statistical purposes (Art. 89 (1) GDPR). The exact conditions and their relationships are rather complex and therefore summarised in Fig 4.2.

Advertising Blacklist A somewhat more difficult question concerns the practical implementation if a data subject objects to receiving advertising. Of course, you can just delete the person from the relevant current directories, but what happens the next time a set of addresses is purchased, as is customary and generally permitted in advertising, if it contains the address just deleted? In this case, you do not want to (and are not allowed to) send the person advertising again despite their objection. In order to be able to identify

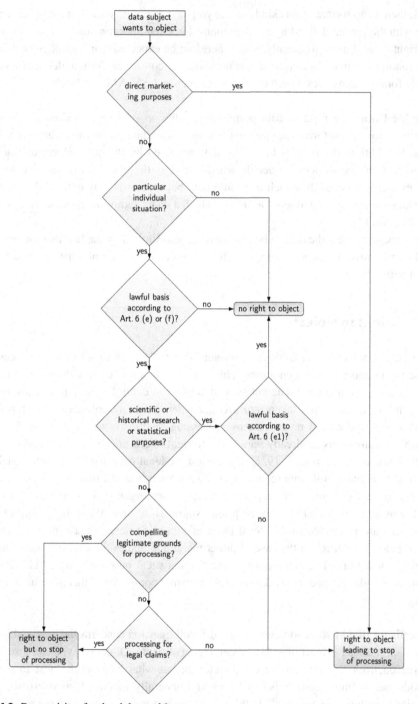

Fig. 4.2 Prerequisites for the right to object

this situation and handle it adequately, the most common solution is to keep an advertising blacklist with the contact details of those data subjects that have lodged such an objection, but of course this in itself is a form of processing of personal data, which needs a legal basis.

The German Data Protection Conference has described the use of a blacklist in [Kon18, p. 13] as an adequate tool in such cases. However, the person must be informed of the implementation of their objection when they are notified, with the information that the sending of advertising cannot be permanently prevented if they object to inclusion in this blocking file.

Public Advertising Opt-Out Lists A related topic are public opt-out lists that need to be considered in advertising. In many countries, there is some form of national opt-out list where consumers (or other data subjects) can register to state their objection to the processing of their personal data for advertising or marketing purposes. This does not only apply within the EU but also in many other countries worldwide, even though the exact rules about objecting or opting out are of course different.

> **Example 4.4 (National Opt-Out Lists)** A company based in the USA called a former customer (based in another state within the USA) via telephone to sell one of their new products. The former customer instigated private litigation because he was registered in the official advertising opt-out list of his home state and the company had not taken that list into account. The customer was eventually awarded a compensation of several thousand dollars.

4.8 Automated Individual Decision-Making

The right to a decision that is not solely automated (Art. 22 (1) GDPR) gives data subjects the right that decisions with legal effect on them, for example, about granting a loan or deciding a job application, are not exclusively automated, but have a manual component. For software development, this means that there must also be the option of manual intervention for all automated decisions, as formulated in the following requirement:

Requirement (F-23 Manual Decision-Making) *If the system makes automated individual decisions with legal or similar effects on the data subjects, then the system shall allow the controller to take these decisions manually instead.*

The system should document such manual decisions including the initial automated decision, if applicable.

Once the system supports such manual decisions, it would of course be possible to simply confirm the automated decision without thinking. Obviously, this is legally not acceptable even though proving it is difficult. If however the documentation in the second part of the requirement shows that the automated decisions are occasionally overthrown by a manual decision, this is an indicator that the manual decision is indeed a serious and separate decision.

In many use cases, allowing such manual decisions is contrary to what one wants to achieve using automation, but this involves a risk to the rights of the data subjects, for example, due to bias and discrimination as discussed in Sect. 3.1.6, and is therefore restricted by GDPR.

> **Case Study 4.4 (Automated Decision-Making at the Online Retailer)** In the online retail shop, automated case-by-case decisions regarding the payment methods offered are made on the basis of simple rules that specify, for example, that new customers can only order with advance payment. It must therefore be possible for employees, for example, from customer service, to change this decision in order to be able to respond to individual cases.

References

BBM18. Benedikt, Kristin, Buckel, Alexander, and Mammen, Jan Hendrik: *DSGVO und ePrivacy-VO auf Websites umsetzen (in German)*. Selbstverlag, 2018, ISBN 978-1720199472.

KB20. Kühling, Jürgen and Buchner, Benedikt (editors): *Datenschutz-Grundverordnung / BDSG. Kommentar (in German)*. C.H. Beck, 3. edition, 2020.

Kon18. Konferenz der unabhängigen Datenschutzaufsichtsbehörden des Bundes und der Länder (Datenschutzkonferenz): *Orientierungshilfe der Aufsichtsbehörden zur Verarbeitung von personenbezogenen Daten für Zwecke der Direktwerbung unter Geltung der Datenschutz-Grundverordnung (DS-GVO) (in German)*, 2018. https://www.datenschutzkonferenz-online.de/media/oh/20181107_oh_werbung.pdf

Pet19. Petrlic, Ronald: *Identitätsprüfung bei elektronischen Auskunftsersuchen nach Art. 15 DSGVO (in German)*. DuD Datenschutz und Datensicherheit, 43(2):71–75, 2019, ISSN 1862-2607.

Data Transfer

5

Abstract

In many cases, the pronounced division of labour in the economy also applies to IT and results in the need to divide the processing of personal data between different parties. IT companies, for example, often act as processors who process certain data on behalf of a customer, and this is also frequently the case as part of software development. Although sometimes difficult to distinguish, the joint controllership of the parties involved for the processing of personal data is a significantly different situation from a legal perspective. Cooperation between different parties becomes particularly complex if the data are transferred to so-called third countries, i.e. outside the territorial scope of the GDPR, and processed or stored there, for example, in the context of cloud usage. This chapter therefore describes the regulations defined by the GDPR under which an exchange of data is permitted and what effects this has on the architecture of ICT systems and their development. As such systems are often used across borders, the chapter concludes with a brief overview of the various data protection regulations worldwide.

5.1 Basic Rules for the Transfer of Personal Data

Software is often designed for different parties to work together, often including the exchange of (personal) data. For example, customers transfer tasks to a service provider that itself uses cloud or other third-party services. Different companies may work together on a task such as a contract. Credit agencies collect data and make it available to their customers for a fee. What all these examples have in common is that personal data are transferred from an organisation responsible for the data to a third party that is neither the original controller nor the data subject. This "third party" may belong to the same company group, for example, when legally separate companies within a company group carry out development or support together or if one company acts as a service provider for the others in the group.

Two fundamental conditions must be met before personal data can be transferred to any such third party, independently of whether they belong to the same company group or not: firstly, this transfer constitutes a form of processing for which there must be a legal basis. In addition, it must be ensured that the data are adequately protected by the recipient, i.e. that an appropriate level of data protection is in place at the recipient, which to some extent depends on the recipient's location. These two requirements are illustrated in Fig. 5.1 and will be considered in more detail below.

In addition to the legal bases already considered under Art. 6 (or Art. 9, if special categories of personal data are included), another possible legal basis for data transfer to a third party is commissioned processing, called *processing on behalf* of a controller or processor in GDPR, which will be discussed in Sect. 5.2. Another special case of processing is *joint controllership*, which will be explained in Sect. 5.3.

Requirement (C-08 Data Transfer from or to Third Parties) *Any transfer of personal data to or from third parties shall be identified in advance. For any such data transfer, the legal basis shall be identified and documented. In case the legal basis is a controller-processor relationship, a legal contract according to Art. 28 GDPR shall be agreed.*

Data Transfer Outside the EEA A distinction must be made between two main cases when it comes to the question of an appropriate level of data protection at the site of the recipient of the data. If the data remain within the European Economic Area (EEA) during the transfer and thus within the scope of the GDPR, such a level of data protection is generally assumed. If this is not the case, the adequate level of data protection must be proven by some other means, for which the GDPR offers several options (see Sect. 5.4).

Regardless of the legal basis for the data transfer and the proof of the adequate level of data protection used, it must always be ensured that the data exchange takes place in a secure manner (see Sect. 7.4.6).

If personal data are transferred outside the European Economic Area (EEA) where the GDPR is directly applicable, several additional requirements apply to ensure that an adequate level of data protection is in place at the destination, comparable to that within the territorial scope of the GDPR.

In order to assess whether there is an adequate level of data protection at the destination, the GDPR defines a number of criteria in Art. 44–50, which are considered in more detail in Sect. 5.4.

Unintentional Data Transfer Particularly in the area of software development, it is important to remember that such data transfer can also occur unintentionally, possibly even without the organisation or software developers being aware of it. This primarily concerns the use of cloud services as well as SDKs and SW libraries, where user data are

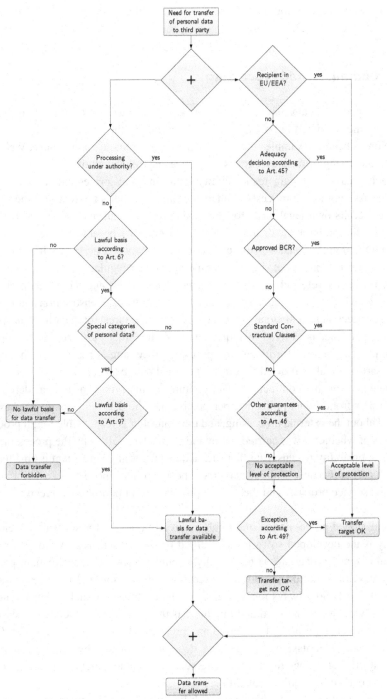

Fig. 5.1 Prerequisites for transferring personal data to third parties. Similar to BPMN, the "+" diamond is used as a parallel gateway, i.e. both branches must successfully be run through and combined at the parallel join in order to reach "Data transfer allowed"

sometimes transferred to the provider of the service, etc. This topic will be discussed in more detail in Sect. 6.6.2.

5.2   Commissioned Processing

Transfer of personal data may also be necessary if an organisation (the controller) does not process the data itself but uses a service or contractor (the processor) who will process the data on its behalf. Examples include cloud services, remote maintenance, Web hosting and the outsourcing of business processes such as payroll accounting.

In such a case, the main responsibility regarding data protection remains with the controller. As long as the processor adheres to the controller's instructions, the processor does not need its own legal basis for processing the data but may do so on the basis of a corresponding contract with the controller. In order to be able to use this privilege, Art. 28 GDPR requires that a contract is concluded between the controller, in this case the client, and the processor, i.e. the contractor, which regulates the cooperation. This contract is usually referred to as a *data processing agreement (DPA)*. In particular, it must be agreed that the processor is bound by the controller's instructions and will take appropriate (technical and organisational) security measures for handling the personal data. The controller is obliged to require and monitor this. Furthermore, the processor may not process the data for its own purposes. If processing is based on such a contract, the two parties are also allowed to transfer personal data between them as needed for the implementation of this contract. In such a situation, the processor is considered part of the controller from a data protection perspective, i.e. the data subjects do not have to be informed about the external processing, and the controller is responsible for all processing, regardless of whether it was carried out by the controller itself or by the processor.

The responsibility for ensuring that such a data processing agreement is concluded lies with both parties, because without a contract, the controller is not authorised to transfer the data to the service provider and the service provider is not permitted to receive or process the data.

Commissioned processing is often only indirectly relevant for software development, primarily if the developed software uses cloud or similar services. Although a contract for commissioned processing is not usually required during the development phase, the software developer should provide the necessary information and prepare the contract. In particular, it is not always recognisable for the customer of such a development that external services are being used and that there is therefore commissioned processing and which specific data are being transferred and processed by the service provider. Overall, this means that commissioned processing does not result in any requirements for the software itself, but it does result in requirements for the documentation of the software, as already covered by requirement C-08.

In contrast to this rather indirect responsibility of software development, IT operations usually have a very direct responsibility for the correct implementation of the data protection requirements on commissioned processing, as this is where cooperation with processors is performed in practice. Accordingly, IT operations must ensure that a DPA is in place for all services used to which personal data are transferred. Conversely, the IT organisation may also offer services for third parties, i.e. act as a processor itself, and a DPA must also be in place in this case. This must cover the customer's instructions relatively precisely, and it must be ensured that the data are processed in accordance with these instructions. It should also be noted that a processor may not use subcontractors for processing without the consent of the controller.

In practice, this DPA is often offered as a standard contract by the processor, for example, for a cloud service, so that the client's instructions are limited to providing a certain service or not. However, after that, the processor has little room for manoeuvre for its own decisions in relation to this processing but must adhere to the instructions set out in the contract.

(Remote) Maintenance A special case of commissioned processing is the (remote) maintenance of ICT systems. Although the provisions of the GDPR are only relevant here if personal data are processed, this is the case if a maintenance service provider gains access to log files or other personal data available in the ICT system during maintenance. In such a case, maintenance of a system is also a form of commissioned processing, which accordingly requires a DPA.

5.3 Joint Controllership

Joint controllership is characterised by the fact that several parties jointly decide on the processing of the data, in contrast to commissioned processing, where only one party decides and the other party is bound by the resulting instructions. The aim of the corresponding provisions in Art. 26 GDPR is to ensure that in these cases, the cooperation and the division of responsibility is clarified at least internally, i.e. between the joint controllers, while at the same time both are jointly responsible externally, in particular vis-à-vis the data subjects, for the entire processing including the fulfilment of the data subjects' rights.

The controllers can work together on an equal footing, but in most cases, there is a more or less clear division of labour between them, whereby one of the controllers is often in a leading role and defines the manner of cooperation alone. This applies, for example, to a travel agency that primarily collects travellers' data and then passes them on to the hotel, airline, etc. or to a company that reports its employees' data to the relevant health insurance company. More IT-related examples of joint controllership are fan or profile pages of companies in social networks or online advertising with tracking by third parties.

In these cases, the specific form of cooperation, in particular the responsibility for the fulfilment of data subjects' rights, must be defined in a joint agreement. This can be done in an individual agreement or in a standard contract specified by one of the parties involved, such as the airline or the operator of the social network in the examples above.

As far as feasible, it is usually preferable to structure the cooperation in such a way that there is a clear separation of responsibilities between the two parties, in order to avoid being liable for the activities of the other organisation. The prerequisite for this is that the tasks between the parties involved can be clearly delineated, and this can also be made clear to those affected.

Use of External Specialist Services In addition to the forms of cooperation between different parties described here and explicitly named in the GDPR, there is also the variant of *utilisation of third-party specialist services* (transfer of functions) already introduced in Sect. 2.7.4, in which the recipient of the data processes it on its own responsibility and separately from the sender. A typical example is a tax consultant who prepares the necessary tax documents for a company on behalf of the company, but under their own responsibility and not bound by instructions. The main difference to joint controllership is that each of the parties involved is responsible for their own processing.

The following Table 5.1 provides a brief overview of the forms of cooperation considered and the legal bases required for this.

Table 5.1 Forms of cooperation and their required legal bases

	Processing by data owner requires legal basis	Data transfer requires legal basis	Data recipient requires own legal basis for processing
Commissioned processing	Yes	Provided by DPA	Provided by DPA; bound by instructions
Joint responsibility	Yes	Yes	Yes
Utilisation of third-party specialist services	Yes	Yes	Yes

Processing of Prompts in Machine Learning Machine learning system often contain a model provided by some external provider. If this provider uses data from operating the system, for example, input prompts, to further train the system, then both parties act as controllers: the organisation using the model acts as controller for processing personal data using the machine learning model. The provider of the model acts as controller for the processing involved in training the system. Depending on the setup used, both may be separate controllers, or they may be joint controllers.

5.4   Transfer of Personal Data to Third Countries

In this context, the term "third countries" refers to countries outside the EEA that are not subject to the GDPR but have other legal regulations on data protection. If personal data are transferred to any of these countries, for example, as part of outsourcing or cloud computing, it must be ensured that the data are still adequately protected:

Requirement (C-09 Data Transfer Outside the EEA) *If personal data are to be transferred outside the European Economic Area, an adequate level of data protection must be ensured by the recipient.*

For the assessment of whether an adequate level of data protection is available, the GDPR provides, in Art. 44–50, a number of conditions as to how this proof can be provided. The most important of these conditions are:

- On the basis of an *adequacy decision* according to Art. 45 GDPR: Such an adequacy decision of the EU commission states that the level of data protection in the respective country is considered adequate. According to the list published by the European Commission [Eur], such adequacy decisions exist (as of August 2024) for Andorra, Argentina, Canada (commercial organisations), Faroe Islands, Guernsey, Israel, Isle of Man, Japan, Jersey, New Zealand, Republic of Korea, Switzerland, the UK, the USA (commercial organisations participating in the EU-US Data Privacy Framework; see below for more explanations) and Uruguay.
- On the basis of binding internal rules on data protection within a corporation (*Binding Corporate Rules BCR*) according to Art. 47 GDPR: companies generally have the option of adopting internal data protection rules as a basis for the transfer of data. These rules must be approved by the competent supervisory authority in consultation with the other supervisory authorities and must be legally binding. Due to these rather strong requirements, they are primarily suitable for large international corporations.[1]
- On the basis of *Standard Contractual Clauses*) according to Art. 46 (2)(c, d) GDPR, which are provided by the EU: There are four such sets of standard contractual clauses, based on the different roles involved in the transfer:[2]
  - Transfer controller to controller
  - Transfer controller to processor
  - Transfer processor to processor
  - Transfer processor to controller

---

[1] A list of such BCRs approved by the supervisory authorities is available at https://ec.europa.eu/newsroom/article29/item-detail.cfm?item_id=613841.

[2] These are available from https://eur-lex.europa.eu/eli/dec_impl/2021/914/oj.

- In addition, the GDPR allows a number of exceptions in Art. 49, for example, if explicit consent has been given for data transfer or if this is necessary to fulfil a contract.

If proof of an adequate level of data protection is provided on the basis of these rules, then personal data may be exchanged according to the same rules as within the EEA, for example, on the basis of an commissioned processing contract.

Representative Within the EU For organisations in third countries that process the data of EU citizens, there is an additional requirement, namely, the appointment of a representative within the EU (Art. 27 GDPR), in order to provide data subjects and supervisory authorities with a point of contact within the EU.

Data Exchange Within a Company Group It is important in this context that the regulations described also apply within a group. For example, if the parent company of a Swedish company is based outside the EU, personal data (e.g. employee data) may only be transferred to the parent company if the above conditions are met.

Case Study 5.1 (Matomo Hosting at the Software Company) The software company wants to use the tool Matomo to analyse the use of its Web site (Web analytics). Matomo is available as open-source software and can therefore be installed on the company's own server. However, the company has decided to use a hosting solution from the software provider. Since the provider is a company from New Zealand, the legal basis for this must first be clarified:

As there is an EU adequacy decision for New Zealand, cooperation with the provider is basically possible under the same rules as within the EU. This requires a commissioned processing contract in which the cooperation and compliance with the relevant rules are defined. This contract also stipulates that the provider appoints a representative within the EU. Although this provision is not necessarily contained in the contract, as it relates to a legal obligation of the provider and not the software company, it gives the software company additional security that the provider fulfils its obligations under data protection law.

Transfer of Personal Data from the EU to the USA The USA is a particularly important third country, as many providers of cloud and other services such as social networks are based there and there are also other close economic ties between the EU and the USA, which also lead to an exchange of personal data. At the same time, it is particularly controversial in the case of the USA whether there is an adequate level of data protection there, as legal regulations such as the US Cloud Act allow the US intelligence services to collect and analyse data from non-Americans to an extent well beyond what is considered adequate in the EU, with no legal remedies possible against this.

Safe Harbor   To resolve this complex situation, the EU and the USA agreed on a framework for data protection in the so-called Safe Harbor Agreement. US companies were able to register under this agreement if they confirmed that they complied with the defined data protection requirements, and the EU adopted an adequacy decision stating that these companies had an adequate level of data protection. However, this decision was declared invalid by the European Court of Justice (ECJ) in 2015 due to the above-mentioned concerns after the Austrian Max Schrems lodged a complaint against the transfer of his data at Facebook to Facebook headquarters in the USA.

Privacy Shield   After Safe Harbor was declared invalid, the EU and the US negotiated a similar new agreement with somewhat stricter rules, the so-called EU-US Privacy Shield. Nevertheless, this new agreement did not solve the fundamental problem either, and in July 2020, again following a complaint by Max Schrems, this agreement was also declared invalid by the ECJ ("Schrems II judgement").

Trans-Atlantic Data Privacy Framework   In 2022, a new agreement between the EU and the USA was formed to address the criticisms stated in the Schrems II judgement and to make data transfer between the EU and the USA easier. This "Trans-Atlantic Data Privacy Framework" included certain restrictions on the powers of intelligence services in the USA, which were implemented via a presidential executive order in October 2022. Based on that, the EU Commission adopted a new adequacy decision in July 2023.[3] Again, this decision is expected to be challenged in court, and it remains to be seen what the ECJ will eventually decide.

The new framework also set up some additional requirements on companies that want to join it and to confirm that they provide an adequate level of data protection. In order to do so, they have to self-certify that they adhere to the principles of the framework, based on a self-assessment or an outside compliance review. Although joining is voluntary, once an organisation has joined the framework, it is bound to comply to its requirements under US law.

---

[3] Apart from the EU-US framework discussed here, almost identical agreements exist between Switzerland and the USA, as well as between the UK and the USA. For more information about the framework and its implementation in the USA, see https://www.dataprivacyframework.gov/.

5.5   Use of Cloud Services

In cloud computing, services are provided via the Internet so that they are available from almost anywhere, and it is usually not recognisable to the user where the service is provided.[4] The different variants of cloud computing cover a wide range and include, for example, the storage and possibly synchronisation of data, such as the synchronisation of files, appointments and addresses and the provision of computing capacity for complex calculations.

From a data protection perspective, the following issues must be considered when using cloud services:

- *Form of collaboration*: this usually involves commissioned processing, particularly in the case of the service models "Platform as a Service (PaaS)" and "Infrastructure as a Service (IaaS)", where the service provider provides a platform or infrastructure for use. With the "Software as a Service (SaaS)" service model, shared responsibility may also be an option depending on the constellation.

  Accordingly, when using cloud services, a commissioned processing agreement is required with the service provider as described above or, in some cases, an agreement on joint controllership instead.

- The *location of service provision* is usually not relevant for cloud computing from a technical perspective and can therefore change repeatedly, especially for large providers with globally distributed data centres. From a data protection perspective, however, this location is very relevant, as otherwise an appropriate level of data protection cannot be ensured during processing.

  When using cloud services, it is therefore important that the DPA also specifies where the data are processed and from which countries the data can be accessed. At least the major providers have now adapted to this requirement and offer cloud services, for example, where data are only processed at predefined locations, e.g. within the EU. It is important that all forms of processing are taken into account, even if, for example, the data are stored in a different country than where it is later analysed or otherwise processed.

- Finally, *information security* must be taken into account, both for the transfer of data between the user and the service provider and for processing by the service provider. In order to demonstrate adequate security, most cloud providers have one or more relevant certifications, for example, according to ISO/IEC 27018 or other relevant norms and standards (see Sect. 1.4).

---

[4] This description is based on the widely accepted definition of cloud computing published by the US *National Institute of Standards and Technology* (NIST), which can be found at http://nvlpubs. nist.gov/nistpubs/Legacy/SP/nistspecialpublication800-145.pdf.

The user of cloud services is usually neither interested in checking the information security and appropriate implementation of data protection with a cloud provider themselves, nor able to do so. It is therefore usually best for both contracting parties if the review of the cloud service provider required by the GDPR is limited to checking the existence of relevant certification.

Encryption for Cloud Services As far as possible, data stored with a cloud service provider should also be encrypted, but this only works for the pure storage of data and not if it is also processed by the service provider.[5]

It is important to consider when and where this encryption takes place. Some cloud providers offer to encrypt the data and then store it in encrypted form, but this means that at least the cloud provider still has access to the data. Even if the provider itself does not access the data, there is still a risk that the provider's employees will do so. Furthermore, in such a case, the provider is a worthwhile target for attackers who, once they have cracked the provider's protection mechanisms, can gain access to the data of all customers. Therefore, if possible, the data should be encrypted by the customers themselves before it is transferred to the service provider and stored there.

Cloud Services Offered Free of Charge Many providers offer their cloud services free of charge, at least for private users. It should be borne in mind that, with rare exceptions, they do not do this out of generosity but that the services have to be financed in some other way, often by using the data for advertising purposes. So you have to be very careful what the provider's terms and conditions say about the use of the data, and be careful about which data are stored there. For companies, there is the additional risk that their employees may use such free services unofficially, without permission by the company, and store customer data in the form of calendar entries or photos, for example. Even if the direct contact person at the customer has no problem with this and possibly uses the same services, this does not necessarily apply to their legal department, especially since in these cases such data storage is often not just a data protection problem but also a violation of customer contracts or confidentiality agreements.

---

[5] With *homomorphic encryption*, cf. Sect. 7.4.3, there is also an approach for processing data without decrypting it. However, homomorphic encryption is currently still a research topic and cannot be used in practice on a large scale.

Example 5.1 (Use of MS Office 365) The product MS Office 365 is currently used by many companies, but it is currently heavily disputed whether and under which conditions the use of this product is acceptable from a data protection point of view.[6] The main issue in this dispute concerns the transfer of personal data outside the EU. According to the EDPS, Microsoft does not provide adequate transparency about which data are transferred and for what purpose.

In principle, MS Office 365 is a form of commissioned processing within the meaning of Art. 28 GDPR, so that a corresponding contract must be concluded with the provider Microsoft, which contains the relevant assurances with regard to data protection. This is not a speciality for Microsoft but is offered as standard, at least in Europe.

---

[6]Probably the most visible aspect of this dispute is the finding of the EDPS that the EU Commission's use of MS Office 365 infringes data protection law; see https://www.edps. europa.eu/press-publications/press-news/press-releases/2024/european-commissions-use-microsoft-365-infringes-data-protection-law-eu-institutions-and-bodies_en.

Reference

Eur. European Commission: *Adequacy decisions. How the EU determines if a non-EU country has an adequate level of data protection.* https://commission.europa.eu/law/law-topic/data-protection/international-dimension-data-protection/adequacy-decisions_en

Technical and Organisational Implementation of Data Protection

6

Abstract

There is a large number of concepts and frameworks for implementing the data protection requirements into (IT and other) systems. Individual measures to do so are often summarised as technical and organisational measures. Technologies that support privacy, often by allowing to process data while limiting data access, are known as privacy-enhancing technologies. Examples of such technologies include anonymisation, federated learning or synthetic data generation. A very fundamental approach to implementing data protection is data protection by design, as required by the GDPR. This is based on the idea that data protection needs to be implemented in the development of systems from the start. Data protection needs to be integrated into the design of a system from the outset and across the entire life cycle, not as an issue that is implemented at the end through a data protection review and subsequent adaptation of the system.

6.1 Technical and Organisational Measures (TOM)

Technical and organisational measures (TOM) serve to implement the abstract requirements of data protection and are therefore required from different viewpoints in the GDPR. In Art. 24 GDPR, the implementation of suitable TOM to ensure and demonstrate compliance with the requirements of the GDPR is required. Article 25 GDPR adds more detail and requires the use of data protection by design and by default as described in more detail in Sect. 6.5. Additionally, Art. 32 GDPR requires TOM for the security of processing, i.e. protection against external influences, discussed in Chap. 7 of this book. Documentation of the TOM is required "where possible" as part of the RoPA, but

© The Author(s), under exclusive license to Springer-Verlag GmbH,
DE, part of Springer Nature 2025
R. Kneuper, *Data Protection for Software Development and IT*,
https://doi.org/10.1007/978-3-662-70639-8_6

surprisingly, this only applies to security TOM (Art. 30 (1)(g) GDPR). Nevertheless, it is still recommended to get a better overview and as proof if needed to document all TOM within the RoPA.

The GDPR does not generally require any specific measures but requires that controllers select and implement adequate and effective measures to conform to the data protection principles in the specific context. GDPR mentions pseudonymisation and encryption of data as examples of technical measures, and other organisational measures that may be appropriate include the use of process descriptions, the use of suitable criteria for supplier selection or the creation of legal documents such as contracts or confidentiality agreements with clients and contractors.[1]

Integration of TOM into a Data Protection Management System (DPMS) If the TOM are combined into a comprehensive and consistent system that is continuously maintained and improved as required, this is also referred to as a *data protection management system*, analogous to other management systems such as a quality management system.

6.2   Internal Regulations

6.2.1 Basic Rules

No matter how large or small a (software or IT) organisation is, it needs to define a number of basic internal rules on data protection and train all its employees on them, so that all employees know them and are aware of their importance. Obviously, it would be too much to expect employees to be completely familiar with and able to implement the relevant processes, but they need to know when to initiate these processes and contact a central authority in the company such as a data protection officer. For example, employees need to know about those issues for which they may receive requests from data subjects which they should pass on urgently to comply with GDPR deadlines. Additionally, they need to know about those data protection issues that they are likely to come across in their daily work and need to handle adequately.

Therefore, the following basic rules should be introduced:

- If customers or other persons ask for information about or deletion of their personal data, i.e. they assert their right of access, to erasure, etc. they must not be turned away or referred to other contact persons, because the corresponding deadlines (usually one month) begin to run with this first request. Instead, the enquiry, including the relevant contact details, must be recorded and forwarded immediately to the designated authority within the company.

---

[1] Extensive discussions of TOM can for example be found in [EDP20, Fed24].

- In the event of a data breach (or at least the suspicion thereof, e.g. through a corresponding external tip-off), there is a 72-hour deadline for reporting to the responsible supervisory authority (see Sect. 6.2.2). The relevant internal authority must be informed immediately if such a data breach is detected. Examples include the use of an open mailing list and the theft or loss of a laptop.
- When sending emails to distribution lists beyond a team (information, newsletter), the recipients must be set to blind copy (BCC) so that they are not visible to other recipients. The decisive factor here is not the number of recipients but whether this makes personal data known to other recipients of the email.
- When using social networks, photos of employees, customers and others may only be posted with the consent of the persons depicted. As a reminder, such consent must be explicit, voluntary and revocable. Analyses of these networks and their use are also only permitted to a very limited extent, as they usually relate to personal data.

These are just a few, very basic rules, but all employees should know them and be aware of their importance, i.e. appropriate training must be provided and repeated regularly. Depending on the size of the organisation and the type and risk of the data processed, these basic rules should also be described in more detail, for example, in the form of defined processes.

In addition, there are some basic rules that should be defined and implemented regarding the design and development of ICT systems:

- As far as possible, the storage or other processing of personal data should be avoided when developing or operating ICT systems, for example, by anonymising the data if it is not possible to completely avoid using them.
- If personal data are stored or otherwise processed in an ICT system, this processing must be agreed with those responsible for data protection, for example, the data protection officer of your own organisation or of the customer, in order to clarify the legal basis and the appropriate protective measures.
- If libraries, SDKs or similar third-party tools are used, it must be checked whether these tools themselves pass on data, even without the organisation's own software being actively involved (see Sect. 6.6.3 for more detail).

6.2.2   Handling of Data Breaches

If any data protection requirements are not met, this is referred to as a data breach. In addition to the use of an open distribution list or the theft or loss of a laptop or smartphone mentioned above, examples of such data breaches include errors in the disposal of printouts or data storage medium, as well as unauthorised access to data due to deficiencies in information security, which may also be noticed and reported by external parties.

Notification and Communication Requirements If a data breach poses a risk to data subjects, the GDPR requires a corresponding notification to the competent supervisory authority, which must be submitted within 72 hours of becoming known (Art. 33 (1) GDPR). Of course, it is unpleasant having to inform the supervisory authority about problems that have arisen in one's organisation. However, it is at least true that (in many countries, e.g. Germany) such a report may not be used in criminal or fine proceedings.

If the risk to the data subjects caused by the data breach is high, the data subjects themselves must also be informed (Art. 34 (1) GDPR). Whether this is the case should be decided in consultation with the supervisory authority. As data breaches often affect many data subjects, this information may involve considerable effort. Depending on the industry sector and type of application, additional reporting obligations may also be relevant, but these will not be discussed further here.

If a data breach does not cause any risks to the data subjects, there are no notification or communication obligations, for example, in case of a power failure that makes the data temporarily unavailable or the loss of a USB stick with encrypted data. Even in such cases, however, the data breach should be handled in accordance with the procedure described below in order to prevent future recurrences with potentially greater damage.

Organisational Implementation In order to meet the 72-hour deadline, it must be ensured that the information is not delayed for long before it reaches the responsible persons within the organisation. It must therefore be clarified in advance who is responsible for handling such data breaches, and this must be known to all employees. Figure 6.1 provides an overview of the measures that are required once a (suspected) data breach becomes known.

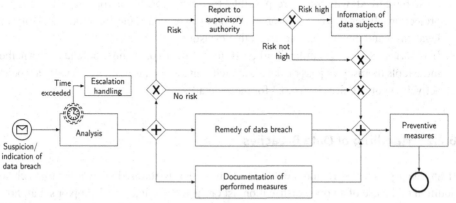

Fig. 6.1 Handling of data breaches (in BPMN format)

Analysis   As soon as the information about a suspected data breach reaches the defined responsible parties, a quick and comprehensive assessment and response to the following questions is required:

- What exactly happened? What countermeasures should be taken?
- Is it a data breach within the meaning of the GDPR or a reportable incident under some other set of regulations?
- If so, does this data breach result in no risk, a medium risk or a high risk for the data subjects?
- What information needs to be provided to the competent supervisory authority? On the one hand, all legally required information must be provided; on the other hand, you naturally do not want to provide more evidence than necessary for an investigation by the supervisory authority with possible sanctions.
- What information may have to be communicated to data subjects, and which data subjects are affected?

You should be well prepared for such an analysis in order to be able to work through these questions (with the exception of the last one) within the required 72 hours if necessary.

Further Handling of Data Breach   Depending on the results of the analysis, the competent supervisory authority may need to be notified, and after consultation with the authority, the data subjects may need to be informed. At the same time, the data breach itself must be remedied, insofar as this is possible retrospectively, and care must be taken to minimise the damage caused. It is also important to document the corresponding measures in order to be able to prove later that the data breach was dealt with appropriately. You should also keep an eye on the extent to which there are public reactions to the data breach, for example, in the press or social media, and how you deal with them if necessary. And finally, once the urgent measures have been taken, you should clarify what caused the data breach and how you can prevent it from happening again.

The Role of Software Development and IT   Software development and IT are not directly responsible for reporting and handling data breaches; this is the responsibility of the controller. In practice, however, the controller usually requires appropriate information and support in order to be able to fulfil this responsibility adequately.

Data Breaches and Commissioned Processing   A particular challenge arises in the event of data protection breaches in the context of commissioned processing. As the 72-hour deadline also applies in this case, it is particularly important that the processor forwards the information to the controller quickly. The responsibility for the notification and further processing also lies with the controller for the entire processing in the case of order processing, but the processor must support this accordingly, in particular by providing the relevant information.

Example 6.1 (Data Breach Due to a Missing Update of Access Rights) In the company discussed in this example, temporary external employees were sometimes used to take on tasks within the company for a limited period of time to cope with major fluctuations of the work load.

One employee, who frequently supervised such external staff and sometimes maintained contact even after the end of their temporary contract, was repeatedly informed by former external employees that they still had access to internal systems. He passed this information on to superiors and IT in each case, but sometime later, a former external employee approached him again because he had received another automatically generated request to process certain tasks, including access information to the relevant (personal and confidential) data.

This time, he reported the problem to the company DPO and a few days later received a call from IT, which referred to that report and wanted to know additional details in order to rectify this data breach. The process for dealing with former employees was then revised to ensure that the access rights for all relevant systems were deactivated but could be reactivated with little effort in the event of a follow-up contract.

From a data protection perspective, this situation involved two serious problems:

- The DPO did not comply with his duty of confidentiality (towards the employee) but passed on the information including the identity of the employee to IT without asking this employee first. This is a serious breach of trust and contradicts the GDPR requirements for data protection officers (Art. 38 (5) GDPR).
- The company did not adequately address the repeated minor data breaches and in particular did not adapt the process for revoking access rights for external employees leaving the company. It was only after a more serious data breach occurred, and the DPO was involved that the problem was finally addressed.

6.2.3   Training and Commitment of Employees

Training on Data Protection In order for employees to be able to implement the relevant data protection requirements, they must be familiar with them, i.e. appropriate training (whether in the form of Web training, classroom training or any other form of training) is required. This is usually implemented as short, regularly repeated training for all employees, supplemented as required by more in-depth training for those employees who deal with personal data on a larger scale, for example, in a human resources department.

Commitment to Confidentiality In order to ensure that employees adhere to the relevant rules, some form of employee commitment to maintain data confidentiality is required following the training. In other words, in order for the organisation to implement the data protection requirements, it must ensure that employees also do their part and explicitly commit to complying with the relevant data protection regulations. Although this is not an explicit requirement of the GDPR, it is implicit in the requirements regarding TOM and the security of processing (Art. 24 and Art. 32 (4) GDPR).

6.3 Anonymisation of Data

Depending on the task, the connection between data and the person that these data refer to may or may not be required for an application. For example, while the identity of the customer must in general be known for processing orders, this is usually not the case for statistical analyses of orders. In the latter case, anonymisation of the data is appropriate, especially if the original data are no longer required for operational purposes but data analyses are still desired. The same applies if data are to be published, for example, for research purposes or to fulfil freedom of information requests.

However, simply omitting identifiers such as name or customer number is usually not sufficient for anonymisation. With the help of a combination of other data fields such as postcode, date of birth or gender, the so-called quasi-identifiers, the relevant person can often still be identified or at least restricted to a small group of candidates (see Sect. 2.3). The following description is intended to provide an initial insight into anonymisation so that suitable methods and algorithms can be selected as necessary. Similar to the encryption of data, it is strongly discouraged to use your own methods for anonymisation; instead, proven and tested methods should be used.

From a data protection perspective, it must be taken into account that anonymisation is also a form of processing personal data, i.e. there must also be a legal basis for this. However, this will usually be provided by the "legitimate interest" of the controller, especially as anonymisation is usually also in the interest of the data subjects.

6.3.1 Basic Concepts

Attribute Types To evaluate the anonymity of data, different types of data need to be distinguished:

- *Identifiers* are used to assign data records (also referred to as tuples in a database) to a specific person. These include the name as an obvious identifier, even if it is often not unique in practice, as well as artificial identifiers such as customer, matriculation or tax numbers. As identification is to be prevented in anonymisation, the identifiers need to be removed for anonymisation and are therefore not considered further below.

- In addition to intended identifiers, there often are many more attributes that can serve as identifiers, at least in combination, and which are therefore referred to as *quasi-identifiers*.
- Identification, i.e. the assignment of a tuple to a person, is only problematic if the tuple also contains confidential or *sensitive data*. Depending on the specific situation, these may overlap with the quasi-identifiers. The sensitive data are the data to be protected, and their assignment to a person is to be prevented by anonymisation.
- Finally, there may also be *non-sensitive data* that would be unproblematic to assign to a person. However, it is usually not easy to assign the non-sensitive data alone, so they are usually protected or anonymised together with any sensitive data. Since the non-sensitive data are not relevant in the context of anonymisation, they are not considered any further below.

Threats to Anonymity Once data have been anonymised, the following threats to anonymity may arise:

- Re-identification (de-anonymisation) may be possible, i.e. the anonymised data can, at least partially, be assigned to specific persons again.
- Attribute derivation: information about individuals can be derived, for example, because their identity can be restricted to a group that all have the corresponding attribute.
- Membership derivation: it may be possible to derive whether a certain person belongs to a dataset under consideration. This information can be problematic sensitive by itself if, for example, it concerns visitors to a counselling centre. Just like membership, non-membership can also be sensitive information.

Additionally, such a break of anonymity is not the only potential problem, but sometimes sensitive information can be derived with a high degree of probability though not certainty.

A similar definition of threats to anonymity is given by [Art14, p. 11f]:

- Singling out: "possibility to isolate some or all records which identify an individual in the dataset"
- Linkability: "ability to link, at least, two records concerning the same data subject or a group of data subjects"
- Inference: "possibility to deduce, with significant probability, the value of an attribute from the values of a set of other attributes"

Different techniques can be used to implement these threats to anonymisation, including the linking of different data records, each of which may be unproblematic on its own but which together allow sensitive information to be assigned. For some examples, see the processing of health insurance data in Massachusetts and the case of Netflix, both described in Sect. 2.3. The publication of different analyses of the same dataset may also allow undoing anonymity by creating differences (e.g. "Number of examinees who have passed the exam" vs. "Number of examinees other than Ralf Kneuper who have passed the exam"), similarly the same analysis of different levels of a dataset ("At the end of May, 120 out of 131 examinees passed the exam" vs. "At the end of June, 120 out of 132 examinees passed the exam". Anyone who happens to know—by chance or through research based on this information—that a particular student took the exam in June also knows that they did not pass).

The methods and anonymity models described below help protect against these threats. First, however, the scenarios in which anonymisation is used should be introduced.

Anonymisation Scenarios There are various scenarios that need to be considered when discussing anonymisation. In the first scenario, a trustworthy trustee collects the data of the data subjects and anonymises or at least pseudonymises them. He then makes them available to third parties (data users) for evaluation (see Fig. 6.2). This gives the data users considerable freedom to analyse the data as desired. However, this scenario requires a great deal of trust from the clients in the trustee. Additionally, it places high demands on the quality of anonymisation, as the trustee also has little or no control over how the data are subsequently evaluated or combined with other data once they have been provided. In addition, the data are still personal data, and the trustee must protect them accordingly, which would not be the case with anonymised data.

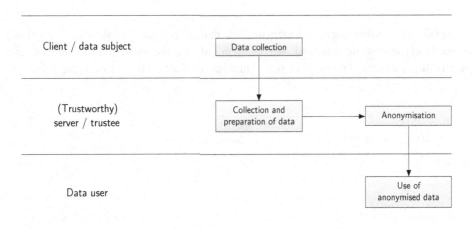

Fig. 6.2 Anonymisation scenario 1: using a trustworthy trustee who provides the anonymised data to the data users

The second scenario also assumes a trustworthy trustee who stores the personal data, but in this scenario, the trustee only releases anonymised evaluations and no raw data, not even in anonymised form (see Fig. 6.3). This reduces the risks involved, and especially in the context of differential privacy described below, there are some algorithms that are particularly suitable for this case.

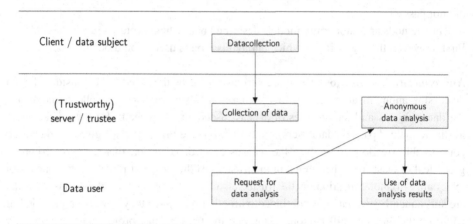

Fig. 6.3 Anonymisation scenario 2: using a trustworthy trustee who provides anonymised data analyses

Finally, the third scenario considers the case that data are anonymised at the client site immediately after collection, and only anonymised data are passed on to the server and finally the user of the data (see Fig. 6.4). This way, no trustworthy trustee is required.

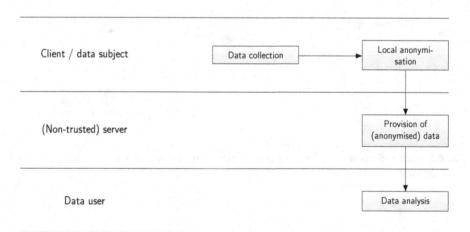

Fig. 6.4 Anonymisation scenario 3: no trustee, anonymisation at client site

6.3.2 Anonymisation Procedure

Even if there is no widespread standard procedure for anonymising personal data, the following steps should generally be taken into account:

1. Identification of affected data and their intended use
2. Initial risk assessment
3. Basic anonymisation
4. Repeat risk assessment
5. Further anonymisation as needed, based on anonymity model

In the following, these steps will be explained in more detail.

Identification of Affected Data and Their Intended Use First of all, it is important to identify the data involved, which purposes they are still needed for and what use they will be put to. (If the data are no longer needed, they should be deleted, and anonymisation is superfluous). It must also be ensured that the planned anonymisation and, in particular, the subsequent use and possibly publication of the data are based on a suitable legal basis.

In this context, the types of the attributes contained in the data must be identified, i.e. to what extent they are identifiers, quasi-identifiers, sensitive data or other data. In particular, in the case of quasi-identifiers, it is also relevant to know which other data records exist that could be used for re-identification.

Initial Risk Assessment In this step, the risks associated with the data are identified and evaluated, as usual by evaluating the potential damage and the probability of that damage occurring:

- *impact:* What is the potential impact on the data subjects if anonymity of the data is partly or even fully breached, and what protection is therefore required? If special categories of personal data are affected, a (at least) high risk should normally be assumed. In this analysis, the most unfavourable case must always be considered, i.e. what is the maximum damage that could possibly occur.
- *probability of damage:* As the probability of damage depends heavily on the measures used, this initial consideration should only take into account the availability of the data, considering who or how many users have access to the data. For example, if the data are to be made publicly available, the risk of misuse is much greater than if the anonymised data are only available to a narrowly restricted group of users.

Basic Anonymisation (Using Generalisation and Suppression of Data) Before using more complex approaches to anonymisation as described below, basic steps should be carried out, starting obviously with the deletion of identifiers. The *US Department of*

Health & Human Services has, as part of the HIPAA regulations and called *Safe Harbor*,[2] defined a list of information items which are considered as (quasi-)identifiers and must be removed to anonymise the data [Off12]. This list comes from the healthcare sector but can also be applied to other areas after slight adjustments. For less critical data, it may be possible to relax these rules, but for very sensitive data, it may be necessary to tighten them.

The HIPAA Safe Harbor Rules for Anonymisation The following information must be deleted for anonymisation according to Safe Harbor:

- *Names* of individuals
- *Geographic subdivisions*, which refer to units of less than 20,000 people. In many countries, this implies that the ZIP code may not be kept fully but only in abbreviated form, leaving out at least one sign.[3]
- *Dates* (except year) that relate to an individual, for example, a birth date or the admission date to a hospital. Additionally, ages over 89 years should only be kept in an aggregated category "90 years or older".

   In contexts other than hospitals or health services, this upper age limit should usually be reduced, and an additional lower limit may also be needed. For example, in a list of employees, the upper limit should usually be set below the retirement age.
- *Telephone numbers* and *telefax numbers*
- *Email addresses*
- Unique identifiers such as *social security numbers, medical record numbers, health plan beneficiary numbers, account numbers* and *certificate or license number*
- *Vehicle identifiers, license plate numbers*
- *Device identifiers and serial number* such as the IMEI number of a mobile phone or the tracking ID of Android or iOS devices
- *Web Universal Resource Locators (URLs)*
- *IP addresses*

   When analysing the use of Web sites (Web analytics), however, the IP addresses of visitors are still required. Safe Harbor does not consider this case as it is not normally relevant in the context of health data.

   Analogous to the shortening of ZIP codes, at least the IP address should be shortened in order to reach units with at most around 20,000 persons. Somewhat simplified, we assume that an IP address can be uniquely assigned to a person, and therefore units of at least 20,000 IP addresses are required.

---

[2] Not to be confused with the former contract of the same name between the EU and the USA (see Sect. 5.4).

[3] For example, in Germany, Austria and Switzerland, a ZIP code typically refers to about 2,000 to 4,000 people.

In order to form units of about 20,000 people based on a current world population of about 8 billion people, a maximum of 400,000 ($\approx 2^{18}$) such units may be distinguished, assuming an approximately even distribution of people across the units for the sake of simplicity (but not entirely correct). In other words, the identification of the unit, in this case the IP address, may be specified to a maximum of 18 bits, i.e. IP addresses must be shortened to a maximum of 18 bits for anonymisation, regardless of whether it is an IPv4 address with 32 bits or an IPv6 address with 128 bits.

The implementation of this regulation can be difficult, as the most widely used system for Web analytics, Google Analytics, only deletes *one* octet of an IPv4 address, i.e. shortens the address to 24 bits, corresponding to units of just under 500 persons, even in the case of "anonymisation". With Matomo, on the other hand, the number of octets to be deleted can be set as a parameter and should be set to 2. However, since Web analytics does not normally involve health data—as assumed in Safe Harbor—a reduction to 24 bits may be justifiable as long as it does not involve Web sites with particularly sensitive data and no other parameters are recorded that can be used in combination with the (shortened) IP address for identification.

- *Biometric identifiers*, including finger prints
- *Full-face photos*
- *Other unique identifiers, characteristics of codes*

Generalisation and Suppression The described adjustments are special cases of the general concepts of *generalisation* and *suppression*:

- *Generalisation*: if there are many different possible values of a quasi-identifier, the information content of a specific value is high, and each value severely restricts the number of possible persons. To reduce this effect, the number of values can be reduced by generalisation, i.e. by aggregating or summarising them. For example, according to the rules described, only the year of birth is given instead of the exact date of birth, and postcodes or IP addresses are stored in abbreviated form.
- *Suppression* refers to the deletion of certain data, for example, complete attributes such as name or national insurance number. Alternatively, individual fields can also be suppressed, for example, whenever a certain value occurs only rarely (outliers). For example, in many cases, the specification of the occupation is unproblematic. However, if the occupation in an employee database is "Chief Executive Officer", this no longer applies, and the field with this value must be suppressed.[4]

---

[4] Of course, it is not enough to suppress just this one field of a data record, but an appropriate number of other fields must also be suppressed, as otherwise the suppression itself would represent a unique marking.

Repeat Risk Assessment The aim of repeating the risk assessment is primarily to estimate the probability of a breach of anonymity, and thus the remaining risk after basic anonymisation has been carried out. This includes an assessment of how well a dataset allows to identify individuals and what other data are available that could be linked to remove anonymity.

In particular, any steps of basic anonymisation that may have been excluded from the list above must be taken into account, for example, if certain quasi-identifiers are required for the application and therefore not generalised or suppressed. The risk involved may also change over time, for example, due to new methods of data analysis. Therefore, if anonymous data are published repeatedly, the risk assessment must also be updated regularly.

It may also be necessary to reassess the need for protection in order to take changes of the environment into account.

Further Anonymisation Depending on the remaining residual risk, further anonymisation based on the anonymity models introduced below may be appropriate. These models primarily help quantify the degree of anonymity achieved and the degree of anonymity required in order to decide on further anonymisation steps.

Apart from generalisation and suppression, other common techniques are the permutation of data and the addition of noise. (The following explanation assumes that data are structured in a database table where each row represents one person.)

- *Permutation* of data within a column is a useful measure if the relationship between the values in that column and the values in other columns is not important, but statistical analyses such as mean value and variance over the values in the column are performed. In this case, values in that column can be swapped between different rows.
- *Adding "noise"* describes the process of systematically adding small errors that do not or at least only slightly affect the results of the required analyses but at the same time modifying statements about individuals in such a way that they are no longer useful. If, for example, random numbers are added to the individual values according to a known probability distribution, the individual values can hardly be used, but thanks to the known distribution, this "noise" can be eliminated when calculating parameters such as the mean value.

6.3.3 Anonymity Models

If anonymisation is insufficiently well thought-out, it can be reversed, as the examples in Sect. 2.3 show. The most promising approach to such re-identification (also known as de-anonymisation) consists of linking [5] the anonymised data with other, (publicly) available data. In order to prevent such re-identification, various anonymity models have been developed that assess the degree of anonymity and thus quantify the difficulty of re-identifying anonymised data. Closely related, there are suitable algorithms that help achieve anonymity according to these models. The best-known anonymity models are k-anonymity (with various additions) and differential privacy, both explained in more detail below. An overview of these methods and their strengths and weaknesses can be found in [GDLS14].

All of these models relate to analyses of large amounts of data where the identity of individuals is not important, but where statements are to be made about a large set of people. At the same time, there is often a need to relate different data points referring to the same person. One example is the analysis of the success of advertisements, i.e. the question of what proportion of people that were shown a particular advertisement bought the advertised product. Similar analyses deal with health data, for example, the success of certain therapies or certain hospitals.

In this context, it is important to understand that the aim of such anonymity models is to evaluate and quantify the anonymity achieved. How a certain degree of anonymity can be achieved is not part of the model itself. In the following, k-anonymity and differential privacy are therefore presented as the best-known anonymity models, but only with brief references to the associated algorithms and procedures.

6.3.4 *k*-Anonymity

The concept of k-anonymity was developed by Samarati and Sweeney to assess the degree of anonymity of a set of data [Sam01, Swe02], usually represented as a (database) table with the identifiers (keys) already removed. This approach primarily supports the first of the anonymisation scenarios described above (see Fig. 6.2).

Anonymity Measure A set of data is called k-anonymous if, for any information (values of quasi-identifiers) available about a certain person, there are at least $k - 1$ other persons which, based on the given information, cannot be distinguished from that person. Such a group of k (or more) members is called an equivalence class.

Definition 6.1 A table is called k-anonymous (for some value $k \in \mathbb{N}$) if any combination of values of the quasi-identifiers in the table occurs at least k times (or not at all).

The parameter k defines the degree of anonymity, where however a large degree of anonymity usually leads to a low degree of accuracy of the results of any evaluations.

---

[5] "Joining" the data, as it is called in database terminology.

Implementation The most important measures to achieve k-anonymity with an existing set of data are *generalisation* and *suppression* of data as described above [Sam01]. The measures described by Safe Harbor thus help achieve a higher degree of k-anonymity, even though no specific value $k > 1$ can be guaranteed.

In order to implement these approaches with large sets of data, appropriate software support is necessary, where the use of suitable code libraries is recommended. Apart from the fact that this saves development effort, the use of such libraries also helps make use of the experience of specialists in the field of anonymisation and to avoid errors that might otherwise cancel out the desired anonymisation.[6]

Evaluation The use of k-anonymity (with a sufficiently high value k) provides good protection against the re-identification of data, but little protection against the derivation of attributes or group membership. Especially with a small k, it may still be possible to derive sensitive attributes if all members of the equivalence class have the same or at least similar values for this attribute. Background knowledge can also help exclude certain members of an equivalence class. For example, if you happen to know that the person you are looking for belongs to a certain equivalence class and is only 7 years old, it cannot be one of the members with pregnancy problems.

Since the definition of k-anonymity is based on the values of the quasi-identifiers, an incorrect list of quasi-identifiers can lead to k-anonymity not providing the expected protection. To reduce these problems, there are a number of extensions to k-anonymity, in particular l-diversity and t-closeness [GDLS14, Art14].

6.3.5   Differential Privacy

Differential privacy attempts to overcome the limitations of k-anonymity by taking a completely different approach, limiting the amount of *knowledge that can be gained* from a single additional or modified dataset. Informally speaking, differential privacy describes that the results of analyses are changed only slightly by the inclusion of an additional person, so that very little information about this person can be inferred. Differential privacy is usually considered in the context of anonymisation scenario 2, i.e. with the use of a trusted server or trustee. However, the approach is also suitable for scenario 3 and is then also referred to as *local* differential privacy (see below).

The following description gives a first introduction to differential privacy; for a comprehensive discussion including the associated algorithms, see, for example, [DR13] or [WAB+18].

---

[6] An example of an open-source library for implementing k-anonymity and related approaches is ARX; see [ARX, PKLK14].

The central idea of differential privacy is that statistical noise with a known distribution is added to the original data. For each individual dataset, it is then no longer possible to recognise the extent to which the data have been distorted by this noise. For statistical analyses on the level of the entire dataset, however, the noise can be removed, thanks to the known distribution (given a sufficiently large amount of data). The simplest form of adding such noise is the so-called randomised response, but the Laplace distribution is also widely used.

Randomised Response   The principle of randomised response was originally developed in the social sciences and is used in surveys for questions in which the correct answer may be unpleasant for the respondent, and therefore, the risk of an incorrect answer is high, for example, "Have you stolen anything in the last month?" Algorithm 1 describes a possible implementation of this principle in the case of simple yes-no questions.

Algorithm 1 Example algorithm for randomised response

---
throw coin (unobserved)
if "head" **then**
    return correct answer   ▷ probability 50%
else
    throw second coin (unobserved)
    if "head" **then**
        return answer "no"   ▷ probability 25%
    else
        return answer "yes"   ▷ probability 25%
    end if
end if

By subtracting the inserted statistical noise from the survey result, the correct result is obtained, albeit with significantly reduced statistical accuracy. In the example algorithm, the 25% yes answers and 25% no answers caused by the coin toss need to be subtracted from the collected responses. The main advantage of this approach is that it is no longer recognisable for any given respondent whether the answer received reflects the result of the coin toss or the correct answer to the question. This is also referred to as "plausible deniability" of the answers. Of course, this only works as long as the same people are not asked repeatedly, as otherwise the statistical noise can also be eliminated for a single person.

Measuring Anonymity   Adding statistical noise is modelled by a "randomised function", i.e. a function whose result depends on one or more integrated random events. In the example of algorithm 1, these random events are the two coin tosses.

In order to measure the increase in knowledge that can be achieved by *one* record, the result of this randomised function is considered for different data collections that only differ in one record, and the difference is described as follows by a parameter $\epsilon \in \mathbb{R}^+$:

Definition 6.2 A randomised function f allows ϵ-differential privacy if for all datasets D_1 and D_2 which differ by at most one record and for all $S \subseteq \text{image}(f)$, the following condition holds:

$$P[f(D_1) \in S] \le e^\epsilon \times P[f(D_2) \in S]$$

Here $P[X]$ describes the probability of a random event X according to the distribution contained in f. If ϵ is small, ideally close to zero, then the factor e^ϵ will be close to 1, showing that there is little difference between the two probabilities.

This definition formalises the property that the increase in knowledge and thus the change in evaluation results is low if a single data record (i.e. information about one person) is changed or added. The meaning of "low" is quantified by the parameter ϵ, which thus describes the degree of anonymity achieved. In contrast to the parameter k in k-anonymity, a *small* value of ϵ describes a *high* degree of anonymity.

In the above example of randomised response, f is the algorithm, image(f) describes the set {yes, no} of possible values and f allows ϵ-differential privacy if ϵ is selected as $\ln 3 \approx 1.1$ (or larger) [DR13, Claim 3.5].

Differential Privacy Differential privacy normally assumes that there is a trusted server or trustee that ensures the differential privacy of the analyses. For many applications, this is not adequate, for example, for analyses of individual client applications such as Web browsers. In this case, *local* differential privacy [NXY+16] is introduced in which the statistical noise is not added to the totality of the data but to the data about individual clients. This increases the level of protection but leads to the difficulty that in total, the noise can become very large across all clients and impair the analysis of the results.

There are some open-source libraries for (local) differential privacy such as those published by Google[7] where the library for local differential privacy implements the *RAPPOR* method [EPK14] also developed by Google.

Evaluation Differential privacy offers (if implemented correctly) a mathematically verifiable degree of anonymisation, in which the amount of information flowing is restricted at the semantic level and therefore independent of any other prior knowledge of an attacker. This is a significant improvement over k-anonymity and related models, where certain

---

[7] https://github.com/google/differential-privacy, https://github.com/google/rappor

information flows are restricted at the syntactic level, allowing an attacker with prior knowledge or with a different form of attack to potentially break the anonymisation.

Differential privacy is therefore currently considered the best approach to anonymisation, and companies like Apple, Google and Uber stated that they use differential privacy. However, few details about their actual use of differential privacy are publicly known.

The downside of the high level of protection by differential privacy is that its application is complex and requires in-depth study of the topic. Depending on the context, differential privacy may require a large amount of noise to be added to the initial data so that the benefit of the anonymised data is significantly reduced.

Additionally, there are limitations to the degree of anonymity that can be achieved with differential privacy:

- The data of any individual person still have an influence on the overall result, because otherwise they could be omitted completely (as could the data of all other persons). Differential privacy with a sufficiently small value for ϵ does however ensure that this influence is small and that it is hardly possible to draw conclusions about any individual person.
- Results can still make statements about people as a group, even though no longer about any specific individual.

6.4 Privacy-Enhancing Technologies (PET)

As the name suggests, privacy-enhancing technologies (PET) are technologies that help promote and implement data protection in ICT systems. The basic idea of most PETs is to make (confidential or personal) data available for processing in such a way that the entity processing the data will learn little or nothing about the data they process, apart possibly from the result of the processing. These technologies thus focus on data *in use*, while data at rest or in transit can usually be adequately protected by encrypting them.

In [OEC23], different categories of PETs are defined:

- Data obfuscation tools such as anonymisation, pseudonymisation and synthetic data
- Encrypted data processing tools such as homomorphic encryption (see Sect. 7.4.3)
- Federated and distributed analytics, for example, federated learning (see Sect. 6.4.4)
- Data accountability tools, for example, personal management information systems (PMIS; see Sect. 3.1.2) or access protection

However, there is no unique definition of the concept of PETs, and more general topics such as data protection principles and their embedding in the life cycle of ICT systems are sometimes also considered as PETs (e.g. in [vBBO03]).

6.4.1   Confidential Computing and Trusted Execution Environments

Confidential computing can be defined as "the protection of data in use by performing computation in a hardware-based, attested Trusted Execution Environment" [Con22, p. 5]. It is mainly but not only used in the context of cloud computing and, in this case, addresses the problem that cloud users need to trust the cloud provider not to misuse their data. Encrypting the data would help protect them while they are at rest or in transit but would prevent processing the data. (With homomorphic encryption, there is a PET that overcomes that restriction to some extent; see Sect. 7.4.3.)

Since any layer of the compute stack could be circumvented if the layer below it is compromised, confidential computing places its security features on the bottom layer the hardware used. A central component of confidential computing therefore involves a trusted execution environment (TEE) built including specific processors designed for that purpose.

When a TEE is used, even the owner or operator of a platform or a user with root privileges should not be able to access the data or code. Additionally, confidential computing involves a remote attestation mechanism, which allows users to verify the security of the environment as well as the integrity of the code behind it. The customer will still have to address the security of data while they are transferred to and from the TEE but can trust that not even the cloud provider will be able to access them during processing.

6.4.2   Synthetic Data Generation

In certain use cases, data are needed for purposes such as machine learning or software testing, but the available data may not be used due to data protection or more general confidentiality concerns. In such use cases, synthetic data generation may help, which is based on artificially created data that try to simulate real-world data regarding their central properties but without reference to real persons or use of confidential information.

Prevention of Bias in Machine Learning   In addition to allowing to train or test systems without the need for confidential data, synthetic data may help prevent bias in machine learning. To prevent bias, alternative categories of objects should occur roughly equally often in the data. However, this is often not the case in real-world data. Consider, for example, a system that is supposed to evaluate job applicants according to their suitability for given job offerings. In the real world, some jobs are female-dominated, and others are male-dominated. If nothing is done about it, the system will re-enforce such bias and usually select females for female-dominated jobs and males for male-dominated jobs, based on the existing real-world data. In such a case, synthetic data may provide an equal amount of training data in the various combinations and thus hopefully evaluate job applicants fairly, solely based on their merits for the job.

Generation of Synthetic Data In order to generate adequate synthetic data, it is first of all important to identify what properties are needed in the data. Usually, they will be expected to represent a certain population (not necessarily of humans) and its statistical distribution. In simple cases, generating random values according to some predefined statistical distribution will be enough. In more complex cases, machine-learning models and methods will be used to generate adequate synthetic data. It is also possible to generate partially synthetic data based on real-world data, for example, by replacing identifying information in a dataset by synthetic information.

There are several challenges involved in generating synthetic data: first of all, it is important to ensure that the synthetic data are indeed synthetic and not too close to the real-world data used in their generation. This applies in particular to the case where synthetic data are generated using machine learning, which was initially based on real-world data to learn the relevant properties of the data to be generated, as well as to the generation of partially synthetic data. At the same time, the synthetic data must follow the required structure and distribution to be adequate for their purpose. If this is achieved, synthetic data generation can be very helpful to get sufficient data without conflicts with data protection.

6.4.3   Secure Multi-party Computation

Secure multi-party computation is a technology to address a seemingly impossible task: how can several parties jointly compute a function on data they each control without making those data available to the other parties?[8] This technology was first introduced by Yao as the "millionaires' problem", which describes two millionaires who want to find out who is richer without telling each other (or anyone else) how rich they are. In other words, they want to compute the maximum of two numbers, but each know only one of them [Yao82]. A more practical example concerns a group of hospitals who want to report their total number of patients that were treated for a certain disease within a certain time frame. Duplicates (patients who have been to several hospitals because of the same disease) are to be excluded, but due to data protection constraints, they are not allowed to tell anyone the identity of their patients. A similar example of secure multi-party computation is known as the *private set intersection* problem where two parties each hold a set of data and want to know the intersection of these sets without revealing anything about the data they hold that are not in the intersection. For example, a social network might want to give its members

---

[8] This technology is related to zero-knowledge proofs, and there is some overlap between the two, although they address different use cases: in zero-knowledge proofs, one party tries to prove to another that it knows a certain secret (such as an access code to some service), without releasing any information about that secret. In secure multi-party computation, one party wants the other party (or parties) to perform a computation based on a secret without releasing any information about that secret.

the opportunity to find out which entries in their address book are also members of the network without the members having to share their address book with the network.

In secure multi-party computation, this type of problems can be resolved by using cryptographic techniques based on one-way functions. In other cases, the computation is distributed over several parties in such a way that no party learns anything about the data of the other parties, apart from the result of the overall computation. More advanced algorithms for secure multi-party computation can also prevent or at least identify certain forms of cheating of some of the parties involved.

6.4.4 Federated Learning

Federated learning addresses a similar situation to multi-party computation: different parties each have a collection of data concerning the same topic, and they want to jointly use these data for machine learning. However, they do not want to or are not be allowed to share their data for this purpose. Federated learning is a technology that allows the different parties to each build a model based on machine learning from their own collection of data and then bring these models together and build up a joint model without having to share the underlying data between the parties. The different models usually need to have the same structure of nodes in their neural networks, and the parties then exchange the parameters they learned in their models. The resulting model is likely to be not quite as good as could be achieved by learning directly from a combined collection of all data but much better than each of the individual models trained from just one collection.

A common use case of federated learning concerns learning from data collected on data subject's devices such as mobile phones or PCs. If an organisation wants to learn from these data without actually collecting the data from the devices due to data protection constraints, federal learning may help by only exchanging the trained models rather than the training data. Another use case concerns medical research based on health data collected by different institutions such as hospitals or research institutes. Exchanging such data for research purposes is only legal under strict constraints, and federated learning may help since there is no exchange of health data any more.

Of course, in all these cases, one needs to ensure that no personal health data are exchanged by bringing the models together, and no such data can be extracted from the models any more.[9]

A variant of federated learning was Google's *Federated Learning of Cohorts* (FLoC), which was planned to replace third-party cookies.[10] The idea of FLoC was to group

---

[9] Various studies have shown that extracting training data from a model can be possible; see, for example, [NCH+23, CHN+23].

[10] FLoC eventually was withdrawn since there were many concerns regarding data protection as well as competition law.

browsers into cohorts whose users had similar interests. Targeted advertising was then to be presented on that browser based on the cohort rather than on third-party cookies. Each browser was to "learn" its model of user interests, and the different models were to be combined, at regular intervals, into a common model to refine the definition of the cohorts to be used.

6.5   Data Protection by Design and by Default

As the name suggests, the explicit requirement for data protection by design as set out in Art. 25 GDPR applies in particular to those who design technical systems, such as software developers. In essence, this regulation states that data protection must be taken into account from the outset in the design and development of systems and should not only be incorporated retrospectively on the basis of appropriate checks. Closely linked to this is data protection by default, which requires that systems are configured by default in such a way that the processing of personal data is very restrictive. Any additional processing options, for example, for convenience functions that require the processing of additional data, must be explicitly switched on by the users and not vice versa.

   This section describes these requirements in more detail and also looks at some approaches to implementation, such as *privacy by design* according to Cavoukian.

6.5.1   Data Protection by Design

Data protection by design (Art. 25 (1) GDPR) places requirements on the way in which IT and other technical systems are developed, not on the respective systems themselves. This can be expressed as follows:

Requirement (C-10 Data Protection by Design) *Data protection measures shall be taken into account throughout the entire life cycle of the system, starting with analysis and design.*

The purpose of this requirement is to ensure that appropriate data protection measures are taken into account at an early stage, not as an afterthought when such measures are no longer technically or economically feasible. Taking into account the software requirements for data protection listed in this book as part of the requirements analysis and embedding them in the life cycle as described in Sect. 6.6 are therefore suitable means of implementing data protection by design. It is important to take a proactive approach and not just a subsequent assessment (audit, DPIA) and correction, which then often only consists of informing the data subjects and, if necessary, obtaining consent. A data protection impact assessment (DPIA) is often mentioned in this context, but this only addresses the concept of data protection by design if such a DPIA is performed at all, and this is done early in the development cycle.

The demand for such a proactive approach sounds obvious, but practical experience shows that the initial focus is often almost exclusively on functional requirements, while data protection is not taken into account. (Unfortunately, the same applies to other topics such as the subsequent operation of the software, or information security, which is closely related to data protection.) However, there are now approaches such as Dev(Sec)Ops (see Sect. 6.6.9), which deal with precisely this problem and attempt to improve cooperation between the various parties involved.

The GDPR does not require any specific measures but rather the implementation of *appropriate* technical and organisational measures, whereby the appropriateness is to be assessed on the basis of the state of the art, the costs and the risks. Only pseudonymisation is mentioned as an example of a measure.

A detailed description of how data protection should be embedded in the entire life cycle in accordance with requirement C-10 can be found in Sect. 6.6 or, alternatively, for example, in [FFF14, Ch. 6].

Privacy Patterns Patterns, in particular design patterns, have proven themselves in computer science for describing solution strategies for typical tasks in a subject area. For the area of data protection, so-called privacy patterns have been defined and made available on the Web (see, e.g. [Dro16, Dro, UC]).

6.5.2   Data Protection by Default

Data protection by default is closely related to the concept of data protection by design discussed above and is therefore included in the GDPR in Art. 25 (2), immediately following the concept of data protection by design. In the context of software development, this can be expressed as the following requirement:

Requirement (Q-04 Data Protection by Default) *The system shall be configured in the default settings in such a way that only the data required for the respective purpose are processed. Any processing beyond this is only permitted if the data subject expressly consents to the processing and customises the configuration.*

This requirement is closely related to the requirement for opt-in instead of opt-out for consent. By default, the system must be configured in such a way that the data used are kept to a minimum, and additional data, for example, for convenience functions, are only processed with active opt-in consent.

Note however that the GDPR requirement goes beyond an individual IT system and applies to the entire organisation. The organisation must *ensure through suitable TOM* that all of the organisation's ICT systems use data protection by default.

6.5.3   Privacy by Design According to Cavoukian

The concept of privacy by design was first introduced by Ann Cavoukian, the former Information and Privacy Commissioner of Ontario, Canada. According to Cavoukian, this does not describe any specific procedure but essentially consists of the following seven basic principles for the design of information systems and business processes summarised in [CTA10]:

1. Proactive not Reactive; preventative not remedial
2. Privacy as the default
3. Privacy embedded into design
4. Full functionality—positive sum, not zero sum
5. End-to-end life cycle protection
6. Visibility and transparency
7. Respect for user privacy

While most of these principles have already been introduced in other contexts, principles 4 and 5 will be explained in more detail here. "Full functionality" describes the goal to be pursued by development to simultaneously strive for the desired functionality for the users and the realisation of data protection in full, so that data protection does not come at the expense of the benefit for the users of the system. "End-to-end life cycle protection" emphasises that the security of the data and the entire system must be taken into account by the design over the entire life cycle.

6.6   Embedding Data Protection into the Software Life Cycle

This section assigns the various data protection tasks to the corresponding phases in the software life cycle.[11] The simple software life cycle in Fig. 6.5 is used as a framework, although this is of course only one of many possible software life cycle models (see [Kne18] for a more general discussion of software life cycle models). However, since the basic development tasks are always largely the same regardless of the model used, the data protection tasks described below can also be assigned to the respective phases in other software life cycle models, regardless of whether it is a sequential model or an iterative-incremental model as is common in agile development (see Sect. 6.6.9).

Since at least the details of data protection legislation and its interpretation are constantly changing, you should be prepared for the fact that the resulting software requirements may also change at short notice.

---

[11] Most of this section is taken from [Kne19].

Fig. 6.5 Example software life cycle (Source: [Kne19])

The requirements of information security (see Chap. 7) are only marginally considered here, but they form an important part for data protection and must therefore also be taken into account.

6.6.1   Analysis

As is to be expected, the main task of analysis regarding data protection is to clarify the general setup, answering in particular the following questions:

- Which data protection roles are involved in the processing? Who is the controller, and are there any separate processors? Is there a single controller or joint controllership, that is, multiple controllers who are jointly responsible?
- Who are the data subjects?
- Which data protection legislation is applicable? If processing is to be performed within the EU, this will be the GDPR, but there is likely to be additional legislation such as a national data protection act and/or some industry-specific legislation. If data are to be processed or moved outside the EU, other or additional national legislation will apply.
- Which personal data are needed (not just considered useful) for the intended function-ality? Remember that the answer to this question not only depends on the data needed but also on the relevant legislation and its interpretation of the term "personal data".
  - Do the personal data processed include any special categories of personal data (Art. 9 GDPR) or data of children (Art. 8 (2) GDPR)?
  - Would it be possible to do without these data, at least some of them?
  - If not, would it be possible to turn them into anonymous or at least pseudonymous data?
  - Are there any relevant metadata to be processed, i.e. data about data? For example, even though the contents of a certain message may not be known, date and time of the message or the identity of its sender and receiver still describe personal data.
- Which legal basis according to Art. 6 (1) GDPR is going to be used for processing the personal data? What implications does this lead to—which steps are allowed, required or forbidden?
  - If consent is to be used as the legal basis: what is going to be covered by this consent? What happens if users do not give their consent or only partial consent or withdraw it at a later stage? Consent is only considered as a legal basis for data processing if it is genuinely voluntary, implying that one also has to deal with the case that it is not given. How will the consent that has been given (or refused) managed?

- If the legitimate interests are to be used as the legal basis: which interests of the data subjects are relevant and need to be considered? What does that imply for the design and implementation of the system? Where are the limits of those legitimate interests?
- If relevant, the legal basis must also cover the special categories of personal data and the personal data of children.
- How long will the data need to be retained? Are there any legal retention periods that are applicable?
- Which (functional or non-functional) software requirements resulting from data protection are relevant and need to be considered?
- Based on the data protection roles identified above, to what extent are data going to be exchanged with third parties, for example, by using cloud or other third-party services?
- What need for protection and what risks result from the answers to the previous questions? What data protection damage could be caused by the software system to be developed? The answer to these questions should take into account both the usage as intended and any possible misuse, for example, by an attacker who steals the data. Who can access the data—legitimately or illegitimately, on purpose or by accident? This could include own employees, external suppliers (processors), external attackers and other third parties who happen to run across the data by accident.
- Is the system under development expected to lead to a high risk for the data subjects, which would imply that a DPIA needs to be performed?

The answers to these questions should be used to derive the data protection requirements to be fulfilled, which should be clarified with the customer's data protection officer and possibly also with the data protection officer of the development organisation. This helps with the correct derivation and interpretation of the requirements, and it also helps the data protection officer in their work if they are informed about upcoming changes in good time.

6.6.2   Design and Architecture

The main task in design regarding data protection is to define suitable technical and organisational measures (commonly known as TOM) to adequately implement the requirements identified in analysis. In particular, the following questions need to be addressed:

- What implications does the selected legal basis have on the design? For example, if user consent is to be used, how will this be implemented? One approach that is sometimes recommended for this purpose is a privacy layer in the system architecture that queries the authorisations granted and grants or denies access accordingly.
- If additional data are collected that were not identified as necessary in the analysis: are these really necessary for the system to be developed? For example, time stamps are

often used in applications that allow conclusions to be drawn about the user (working times, working speed, etc.) but are not required for the application [BF19].

- An aspect that is easily overlooked: what personal data are transferred to third parties by the libraries, SDKs and other tools or services planned to be used? This is closely related to the question regarding data exchange with third parties in analysis, but while in analysis the focus was on deliberate sharing of data, design also has to identify the data sharing that is not needed to provide the intended functionality but introduced by the tools used. See below for more detail.
- Are there any existing frameworks or other information that should be taken into account? In the case of Web tracking, this includes, for example, the do-not-track flag and the *IAB Transparency & Consent Framework*.
- Which privacy-enhancing technologies (PET) should be used, such as encryption, anonymisation or pseudonymisation?
- How can you achieve the required security of the data? (This topic will be discussed in more detail in Chap. 7.)
- What do you need to do to achieve transparency about the processing of the data? (information of data subjects, RoPA)
- Are the results of analysis regarding data protection still up to date and complete, and are they fully addressed by the design?

Similar to the analysis phase above, the answers to these questions should be discussed with the customer's data protection officer, possibly also with the DPO of the development organisation itself, to ensure that the answers are appropriate from a data protection perspective.

It should also be clarified with the data protection officer whether a DPIA is required to finalise the design. This requirement applies in particular for new technologies that are "likely to result in a high risk to the rights and freedoms of natural persons" (Art. 35 (1) GDPR). If this is the case, the DPIA must be carried out by the controller, but the controller will usually require appropriate support from the development organisation.

Identification, Authentication and Authorisation Performing identification (who is the user?), authentication (is he really the user he claims to be?) and authorisation (what rights does the user have?) is a standard task of information security which needs to be integrated into the design of almost any system (see Sect. 7.3) and forms one basis for data protection. Data protection puts additional restrictions on the authorisation step, requiring restrictive handling of authorisations for the processing of personal data.

Using Code Libraries, SDKs and Web Services A major challenge may be the selection of libraries, SDKs etc., in the following just summarised as "libraries". This mainly applies to the development of mobile apps and of services and plug-ins for Web applications, where it is quite common to use external libraries which sometimes share data with their provider and other third parties, often without the developer knowing about it [EAN18, Lin19].

Even if the library does not include any explicit functionality to share personal data, just calling it at runtime will, if no explicit steps are taken to prevent this, usually pass at least the IP address of the user to the provider of the library.

To address these issues, the following steps are needed when using any third-party libraries (or SDKs or other run-time services):

- Find out about any personal data passed on by the library to any third parties.
- Check whether the library can be configured such as to prevent or at least reduce this passing on of data. Often, the libraries support suitable parameters, even though these may be well hidden. According to the principle "data protection by default", the default library configuration should be such that a high level of data protection is ensured, but in practice, this often is not the case, in particular when the library was developed outside the EU.
- When a library is called at runtime, it may be possible to deploy this library on one's own server rather than call it from somewhere else.
- Analyse and decide whether the remaining passing on of personal data is acceptable and covered by the legal basis used for the processing (cf. Chap. 5). A new analysis of the legal basis used may be needed, in particular if the "legitimate interest" is used, which requires a weighing of interests. In some cases, this will lead to the decision that the legal basis is no longer adequate, and the functionality planned must be based on a different library or reduced or even withdrawn altogether.
- Check whether any legal agreement with the recipient of the data is necessary, such as a commissioned processing contract or a joint controllership agreement.
- Document your decisions including the reasoning used. Ensure that the users (data subjects) are informed about any data still passed on.

The same is true when embedding information from other Web sites such as videos, fonts or social media buttons. If no suitable steps are taken to prevent this, at least the IP address of the user will be transferred to the provider, often more.

So far, this discussion assumed that the developers under consideration *use* the libraries. Of course, someone has to develop these libraries in the first place. Developers creating libraries, SDKs, etc. to be used by someone else also need to address data protection and make life easy for their colleagues using their libraries, e.g. by allowing a data protection-friendly configuration and making this the default.

6.6.3 Implementation

The main task regarding data protection in the implementation phase is to ensure that the analysis and design results are correctly incorporated into development. Any revisions and extensions of these results need to take into account the data protection issues discussed above. In particular, this applies to the decision to use a certain SDK or to embed any third-party services.

6.6.4 Test and Acceptance

The main task of test and acceptance of ICT systems is to check whether the specifications defined in the analysis and design phases have been correctly realised in the implementation, including the specifications regarding data protection. This applies not only to plan-driven process models but also to agile development, where these requirements are often formulated in the form of user stories and a definition of done (see Sect. 6.6.9). Depending on the type of system to be developed, it may be helpful to involve the data protection officer or other specialists for this topic, as is now also common in information security.

In addition to testing whether the system to be developed fulfils the data protection requirements, it is also important to ensure that these requirements are adhered to during the test itself and, for example, that original data are only used to a very limited extent for the test, as was described in Sect. 3.2.4.

6.6.5 Transition to Operations

The transition phase must ensure that the previously defined data protection measures are actually transitioned into IT operations, including the necessary documentation. In particular, this includes:

- Training users with regard to data protection so that they use the existing functionalities appropriately
- Creating transparency for data subjects, for example, by documenting the system in the relevant privacy policy
- Inclusion of the system and the processing contained therein in the record of processing activities
- Setting up data processing agreements with external suppliers and own clients for any relevant commissioned processing
- Setting up processes for dealing with incidents and data breaches
- Implementing further technical and organisational measures for data protection and information security as defined

6.6.6   IT Operations

From a data protection perspective, the IT operations phase plays the most important role, as the processing of personal data largely takes place in this phase. However, the way data are processed is already largely determined in the previous phases, and IT operations has only limited influence on that processing. Nevertheless, some data protection tasks also arise for IT operations itself and will be briefly explained below. The change control considered in Sect. 6.6.7 below usually runs in parallel to IT operations as part of maintenance and further development of the ICT system.

Implementing Information Security   One of the most important tasks of IT operations is to implement appropriate information security to support data protection, for example, by ensuring access restrictions. For the most part, this is done across the entire IT infrastructure and not specifically for individual applications to implement data protection.

Data Collection Within IT Operations   In addition to the processing of data for the original purposes of the ICT systems, IT operations also collect their own data, for example, in the form of log files, which also contain personal data in addition to various other data. This sometimes results in a conflict of interest between data protection and information security, as it may be adequate, from an information security perspective, to log many user activities, but this is not desirable from a data protection perspective. In this case, a comparison of legitimate interests (according to Art. 6 (1)(f) GDPR) is required in order to find a compromise and to limit the collection of data to what is really necessary for security purposes. In particular, it must be clarified who needs access to these log files and how long these data are required and stored. There are no clear guidelines in this regard, but the Liechtenstein supervisory authority has described storage for up to 1 year or until the end of the following year as appropriate. [12]

Handling of Data Breaches   As already discussed in Sect. 6.2.2, data breaches sometimes occur that must be dealt with appropriately and, in particular, reported to the competent supervisory authority at short notice. For IT operations, it is particularly important to identify such data breaches quickly and to pass them on to the responsible parties, as well as to support the subsequent analysis and rectification.

Performing Regular Reviews   In order to prevent data protection breaches and ensure that data protection management works as required, it is necessary to regularly check whether the selected measures are still sufficient and effective. This also addresses the fact that new threats are constantly emerging in information security, and it is important to keep an eye on these and respond to them. The regular performance of such reviews is

---

[12] See https://www.datenschutzstelle.li/download_file/view/510/299 (in German), p. 23f.

often defined as responsibility of the data protection officer, who then carries out a review of data protection management and its effectiveness typically once a year.

Web Site Audits and Reviews   Regular audits or reviews of Web sites are particularly important since Web sites typically undergo continuous changes, increasing the risk of introducing data protection problems, while at the same time such problems on a Web site are publicly visible. To perform such reviews, the author uses the following checklist:

- *External services and plug-ins*: most modern browsers support a network analysis that shows which external services are called by a Web site, leading to data transfer to a third party. In the next step, a manual analysis is necessary to check whether there is a legal basis for this data transfer, and the visitors to the Web site are adequately informed.
- *Cookies*: for most browsers, plug-ins are available for managing cookies, supporting the identification of cookies set by a Web site. Again, a manual analysis then needs to check that only technically necessary cookies are placed without consent, and Web site visitors are adequately informed.
- *Web server security*: secure configuration of Web servers is needed for data protection as well as information security, including the use and secure configuration of `https`, the use of up-to-date versions of relevant software (e.g. content management systems) and opening only ports that are genuinely needed. There are many tools available from the information security community that can help with these checks, e.g. ZAP[13] and Nikto. [14]
- *Data protection statement*: this check must largely be performed manually and concerns questions such as the following: is the data protection statement easy to reach (no more than one click from anywhere on the Web site), does it correctly address all processing performed/all services used on the Web site and does it contain all general information required such as the data subjects' rights?
- *Other services*: finally, depending on the contents of the Web site, additional services may be relevant that need to be checked, such as a newsletter service.

There are many tools that support performing such a Web site review, some of them automating those checks where this is possible.[15]

---

[13] https://www.zaproxy.org/

[14] https://cirt.net/nikto2

[15] For example, the EDPB offers a "Web site auditing tool" that helps perform and document Web site audits; see https://edpb.europa.eu/news/news/2024/edpb-launches-website-auditing-tool_en. The Swedish supervisory authority has developed a tool that automatically runs certain checks and made it available under https://webbkoll.5july.net/.

6.6.7 Change Control

Change control deals with the management of changes to the ICT system under considera-tion. From a data protection perspective, it must be ensured that no new problems arise as a result of the changes, i.e. data protection must also be taken into account when analysing the effects of the changes. More specifically, this means that when changes are made, the extent to which these changes affect the answers to the above questions on analysis, design and implementation must be checked.

6.6.8 Withdrawal

Once a system gets withdrawn, the following question regarding data protection remains:

- What will happen to the data that were stored in the system? Are they still needed elsewhere?
    - If not, then they must be deleted or, depending on circumstances, at least be archived or anonymised. In case the data are deleted, secure and complete deletion of the data must be ensured.
    - If the data are still needed, in a successor system or elsewhere, then they must be migrated in a secure way, ensuring that no data errors occur and no data are lost.
    It is not unusual for some of the data to still be needed, but not others. Such a withdrawal is a good opportunity to check which data are actually still needed and to migrate only these data to the new system.

6.6.9 Agile Development

Regardless of the life cycle model used, the questions described for the individual development phases must of course be answered, or, put differently, they describe non-functional requirements that need to be addressed. Such non-functional requirements are difficult to describe as user stories or in a similar format, and due to the lower emphasis on architecture and design, there is a significant risk in agile development that these will not be sufficiently taken into account.

To deal with this appropriately, the following approach may be used:

- As far as functional requirements are concerned, which includes most of the require-ments on software introduced in this book, these requirements should be expressed in the agreed standard format such as user stories.
- Other requirements should firstly be clearly communicated within the team and then integrated into the quality assurance measures used from the outset, for example, as part of the *definition of ready* and *definition of done*. The definition of ready should contain

checkpoints that are derived from the questions mentioned above for the early phases
and are checked for each functionality before it is included in a sprint, for example,

- Have the roles involved been clarified? (data subject, controller, processor)
- Has it been clarified which personal data of the data subjects are to be processed?
- Has it been checked that these only include the necessary data?
- Has the legal basis for processing been identified? What exactly is included and what
  is not?
- ...

Similarly, the definition of done should include check items such as:

- Has it been clarified and documented which personal data are exchanged with other
  systems?
- Has it been documented which personal data are processed for which purpose? Does
  this correspond to the identified legal basis?
- ...

An important concept of agile development is to obtain early and frequent feedback on the
results produced. This does not only relate to the functionality and usability of the system
to be created, but to all of its relevant properties, in this context in particular data protection
and information security. In concrete terms, this means that regular feedback should also
be obtained from specialists for these topics, for example, by involving the customer's data
protection officer in the sprint reviews.

Dev(Sec)Ops The same applies to the DevOps approach, which places particular emphasis on good collaboration between development and IT operations, using mainly automated
processes from the completion of software development through the various test and
acceptance steps to transition (deployment) in the production environment. However, it has
been shown that the information security requirements of the developed system were often
not sufficiently taken into account, which then led to extend the concept to *DevSecOps*. In
DevSecOps, information security is also integrated into the close collaboration, and data
protection should be integrated in the same way.

Example 6.2 (Implementing Data Protection in a Scrum-Based Project) At a
large financial services provider, essential parts of the described procedure were
used in a Scrum project in order to adequately take data protection into account.

At the beginning of the project, the questions mentioned in Sect. 6.6.1 were
considered. For the most part, the questions were answered, with a few exceptions.
In particular, it later emerged that the handling of different legal bases for storage and
processing had not been sufficiently clarified. Instead, it was assumed that the same

(continued)

legal basis always applied to different forms of processing the same data, which turned out to be incorrect.

The questions listed in Sect. 6.6.4 were largely adopted in the "definition of done". This helped ensure that data protection was seen by the developers as an ongoing part of the project, not as a control instance at the end. The lists of questions were considered particularly helpful for project staff with no prior knowledge of data protection to understand and implement the GDPR requirements.

In contrast, it was difficult to clarify the specific data protection requirements from the user stories, as both concepts operated at very different levels of abstraction. One of the consequences of this was that many new requirements relating to data protection were only identified at a relatively late stage; for example, the need for a deletion concept was only recognised very late.

In addition, the effects of the highly iterative approach were underestimated, which meant that some data protection concepts were originally implemented, but the effects of subsequent changes to the overall system on these concepts were not recognised in good time.

Overall, however, the question lists were seen as helpful because they made it possible to integrate the data protection requirements into the project with a manageable amount of effort. It was also easy to assign the checklists to the project activities, even though the project was carried out according to Scrum. However, it was difficult to implement the relatively abstract data protection requirements, in particular the data protection principles, in the agile environment, which was more orientated towards the incremental implementation of many small and independent individual requirements. It was therefore recommended to include the data protection requirements as epics in future projects and also to consider the checklists for all phases at a very early stage, which is in line with agile thinking.

6.7   Data Protection in Platforms and Software Ecosystems

Software ecosystems and platforms are a metaphor for the interaction of various participants in a shared market in which software solutions and services are offered on a common technological platform, for example, Eclipse or Google's Android platform, to which many different participants contribute their own apps. The following brief overview of the implementation of data protection in such ecosystems is based on [VKR20]. As the difference between platforms and ecosystems is relatively small, only software ecosystems are mentioned below, and platforms are not considered separately.

Due to the large number of (often independently operating) participants and the various software components and services, the first question that arises is who has which role from a data protection perspective. It must be clarified in each individual case who, as a controller, is responsible for the processing, who is the service provider acting as a processor and how, in the case of joint responsibility, cooperation can be structured in such a way that each party can fulfil their own responsibilities.

This situation leads to some particular challenges in terms of data protection:

- *Identification* of personal data collected in the software ecosystem is difficult due to the many parties involved, each of which collects and processes different data, sometimes consciously or unconsciously accessing data collected by other parties or providing data to others.
- *Data minimisation*, i.e. the task of ensuring that only personal data that are actually needed are collected, is a particular challenge that is even more than usual in conflict with the business goal of providing data for new, previously unknown applications.
- *Access* to personal data must be controlled so that each participant in the software ecosystem technically only has access to those data that they are authorised to access from a data protection perspective.
- From the perspective of the controllers, this raises the question of how they can control and limit access to data that they introduce into the software ecosystem.
- At least in some cases, the processing of personal data will require *consent*. However, it would not be appropriate for each party involved in the software ecosystem to obtain and store the required consent individually, with different structuring of the required rights, different appearances, separate storage and so on. A software ecosystem should therefore provide a common framework for managing these consents. In such a framework, sometimes called a "privacy cockpit", the data subjects can individually manage their consents for the various individual processing operations.
- *Transparency* about the processed personal data for the data subjects, but also for the other parties involved in the software ecosystem, is a considerable challenge. However, such transparency is a key requirement of GDPR (as well as many other data protection regulations), with the resulting rights to information and access for data subjects.
- So far, we have only talked about legal requirements resulting from the *GDPR*. However, this is not sufficient, especially in the context of international software ecosystems, as some of the parties involved and the data subjects may be active outside the territorial scope of the GDPR and are therefore subject to other legal regulations that may define significantly different rules. In the worst case, these could even contradict the rules of the GDPR.

6.8 Developing and Operating AI Systems

When developing and operating AI systems, a number of additional topics have to be taken into account beyond the general aspects discussed above. Some of these have been addressed in the relevant sections of this book:

- Need for a legal basis for machine learning (see Sect. 3.1.4)
- Need for a legal basis for the change of purpose that is typically involved (see Sect. 3.2.5)
- Accuracy and bias in machine learning (see Sect. 3.4)

Additionally, the following questions and issues need to be addressed:[16]

- Is the application legally acceptable? (e.g. no social scoring)
- Is the application possible without personal data? (e.g. with anonymised data)
- Is there a legal basis for the use of personal data for training? (In many cases, this will require explicit consent by the data subjects.)
- How are responsibilities (controllership, etc.) split between the different parties involved, in particular if an AI system is built on top of a model that has been built and/or trained by some other entity?
- Have suitable internal regulations on use of AI tools been set up, for example, regulating for which purposes these tools may be used, and which data or prompts may be entered?
- Is a DPIA required because a high risk is involved or the type of application is included on a relevant white list by the relevant data protection authorities?
- Has there been a check for bias and discrimination?

(Web) Scraping Machine learning is based on preferably large collections of data, and organisations trying to set up systems based on machine learning thus are continuously in search of suitable data. Since the Web essentially consists of a large collection of data, an obvious idea is (Web) scraping, which describes the idea of automatically extracting such data from existing Web sites, including social media and similar platforms. However, even though these data are publicly available, they are still subject to data protection and privacy laws in most legislations, apart from the fact that such scraping might be in conflict with the usage terms of the Web sites and with the Web site provider's copyright.

---

[16] More extensive guidelines and checklists have been published by different supervisory authorities, for example, https://www.cnil.fr/en/self-assessment-guide-artificial-intelligence-ai-systems by the French CNIL and https://www.datenschutzkonferenz-online.de/media/oh/20240506_DSK_Orientierungshilfe_KI_und_Datenschutz.pdf (in German) by the DSK, the coordination body of the German supervisory authorities.

Various data protection authorities both within and outside the EU have therefore published statements and guidelines regarding Web scraping, with similar contents. [17] The challenges named in these statements include the following:

- Data subjects lose control over their data if these are scraped from Web sites without their knowledge and against their expectations. Apart from obvious consequences such as direct marketing and spam, this may include the use of scraped data for purposes such as surveillance, for example, based on photos used for facial recognition databases or for identity fraud.
- Scraping data for machine learning leads to a change of purpose (as discussed in Sect. 3.2.5).
- The principles of data minimisation and of accuracy are difficult to conform to if there is no adequate assessment of the reliability of the Web sites used as sources for scraping.

These challenges result in duties for organisations that perform scraping as well as organisations that run Web sites that might be the target of scraping, such as social media platforms. Organisations that (want to) perform Web scraping must ensure that they have an adequate legal basis for their collection, further processing and purpose change of data and that they take any objections by the provider of the Web sites, stated, for example, in a `robots.txt` file, into account. Organisations that run a Web site that might be a target of scraping must adequately protect any personal data on their Web site. On a social media platform, users typically provide their data for use on that platform and for communication with other users, but not for third parties who might scrape their data from that platform Web site and use it for different purposes. Adequate protection measures to be provided by the organisation include technical and organisational measures, for example, the use of a `robots.txt` file, of CAPTCHAs, of monitoring their Web site to identify and block excessive usage and downloads. Depending on the applicable legislation, Web scraping may also constitute a data breach that needs to be reported to the relevant supervisory authority.

6.9   Tools for Implementing Data Protection

To implement data protection in an organisation, the use of suitable tools is often helpful or even necessary. There are many different types of such tools, for very different purposes. This section provides a brief overview over the types of tools that are relevant for software development and IT.

---

[17] For example, the EDPS addressed scraping in a paper on generative AI [EDP24, p. 7], and twelve different data protection authorities, all outside the EU, published a "Joint statement on data scraping and the protection of privacy"; see https://ico.org.uk/media/about-the-ico/documents/4026232/joint-statement-data-scraping-202308.pdf.

According to [IAP22, p. 7], the following categories of privacy tools can be distinguished:

- Assessment managers are mainly a tool for data protection officers or managers to help manage impact assessments.
- Consent managers (addressing the requirements in Sect. 3.1.2)
- Data mapping tools help determine data flows within organisations.
- Data subject request tools for handling requests for access, rectification, etc.
- Incident response to handle data breaches.
- Privacy information managers: note that this category refers to information services about privacy law, rather than PIMS as discussed in Sect. 1.4.
- Web site scanning to identify security risks as discussed in Sect. 6.6.6.
- Activity monitoring.
- Data discovery.
- De-identification/pseudonymity (as discussed in Sect. 6.3).
- Enterprise communication tools that support the confidential communication within organisations.

Using that categorisation, [IAP22] provides a directory of several hundred vendors of privacy tools.

Data Protection Policy Generators A type of tool that many organisations use but usually only once is a data protection policy generator for Web sites. There are many such tools available on the Internet, provided by supervisory authorities, consultancies or law firms. Most of these tools work by asking the organisation about the services and functionality provided by their Web sites and based on this selection collecting standard texts to describe the use of these services and functionality. As a result, such generators work well for Web sites that use standard services and functionality, while Web sites using individual services and functionality are likely to need at least to adapt or extend a generated policy.

The W3C Data Privacy Vocabulary (DPV) The DPV[18] provides a vocabulary of terms and an ontology of their relationships as machine-readable metadata about the use and processing of personal data. To achieve that, it contains concepts such as processes and services, entities (legal roles, authorities etc.), purposes, legal bases and many more, together with their relationships. Thus, the DPV is not a tool for implementing data protection as such but can be used as a basis for developing such tools. For example, the DPV can be used to describe consent records, a RoPA or a data protection notice. [19]

---

[18] See https://w3c.github.io/dpv/2.0/dpv/.

[19] As of October 2024, guides describing these usages are available or in work, see https://w3c.github.io/dpv/.

References

Art14. Article 29 Data Protection Working Party: *Opinion 05/2014 on Anonymisation Techniques*, April 2014. https://ec.europa.eu/justice/article-29/documentation/opinion-recommendation/files/2014/wp216_en.pdf

ARX. *ARX – Data Anonymization Tool. A comprehensive software for privacy-preserving microdata publishing*. https://arx.deidentifier.org/

BF19. Burkert, Christian and Federrath, Hannes: *Towards minimising timestamp usage in application software*. In Pérez-Solà, Cristina, Navarro-Arribas, Guillermo, Biryukov, Alex, and Garcia-Alfaro, Joaquin (editors): *Data Privacy Management, Cryptocurrencies and Blockchain Technology*, pages 138–155, Cham, 2019. Springer International Publishing, ISBN 978-3-030-31500-9. https://svs.informatik.uni-hamburg.de/publications/2019/2019-09-26_Towards-Minimising-Timestamp-Usage.pdf

CHN⁺23. Carlini, Nicholas, Hayes, Jamie, Nasr, Milad, Jagielski, Matthew, Sehwag, Vikash, Tramèr, Florian, Balle, Borja, Ippolito, Daphne, and Wallace, Eric: *Extracting training data from diffusion models*. In *Proceedings of the 32nd USENIX Conference on Security Symposium*, SEC '23, USA, 2023. USENIX Association, ISBN 978-1-939133-37-3.

Con22. Confidential Computing Consortium: *A Technical Analysis of Confidential Computing*, 2022. https://confidentialcomputing.io/wp-content/uploads/sites/10/2023/03/CCC-A-Technical-Analysis-of-Confidential-Computing-v1.3_unlocked.pdf

CTA10. Cavoukian, Ann, Taylor, Scott, and Abrams, Martin E.: *Privacy by design: essential for organizational accountability and strong business practices*. Identity in the Information Society, 3(2):405–413, Aug 2010, ISSN 1876-0678.

DR13. Dwork, Cynthia and Roth, Aaron: *The algorithmic foundations of differential privacy*. Foundations and Trends® in Theoretical Computer Science, 9(3–4):211–407, 2013. http://www.nowpublishers.com/articles/foundations-and-trends-in-theoretical-computer-science/TCS-042

Dro. Drozd, Olha: *Privacy patterns catalog*. http://privacypatterns.wu.ac.at:8080/catalog/

Dro16. Drozd, Olha: *Privacy pattern catalogue: A tool for integrating privacy principles of ISO/IEC 29100 into the software development process*. In Aspinall, David, Camenisch, Jan, Hansen, Marit, Fischer-Hübner, Simone, and Raab, Charles (editors): *Privacy and Identity Management. Time for a Revolution? 10th IFIP WG 9.2, 9.5, 9.6/11.7, 11.4, 11.6/SIG 9.2.2 International Summer School, Edinburgh, UK, August 16-21, 2015, Revised Selected Papers*, pages 129–140. Springer International Publishing, Cham, 2016, ISBN 978-3-319-41763-9. https://www.wu.ac.at/fileadmin/wu/d/i/ec/Research/PPC.pdf

EAN18. Englehardt, Steven, Acar, Gunes, and Narayanan, Arvind: *Website operators are in the dark about privacy violations by third-party scripts*, January 2018. https://freedom-to-tinker.com/2018/01/12/website-operators-are-in-the-dark-about-privacy-violations-by-third-party-scripts/

EDP20. European Data Protection Board (EDPB): *Guidelines 4/2019 on Article 25 – Data Protection by Design and by Default – Version 2.0*, 2020. https://www.edpb.europa.eu/our-work-tools/our-documents/guidelines/guidelines-42019-article-25-data-protection-design-and_en

EDP24. European Data Protection Supervisor (EDPS): *Generative AI and the EUDPR. First EDPS Orientations for ensuring data protection compliance when using Generative AI systems*, 2024. https://www.edps.europa.eu/system/files/2024-06/24-06-03_genai_orientations_en.pdf

EPK14. Erlingsson, Úlfar, Pihur, Vasyl, and Korolova, Aleksandra: *Rappor: Randomized aggregatable privacy-preserving ordinal response*. In *Proceedings of the 2014 ACM SIGSAC Conference on Computer and Communications Security*, CCS '14, pages 1054–1067, New York, NY, USA, 2014. ACM, ISBN 978-1-4503-2957-6. http://doi.acm.org/10.1145/2660267.2660348

Fed24. Federal Data Protection and Information Commissioner FDPIC (Switzerland): *Guide to Technical and Organisational Data Protection Measures (TOM)*, 2024. https://backend.edoeb. admin.ch/fileservice/sdweb-docs-prod-edoebch-files/files/2025/01/17/37a9a545-17d2-41aa-a674-490f6646f268.pdf

FFF14. Finneran Dennedy, Michelle, Fox, Jonathan, and Finneran, Thomas R.: *The Privacy Engineer's Manifesto*. APress Open, 2014, ISBN 978-1-4302-6355-5. http://link.springer.com/book/10.1007%2F978-1-4302-6356-2

GDLS14. Gkoulalas-Divanis, Aris, Loukides, Grigorios, and Sun, J: *Publishing data from electronic health records while preserving privacy: A survey of algorithms*. Journal of biomedical informatics, 50, 2014.

IAP22. IAPP: *2022 Privacy Tech Vendor Report*, 2022. https://iapp.org/resources/article/privacy-tech-vendor-report/

Kne18. Kneuper, Ralf: *Software Processes and Life Cycle Models. An Introduction to Modelling, Using and Managing Agile, Plan-Driven and Hybrid Processes*. Springer, Cham, 2018, ISBN 978-3-319-98844-3. https://link.springer.com/book/10.1007/978-3-319-98845-0

Kne19. Kneuper, Ralf: *Integrating data protection into the software life cycle*. In Franch, Xavier, Männistö, Tomi, and Martínez-Fernández, Silverio (editors): *Product-Focused Software Process Improvement. 20th International Conference, PROFES 2019, Barcelona, Spain, November 27–29, 2019, Proceedings*, pages 417–432. Springer International Publishing, 2019. https://link.springer.com/chapter/10.1007/978-3-030-35333-9_30

Lin19. Lindsey, Nicole: *Popular Android apps are sharing personal data with Facebook without user consent*, January 2019. https://www.cpomagazine.com/data-privacy/popular-android-apps-are-sharing-personal-data-with-facebook-without-user-consent/

NCH+23. Nasr, Milad, Carlini, Nicholas, Hayase, Jonathan, Jagielski, Matthew, Cooper, A. Feder, Ippolito, Daphne, Choquette-Choo, Christopher A., Wallace, Eric, Tramèr, Florian, and Lee, Katherine: *Scalable extraction of training data from (production) language models*, 2023. https://arxiv.org/abs/2311.17035

NXY+16. Nguyen, Thong T., Xiao, Xiaokui, Yang, Yin, Hui, Siu Cheung, Shin, Hyejin, and Shin, Junbum: *Collecting and analyzing data from smart device users with local differential privacy*, 2016. https://arxiv.org/pdf/1606.05053.pdf

OEC23. OECD: *Emerging privacy-enhancing technologies*, 2023. https://doi.org/10.1787/bf121be4-en OECD Digital Economy Papers, no. 351.

Off12. Office for Civil Rights (OCR): *Guidance Regarding Methods for De-identification of Protected Health Information in Accordance with the Health Insurance Portability and Accountability Act (HIPAA) Privacy Rule*, 2012. https://www.hhs.gov/hipaa/for-professionals/privacy/special-topics/de-identification/index.html

PKLK14. Prasser, Fabian, Kohlmayer, Florian, Lautenschläger, Ronald, and Kuhn, Klaus A.: *ARX – A Comprehensive Tool for anonymizing biomedical data*. In *AMIA Annual Symposium Proceedings*, pages 984–993, Washington (DC), USA, November 2014. https://www.ncbi.nlm.nih.gov/pmc/articles/PMC4419984/

Sam01. Samarati, Pierangela: *Protecting respondents identities in microdata release*. IEEE Transactions on Knowledge and Data Engineering, 13(6):1010–1027, 2001.

Swe02. Sweeney, Latanya: *k-Anonymity: a model for protecting privacy*. International Journal on Uncertainty, Fuzzyness and Knowledge-based Systems, 10(5):557–570, 2002.

UC . UC Berkeley School of Information: *Privacy patterns*. https://privacypatterns.org/

vBBO03. Blarkom, G.W. van, Borking, J.J., and Olk, J.G.E. (editors): *Handbook of Privacy and Privacy-Enhancing Technologies*. College bescherming persoonsgegevens, 2003. http://www.andrewpatrick.ca/pisa/handbook/handbook.html

VKR20. Valença, George, Kneuper, Ralf, and Rebelo, Maria Eduarda: *Privacy in software ecosystems – an initial analysis of data protection roles and challenges*. In *46th Euromicro Conference on Software Engineering and Advanced Applications (SEAA 2020), Portorož, Slovenia, August 26–28, 2020*, pages 120–123. IEEE, 2020. https://doi.org/10.1109/SEAA51224.2020.00028

WAB+18. Wood, Alexandra, Altman, Micah, Bembenek, Aaron, Bun, Mark, Gaboardi, Marco, Honaker, James, Nissim, Kobbi, O'Brien, David, Steinke, Thomas, and Vadhan, Salil: *Differential Privacy: A Primer for a Non-Technical Audience*. Vanderbilt Journal of Entertainment & Technology Law, 21(1):209–276, 2018. http://nrs.harvard.edu/urn-3:HUL.InstRepos:38323292

Yao82. Yao, Andrew C.: *Protocols for secure computations (extended abstract)*. In *Proceedings of the 23rd IEEE Symposium on Foundations of Computer Science*, pages 160–164, 1982.

Basic Concepts of Information Security

7

Abstract

Information security is an important basis for data protection, even if the perspective is clearly different: information security focuses on the protection of one's own data and interests, while data protection focuses on the protection of the data subjects and their data and interests, which can sometimes lead to conflicts of interest between data protection and information security. However, the techniques and measures to be applied in both cases overlap in many cases, and this chapter therefore provides an introduction to the relevant aspects of information security. An important part of information security is cryptology, i.e. the science of encryption and decryption, which also plays an important role in data protection, for example, by encrypting data to be protected.

7.1 Information Security

Information security forms an important basis for data protection and is therefore expressly required in Art. 32 GDPR. The meaning of information security is usually broken down into three protection goals which together form the "CIA triad":

- Confidentiality describes the goal that data and systems are only accessible to those that are authorised to have access.
- Integrity describes the goal that modifications of data or services (intentional or accidental) are only possible for those authorised.
- Availability describes that data or services are available at an agreed instant or over an agreed period of time.

If personal data are not protected against attacks and accidental breaches regarding these protection goals, essential elements of data protection cannot be fulfilled. At the same time, however, there is also a significant difference, sometimes even a conflict of interest, between the two areas of responsibility: information security looks at the protection of data and ICT systems from the perspective of the owner of these data or systems and attempts to protect them against potential attacks or accidental interference. Data protection, on the other hand, is limited to personal data and considers the protection of data and systems from the perspective of those affected by the data. From this perspective, protection is also required against the owner of the data who could use them inappropriately. This can mean that data should not be collected in the first place from the perspective of the data subject.

One example of the resulting potential conflict of interest between data protection and information security relates to the logging of events. From an information security perspective, many activities should be logged, and these logs should be kept for a long time in order to be able to better analyse problems that may occur later or perhaps identify them in the first place. From a data protection perspective, you should only log those events that are absolutely necessary and only keep them for a short time.

On the other hand, there are significant overlaps between the objectives of information security and of data protection, and the GDPR therefore requires that personal data be protected using information security measures. Relevant measures include access restrictions, pseudonymisation or encryption. For example, data protection defines which access restrictions (internal and external) are required, and information security implements these requirements through appropriate technical and organisational measures. Information security is usually not limited to the personal data affected by data protection but is also used to protect all other data (and ICT systems) worthy of protection.

How far the protection of personal data should go cannot be defined universally. The GDPR requires a level of protection appropriate to the risks and therefore does not set out specific measures, the specification of concrete measures. For this assessment of the appropriate level of protection, Art. 32 No. 1 GDPR sets out the following main criteria, which the controller needs to take into account when deciding on the measures to be implemented:

- The *state of the art*, which however is constantly changing so that it is always necessary to review and assess whether the current measures are still appropriate.
- The *implementation costs* for implementing the measures. These are also constantly changing, with the costs of technical measures often falling over time, so that measures that were unreasonably expensive in the past may be appropriate today.
- The *probability of occurrence* and *severity* of the risk posed by the processing. In order to stay up to date on which attacks and risks are currently widespread or newly emerged, it is necessary to use appropriate information services such as one of the various Computer Emergency Response Team (CERT) information services.

7.2   Information Security Management

The task of information security management is to plan and control the various information security measures. An information security management system (ISMS) according to the international standard ISO/IEC 27001 is often used for this purpose. Due to the overlaps in content and structure, it often makes sense to combine such an ISMS with the data protection management system (see Sect. 6.1) and other management systems to form an *integrated management system*.

ISO/IEC 27000 The ISO/IEC 27000 series of standards describes the structure of an information security management system. The most important standard in this series is ISO/IEC 27001, which describes the requirements for an ISMS and has established itself internationally as *the* basis for information security certifications. With regard to data protection, the ISO/IEC 27018 and ISO/IEC 27701 standards are also relevant (see Table 1.1), even if these standards are much less well-known and widespread.

In order to set up an appropriate ISMS for the implementation of Art. 32 (1) GDPR, the use of ISO/IEC 27001 is usually recommended, possibly including appropriate certification.

The NIST Cybersecurity Framework (CSF) A similar framework is the NIST Cybersecurity Framework (CSF) which puts a stronger emphasis on the technical implementation of cyber security, while ISO/IEC emphasises the setup of a (information security) management system. Since both models are based on similar fundamental concepts, they can be combined to support each other. In addition to the CSF [NIS24] itself, NIST provides many further resources that help set up a program to ensure cyber security within an information. As a result, it is widely used both within the USA and outside. The CSF in general is a model for voluntary use, except for US federal government agencies which are required to apply it (US Executive Order 13800). In contrast to ISO/IEC 27001, there is no certification based on CSF.

Risk Assessment A fundamental early step in all approaches to information security is an assessment of the risks that need to be considered. In ISO/IEC 27001, this is part of the planning step in the ISMS, while CSF requires a risk assessment as part of the *Identify* function.

Such a risk assessment should be structured according to the CIA triad, assessing risks for each of the protection goals confidentiality, integrity and availability. Again, there are two different but overlapping types of risks that need to be assessed: from the information security point of view, the focus is on risks to the organisation's services and data that may be caused by external attacks or by accidents such as the loss of a laptop or a fire in a server room. From the data protection point of view, the focus is on risks to the data subjects, including, for example, a loss of confidentiality when members of the controller's organisation get access to personal data without a legal basis according to GDPR.

7.3   Identification, Authentication and Authorisation

A core functionality of information security, which is particularly important from a data protection perspective, is the identification, authentication and authorisation of users when accessing data and ICT systems. The first step is identification, in which the user (and possibly the ICT systems) states their identity, usually by providing their username. In the authentication step, the specified identity is verified, in simple cases by entering a password. Finally, authorisation ensures that the authenticated users get exactly the access rights that they should have according to their role, tasks, etc.[1]

7.3.1   Identification

Identifying users when accessing an ICT system, i.e. simply stating the user's identity, is relatively simple. However, care must be taken to ensure that the identification data cannot be intercepted en route, e.g. by using transport encryption as described later in this chapter.

7.3.2   Authentication

In many cases, it is not enough to simply state your identity; this must also be proven and verified in some way, a process known as authentication. In the following discussion, the focus is on authentication as a prerequisite for access to systems, in contrast to Sect. 4.1.2, which dealt with authentication as a prerequisite for exercising data subject rights.

Knowledge, Ownership, Inherence There are three different types of authentication: authentication by knowledge means that you prove your identity by knowing something, for example, a password or a PIN. In authentication by ownership, you prove your identity by having a specific object such as a chip card or a token. Finally, authentication by inherence involves proving your identity using biometric properties, for example, a fingerprint, an iris scan or your face that is recognised. Each of these approaches has its own advantages and disadvantages, especially in terms of security and usability, so it is not possible to say in general that a particular approach is particularly (in)suitable. To increase the security of authentication, several authentication types are often combined to create two-factor authentication (2FA) or multi-factor authentication (MFA). Examples include the use of a bank card plus PIN, the use of a password plus a time-dependent code generated using an authenticator app or a password plus a transaction number (TAN) sent via SMS which requires that the user has access to the phone with the relevant number.

---

[1] For an extensive discussion of these topics, the NIST "Digital Identity Guidelines" in the SP 800-63 series can be recommended; see https://pages.nist.gov/800-63-3/.

Of course, this last form of 2FA only works if the SMS is sent to a previously defined telephone number. The author has actually come across a payment service (!) that allowed users to define a new telephone number which the SMS should be sent to as part of the payment process. This possibility of course makes the second factor worthless for authentication.

Password-Based Authentication The use of passwords is very common for non-critical data, as it is relatively easy to implement. However, as soon as the data or access to a system has somewhat higher protection requirements, it is advisable to combine the password with a second factor to create a 2FA.

Password Policies To ensure the use of secure passwords, password guidelines are necessary which, for example, require a certain minimum length or a certain combination of character types (upper-/lowercase, numbers, special characters). However, what is considered to be adequate password guidelines has changed significantly over time, partly due to new findings, especially about how people handle their passwords and partly due to a changing environment, in particular new algorithms and faster technologies for cracking passwords. Today, organisations are moving away from very complex rules that lead to passwords that nobody can memorise and placing more emphasis on long passwords where brute force methods[2] fail. The US standardisation organisation NIST, in its widely used standard [GFN+17, Sect. 5.1.1], recommends that passwords (here called "memorised secrets") should be chosen by users rather than the *verifier* (the organisation or system that verifies the password) and defined the following mandatory and optional requirements:

- Passwords shall be at least eight characters long (although today, eight characters are usually considered very short).
- If a password is disallowed because it appears on a blacklist of compromised values, the user shall be required to select a new password.
- No further specifications should be required with regard to the complexity of passwords, for example, regarding the use of a mixture of different character types.[3]

In addition to these requirements for the choice of password, [GFN+17, Sect. 5.1.1] contains the following requirements for the verifier:

- A password length of at least 64 characters should be permitted.

---

[2] Brute force methods are methods that essentially try out all possibilities, in this case all possible passwords (up to a certain length).

[3] The reason for this recommendation is that just one or two additional characters usually enable more different passwords than such a required increase in the character set used, which experience has shown often only leads to the character string "1!" being appended to a trivial password.

- All printable ASCII characters including spaces, preferably all Unicode characters should be allowed.
- Passwords must not be shortened by the verifier (even if they are very long—an excessively long password may have to be rejected from the outset).
- No information on the saved password shall be requested from the user or saved by the verifier.
- The verifier must not give any instructions for the choice of password that restrict the selection to certain types of passwords (e.g. "What was the name of your first pet?").
- Selected passwords must be checked by the verifier against a list of known, expected or compromised passwords and rejected if necessary.[4]
- Verifiers should provide users with feedback on the strength of the selected password. However, there are major differences between different systems when evaluating the quality of the same passwords, as described in [FHD20].
- Verifiers shall limit the number of failed login attempts. This can be done, for example, by completely blocking the login for this user after a certain number of failed attempts (for a certain time or until reset by administrators) or by increasing the time period for checking an entered password with each failed attempt. This prevents brute force attacks, at least within the system.
- Verifiers should not require periodic password changes. In the past, such password changes were often recommended, but this recommendation has now been abandoned. The reason is that users are not able to memorise new good passwords so often; therefore, many users have chosen short and insecure passwords, which has reduced security as a result. However, a password change should be requested if there are indications that the password has been compromised.
- Verifiers should support the pasting of passwords from the clipboard to enable the use of password vaults.
- To make it easier to enter the password, verifiers should allow users to display the password they have entered.
- Verifiers must use an encrypted and authenticated channel for the initial transmission of the password. This includes authentication of the verifier to the user, thus ensuring that the password is transmitted to the correct communication partner.

Storage of Access Data Well-chosen passwords that are kept secret by the user are only relevant if the operators of the services concerned also keep these passwords secure. Experience shows that in many cases, the blame for password theft lies with the operators of the services, not the users. It is therefore an important task of service providers to

---

[4] Well-known and well-suited lists of compromised passwords are available from the service *haveibeenpwned*; see https://haveibeenpwned.com/, or via the *NIST Bad Password* tool, see https://cry.github.io/nbp/.

store passwords and other access data securely and protect them against online and offline attacks. The state of the art for secure storage (and therefore required by NIST in [GFN$^+$17, Chap. 5.1.1]) is storage as "salted" hash values (see Sect. 7.4.4). This ensures that even if the stored access data are stolen, they are not directly available to the attacker, but only their hash values, from which the access data themselves can only be recalculated with difficulty. In this way, you at least gain time to change the passwords. However, there are still companies that store passwords in plain text, which is not acceptable from an information security nor from data protection perspective and has in some cases led to fines being imposed by data protection supervisory authorities.[5]

"Forgot Password" Function Instead of trying to find out a user's password for a particular service, in many cases, it is much easier for an attacker to reset the password using the service's "forgot password" function. Of course, authentication is also required in this case, but this is often much less secure than password authentication. Sometimes so-called security questions are used, the answer to which is easy for attackers to find out, such as the mother's maiden name or the date of birth.

The following points must therefore be observed for the secure design of this function:

- Since anyone can trigger the "forgot password" function without any form of authentication and can enter any identification data such as e-mail address or telephone number, no information must be directly visible to the user in this way, not even whether the corresponding account exists.
  - Some services not only indicate that the associated account exists but also display the email addresses and telephone numbers associated with the account so that the user can choose which of these addresses the password reset information should be sent to. An attacker is thus given a choice which of these accounts is easiest to take over, in order to then also take over the account under consideration. Of course, accounts that the user may have given up long ago but forgot to delete as an alternative address and which the attacker can now simply log into themselves are particularly easy.
  - The often-used attempt to make the email address unreadable for attackers by replacing some characters in the display with asterisks does not really help, since the addresses often remain easy to guess (e.g. even an email address of the author of this book like *a**@k***p**.** is no real challenge for an attacker).
- Another method used by some services that only appears secure at first glance is the question "Enter the last password for this account that you remember". So if any of the old passwords for this service have been compromised and appear in one of the password lists published on the darknet, then any new password for this service can be circumvented using the forgotten password function.

---

[5] See   https://www.dataprotection.ie/en/news-media/press-releases/DPC-announces-91-million-fine-of-Meta for an example.

- The most secure method of making an account usable again despite a forgotten password is usually to send a corresponding message to the email address on file. However, as email itself is not a secure medium, such a message must not be permanently valid, but only for a short time (a few hours) and only for a one-off password change.
- If a password or associated contact details such as e-mail address or telephone number are changed, then appropriate information must be sent to the *old* contact details so that nobody can change these contact details inconspicuously and then take over the account using the password forgotten function. For the same reason, the corresponding password should be requested whenever contact details are to be changed.
- The forgotten password function is particularly difficult for email accounts, as sending an email to the account for which the user has lost the password is of no help for the user. For this reason, a second trustworthy channel is required here, such as a second email account or a telephone number, possibly in combination with a good security question.

Authentication Using Biometric Data At first glance, the use of biometric data for authentication appears to be particularly secure, as these data uniquely identify the individual person. However, there are still various attacks that can be used to falsify biometric authentication data, for example, based on a photograph of a fingerprint, and the data cannot simply be changed, as would be possible with a password or other authentication data. In addition, biometric authentication procedures always have a certain error rate, since, e.g. a fingerprint will never be provided exactly as it was originally collected. This leads to authentication attempts that are wrongly accepted (false-positive authentication) or wrongly rejected (false-negative authentication). Frequent false-negative responses lead to user dissatisfaction, while false-positive results lead to a security problem. By selecting appropriate parameters for the strictness of the comparison, the organisation must find a suitable compromise, considering in particular the risk involved with accepting illegitimate users. In summary, authentication using biometric data must be viewed ambivalently, as it has both great strengths and considerable weaknesses.[6]

Data Protection for Biometric Authentication Data When using biometric data for authentication, it should also be considered that these are personal data of *special categories*, which implies that the authentication data require special protection. Furthermore, the biometric data may only be used if there is a suitable legal basis in accordance with Art. 9 GDPR, while the usual legal basis of legitimate interest (Art. 6 (1)(f) GDPR), which is usually adequate for authentication data, is not sufficient in this case. Consent is usually the only option here, but consent must be voluntary, i.e. there must also be an alternative

---

[6] See [Eur20] for more information about using biometric data for authentication.

form of authentication without the use of biometric data. An example of this is the use of a fingerprint scanner on a smartphone, where authentication is also possible with a password or PIN.

7.3.3   Authorisation

The purpose of authentication is to ensure the identity of users in order to assign them the appropriate rights in the system in question, i.e. to authorise them for certain activities. This requires a corresponding rights management system, which is usually based on defined roles, so that the relevant rights do not have to be granted to each user individually and, if necessary, withdrawn again, but this is done automatically according to standardised rules. For example, if you assign a user the role of "employee HR dept.", they are automatically assigned certain rights that are relevant for this role. When they later leave the HR department, these authorisations can then be withdrawn by just removing the role assignment. The basis of such role-based rights management is a *role and rights concept*, in which the roles used and the rights assigned to them are defined.

The definition of such a roles and rights concept is largely a functional task which must then be technically implemented by IT. It is important to bear in mind that access rights and, in particular, their restrictions normally apply to all copies of the respective data. If, for example, a certain role is not to be granted access rights for certain data, it must be ensured that this role is not granted the corresponding rights indirectly, for example, by accessing data backups or archives. In line with the principles of data minimisation and confidentiality, roles should only receive the access rights that they actually need for this role.

Revoking Authorisation In this context, it is often forgotten that role assignments and thus the assigned authorisations may also have to be revoked. This applies, for example, when employees leave a company, as described in the example 6.1, but also a move to another position in the company usually not only means that new roles and authorisations are required but also that old ones are no longer relevant and should be withdrawn. Here too, it is important to ensure that all systems are taken into account. For example, does the former employee also have access to systems run by the customer?

7.4   Cryptology

A protection measure mentioned repeatedly in GDPR is the encryption of personal data. Encryption is primarily used to ensure the confidentiality of data when it is not possible to securely prevent access to the data, for example, when transmitting data via an insecure channel such as the Internet. To a certain extent, encryption can also help prevent unauthorised changes to data, i.e. to ensure its integrity.

This section is intended to provide an overview of the most important concepts of encryption as it is used for data protection.

7.4.1 Foundations

When using encryption for data protection, it is important to bear in mind that encryption does not remove the reference to a specific person. Whoever has access to the key can identify the person concerned, and encrypted personal data thus are still personal data and subject to data protection. Encryption is the transformation of data, usually referred to as plain text, into other data, usually referred to as ciphertext, where this transformation is dependent on additional information known as a key. The aim of encryption is to ensure that the ciphertext can easily be transformed back into plain text with the help of the key, but this transfer is not realistically possible without knowledge of the key.

Encryption can be used on various levels: on the one hand, you can encrypt individual files, for example, to send them from one party to another via an insecure channel such as email or to protect the file on your own computer or cloud storage from unauthorised access. A slightly higher level is the encryption of an entire directory or drive, with a similar area of application. Another application scenario is encryption to secure the communication channel used, where the data are encrypted as part of the communication protocol at the sender and decrypted again at the recipient. Examples of this latter scenario include the communication protocols `https`, `TLS` and `ssh`.[7]

7.4.2 Security of Encryption

As can, for example, be seen from the reports by Edward Snowden, it can currently be assumed that the encryption methods in widespread use are really secure according to the state of the art with the usually recommended key lengths and cannot be defeated even by intelligence agencies. The main risk is that the encryption is circumvented and the key is stolen or the data are tapped before encryption or after decryption. In the day-to-day practice of companies, which must also be taken into account when implementing data protection, the biggest challenge is therefore to keep the keys used secret, which on the other hand must be exchanged (securely) between the communication partners. Particularly with encryption methods in which both communication partners use the same key, the secure exchange of keys is a difficult task, especially as it has to be carried out separately with each communication partner. So-called *asymmetric* encryption methods were developed as a solution to this problem and are discussed in more detail in Sect. 7.4.3.

---

[7] In most cases, it can be assumed that protocol names containing an "s" in the acronym describe encrypted protocols, and the "s" stands for "secure".

Kerckhoff's Principle A basic principle of encryption is Kerckhoff's principle, which states that the security of an encryption method must not be based on the secrecy of the algorithm used but must be based on the secrecy of the key used. There are several reasons for this: first and foremost, an encryption method offers many more starting points for breaking the secret than is the case with a key, and once that has happened, it is much easier to change the key than an entire encryption algorithm. If you want to communicate with multiple partners, it is much easier to generate a new key for each of them than another a new algorithm. Finally, the algorithm can be checked by experts in this way, and experience shows that many seemingly good encryption methods are actually easy to break. It is therefore generally considered a bad idea to keep a cryptographic algorithm secret if one wants to use it for production purposes.

Implementation of Cryptographic Algorithms At least as long as you are not a specialist in cryptology, you should not try to develop cryptographic algorithms yourself (for operational use) and not even implement a known method. Instead, ready-made libraries, preferably open source, should be used to avoid implementation errors, insecure parametrisations and known attack possibilities.

7.4.3 Symmetric and Asymmetric Encryption

Symmetric and asymmetric encryption are two different approaches that are suitable for different application scenarios.

Symmetric Encryption The most obvious form of encryption method, which has been known since ancient times, is the symmetric method, in which the same key is used for encryption and decryption (see Fig. 7.1a).[8] Currently, the most widely used symmetric encryption system is the *Advanced Encryption Standard (AES)*, which was selected as a standard by the US standardisation authority NIST in an open competition process.

Major challenges when using symmetric encryption methods are the exchange of keys, which must be done in a secure way, and the subsequent management of the keys, as a separate key is required for each communication relationship.

Asymmetric Encryption To solve these challenges, the concept of asymmetric encryption methods was developed in the 1970s, in which different keys are used for encryption and decryption (see Fig. 7.1b).

One-Way Functions Asymmetric encryption is based on one-way functions, i.e. functions that are easy to calculate but whose inverse is very complex to calculate. Theoretically, any

---

[8] In accordance with common usage, we refer to the communication partners here as *Alice* and *Bob*.

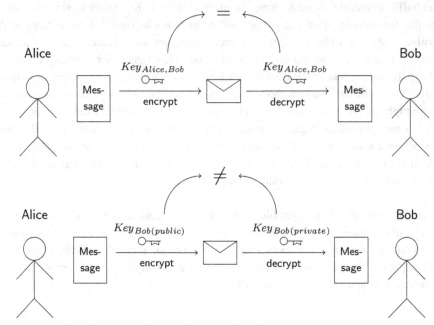

Fig. 7.1 (a) Symmetric encryption. (b) Asymmetric encryption

function can be inverted, even if the result is not always a function, as the initial function may map several different arguments to the same function value. With a one-way function, however, it is so time-consuming to find the right argument for a given function value that inverting the function is practically impossible, at least for large numbers.

A simple example of a one-way function is the multiplication of prime numbers, which is also relatively easy to calculate for large numbers. Conversely, for large numbers, it is practically impossible to split such a product back into its prime factors. This forms the basis for the first and best-known asymmetric encryption algorithm, the *RSA algorithm*.[9]

In an asymmetric encryption method, each communication partner has a *key pair* consisting of a public key (in the case of RSA, this is essentially the product of two large prime numbers) and a secret key (in the case of RSA, essentially the two prime factors). The security of the method is based on the fact that it is practically impossible to calculate the secret key from the public key, which can, for example, be published in a directory. The owner can and must then keep the secret key secret, even from his communication partners.

The main advantages of asymmetric encryption algorithms, also known as *public key encryption*, are the simple key exchange, as no secret key has to be exchanged between the

---

[9] The RSA algorithm was name after its developers Ronald L. Rivest, Adi Shamir and Leonard Adleman.

communication partners, and the simple administration, as all parties involved only need one secret key each, regardless of the number of their communication relationships. On the other hand, asymmetric methods are comparatively slow and require very long keys so that the secret key cannot be calculated from the public key.

Hybrid Algorithms In order to combine the advantages of symmetric algorithms (speed) and asymmetric algorithms (key exchange and key management), hybrid protocols are often used today, for example, in the encrypted variants of the various Internet protocols such as `https` or TLS. In these protocols, a *session key* is exchanged at the start of a communication session using an asymmetric algorithm, while further communication then uses a symmetric algorithm with this session key.

Perfect Forward Secrecy As encrypted communication between two (or more) com-munication partners usually takes place via an insecure channel such as the Internet (otherwise encryption would not be necessary), an attacker can in principle intercept the communication and store it over a longer period of time. If the private key of the asymmetric communication is later broken or stolen, there is a fundamental risk that all session keys and therefore all past communications can be decrypted.

To prevent this, the described key exchange procedure has been expanded so that even if the long-term asymmetric key is lost at a later date, the previously used session keys are not compromised, meaning that the content of any previously stored sessions still cannot be decrypted. This property of key exchange procedures is considered good practice today and is referred to as *perfect forward secrecy*.

TLS and the Selection of a Cipher Suite The protocol *Transport Layer Security (TLS)* uses a hybrid procedure. If two computers want to communicate in a TLS-secured manner, they agree on a *cipher suite* at the beginning of the connection during the *handshake*, which defines which algorithms and key lengths to use for the key exchange and communication.

It is important that these parameters are selected sufficiently secure during the handshake, i.e. you should configure your own systems so that they do not accept any outdated or otherwise insecure protocols. Of course, how strict you need to be depends primarily on the protection requirements of the transmitted data.

To check which parameters a system works with, for example, to check the secure parametrisation of your own system as a DPO, a number of services are offered on the Internet, often under the old name SSL instead of TLS.

Homomorphic Encryption In order to process or analyse encrypted data, it is usually necessary to decrypt these data first. This is a particular challenge in cloud computing, as you have to trust the cloud operators because you are also giving them the opportunity to access the data. If you want to prevent this, you have to transfer the data from the cloud storage to your own computer and process it there, which is just what you want to avoid with cloud computing.

One solution to this problem is the homomorphic encryption, which allows data to be processed without decrypting it first. There are different levels of homomorphic encryption, which differ by the processing that they allow on encrypted data. Fully homomorphic encryption allows any kind of processing steps without limitation of the number of steps, which however comes with certain costs regarding efficiency. Currently, the corresponding processes are in the piloting phase, implying that widespread practical application is not possible for the time being.

7.4.4 Cryptographic Hash Functions

In computer science, a hash function is a function that maps values of arbitrary length to values of a fixed length, for example, as checksums, to make it easier to recognise changes to the original values or to create an index in a database. The cryptographic hash functions relevant in this context are also one-way functions, i.e. mathematical functions that are practically irreversible. This property is used, for example, to check passwords for correctness without storing the passwords themselves. Instead, only the hash value of the passwords is saved and compared with the hash value of the passwords entered. Even if the password database is stolen, this does not allow an attacker to access the associated accounts, as the associated passwords must first be calculated from the hash values.

To make this even more difficult, the hash function can be applied to the password in combination with a *salt*, i.e. a character string whose main task is to extend the initial value and thus make the reversal of the hash function even more difficult.

Since hash functions map values of arbitrary length to values of a fixed length, there are in general more possible input values than output values, and different input values must be mapped to the same output value. Such a combination is called a *collision*, and such collisions are of course undesirable, at least for cryptographic hash functions, because they would allow one value to be replaced by another value without this being recognisable in the calculated hash value. For this reason, cryptographic hash functions are also required to make such collisions—since they cannot be avoided—then at least difficult to find:

Definition 7.1 (Cryptographic Hash Function) A hash function is a function $h : P \to D$ that maps values of arbitrary length to values of a fixed size.

A cryptographic hash function is a hash function h that additionally satisfies the following properties:

- Pre-image resistance: h is a one-way function, i.e. given a value v, it is difficult to find a value x such that $v = h(x)$.
- Second pre-image resistance (weak collision resistance): given an input value x_1, it is difficult to find a value $x_2 \neq x_1$ for which $h(x_1) = h(x_2)$.
- (Strong) Collision resistance: it is difficult to find a pair $x_1 \neq x_2$ of input values such that $h(x_1) = h(x_2)$.

Applications of Cryptographic Hash Functions In addition to the use of cryptographic hash functions for storing and checking passwords, these functions are mainly used to ensure the integrity of data. To check whether certain data have been transmitted unchanged via an insecure channel, i.e. have not been changed due to random noise or to an active attack, the hash value is also transmitted as a checksum and then compared to see whether the self-calculated hash value of the transmitted data matches the transmitted hash value. Compared to the originally transmitted data, a hash value is usually very small, typically in the range of a few hundred bits, so that it is easy and efficient to transmit, perhaps even via a secure channel. This is why cryptographic hash functions are used, for example, for electronic signatures or to verify that a file downloaded from the Internet has arrived unchanged.

Additionally, cryptographic hash functions can be used to create pseudonyms that help protect data, as, e.g. shown in Sect. 2.3 and Example 4.3.

7.4.5 Long-Term Protection of Personal Data

If data need to be kept confidential in the long term, for example, in the case of health data, it is obviously important to ensure that the protective measures used, such as encryption, are also effective in the long term. This applies in particular to data that need to be archived and stored for the long term, e.g. to satisfy legal archiving requirements. In this context, it should also be borne in mind that attackers may be able to steal and store encrypted data in order to decrypt it at a later date using better technology.

When selecting cryptographic systems, it is therefore important to estimate how long the data need to be kept confidential and to take this information into account accordingly, for example when defining the key length. Of course, it is difficult to estimate today what cryptographic options will be available in 10 or 20 years' time, but at least foreseeable trends should be taken into account from the outset. For these reasons, different national information security agencies regularly issue updated recommendations on which algorithms with which key lengths are considered secure for which storage duration.[10]

When transferring data over the Internet, you should also ensure that the connection supports *perfect forward secrecy* in order to protect the transferred data in the long term.

7.4.6 Secure Data Exchange

One of the most important applications of encryption is the secure exchange of data via a channel that is not itself secure and can be intercepted, where an attacker may even be able

---

[10] For example, the US NIST Special Publication 800-57 "Recommendations for Key Management" or the German BSI TR-02102-1 "Cryptographic Mechanisms: Recommendations and Key Lengths".

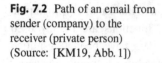
Fig. 7.2 Path of an email from
sender (company) to the
receiver (private person)
(Source: [KM19, Abb. 1])

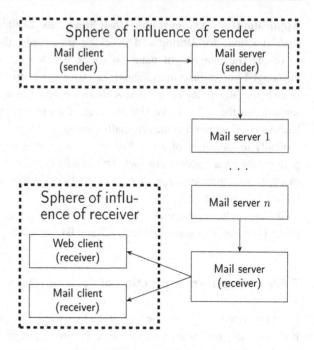

to modify the transmitted data. Examples of this are access to remote computers, whether
in a (wireless) LAN or over longer distances, for example, on the Internet.

If, for example, a contact form is provided on a Web site, the use of this form generates
personal data that must not be transmitted unprotected. The usual way to achieve this is to
combine the transmission protocol http with the encryption protocol TLS to https.

As described above, there are two different approaches when using encryption in the
context of data exchange, namely, transport encryption and end-to-end encryption. This
will be illustrated using the example of sending emails.

Transport Encryption and Transport Layer Security (TLS)   In transport encryption
using the TLS protocol, data are encrypted during transport from one communication
partner to the next, as the name suggests. However, communication partners are not only
the sender and recipient of the message at the end points but also at intermediate stations.
If a message is sent via the Internet, for example, an email, there can be many such
intermediate servers where the message is received, decrypted, re-encrypted and sent to
the next intermediate station until it finally arrives at the recipient of the email, as shown
in Fig. 7.2. At the intermediate servers, the data are therefore available in unencrypted
format before they are encrypted again to be sent to the next server.

Even if this is a significant step forward compared to sending data without any
encryption, there are still some risks involved: first of all, the sender and recipient have
only limited influence over which intermediate servers are used. Even if the sender and
recipient are both based within the EU, it is quite possible that the message will be routed

via a node in the USA or some other countries. However, senders and recipients must trust these intermediate servers not to use the data in an unauthorised manner and to adequately secure the transmission to the neighbouring intermediate servers, including the selection of up-to-date encryption methods with sufficient key length for the transmission.

End-to-End Encryption If the level of security achieved using transport encryption is not sufficient, there is the alternative of end-to-end encryption, in which the original sender encrypts the message and it is only decrypted again at the final recipient. There are two well-known methods for end-to-end encryption of emails, S/MIME and PGP, but neither of these are widespread, and both are difficult for non-experts to use [WT99]. For communication with other companies, this can be implemented to a certain extent, but for communication with private individuals (private customers, applicants, etc.), end-to-end encryption is therefore only applicable to a very limited extent.

Some providers of communication networks, especially messenger services such as Signal or WhatsApp, also use end-to-end encryption. As they work with standardised user interfaces and a communication channel controlled at both ends by the provider, they have been able to make end-to-end encryption easy to set up and use.

Communication with Private Individuals If a company wants to communicate securely with private individuals, for example, to provide them with account statements or to discuss job applications, communication by email is usually not suitable [KM19]. Transport encryption offers a rather low level of confidentiality, and end-to-end encryption is too complicated for widespread use. Table 7.1 summarises various options for securing email communication and the respective area of application. The best and simplest option in cases with high security requirements is usually the use of a Web portal, as is often used by companies such as banks or job portals.

7.4.7 The Way Ahead: Quantum Computing and Post-quantum Cryptography

One technology that poses a significant risk of breaking some of the current asymmetric cryptosystems, in particular RSA, is quantum computing, i.e. computing using quantum computers. Apart from individual tasks specifically tailored to this technology, these are still a long way from being able to compete with conventional computers, but intensive research is currently being carried out on quantum computers, and progress is being made at a correspondingly rapid pace. Probably the best-known algorithm for quantum computers is the Shor algorithm for prime factorisation of numbers, in which the number of calculation steps (the time complexity) increases linearly with the size of the number. However, the security of the RSA algorithm depends precisely on the property that prime factorisation is practically impossible for numbers with only large prime factors,

Table 7.1 Degrees of suitability of email for secure communication (based on [KM19, Table 1])

	Characterisation	Suitable for
A	Simple email without any extra protection	Only messages without requirements on confidentiality and integrity; not suitable for personal data
B	Email with informed consent of the recipient, secure email transport, transport encryption from the sender to the Internet provider	Messages with low requirements on confidentiality and integrity
C	Email with informed consent of the recipient, secure email transport, transport encryption across the entire path from the sender to the recipient, using only trustworthy Internet providers for the entire path	Also suitable for increased requirements on confidentiality and integrity. In practice not applicable for communication to private persons since the path beyond the sender's Internet provider cannot by controlled by the sender
D	Contents end-to-end encrypted using S/MIME or PGP (or similar)	Suitable for high requirements on confidentiality and integrity. In practice not applicable for communication to private persons since these are often not able to handle end-to-end encrypted email. However, it should at least be offered (for both outgoing and incoming email)

as the number of calculation steps required for all known classical algorithms increases exponentially. If this property is no longer given, it may become relatively easy to calculate the corresponding private key from a public key for the RSA algorithm, in which case the security of this widely used encryption method would collapse.

For this reason, research is being conducted into so-called post-quantum cryptosystems, whose security is unlikely to be broken even with quantum computers. To judge the security of these post-quantum cryptosystems and select one or more such systems for standardisation, the NIST has set up a selection and standardisation program which is currently (as of August 2024) coming to an end.[11] For many application scenarios, this is currently not a challenge as it is usually expected that it will take at least another 5 to 10 years before the first quantum computers become available that could break RSA encryption with today's standard key lengths and considerably longer before they become widely available. However, if you work with data whose confidentiality is worth protecting beyond this period, you should already be thinking hard about which other protection mechanisms should be used in addition to encryption and to what extent you should switch to encryption with post-quantum methods. This applies, for example, to certain health data such as information about chronic illnesses, especially if these are also hereditary.

---

[11] See https://www.nist.gov/pqcrypto for up-to-date details.

References

Eur20. European Data Protection Supervisor: *14 misunderstandings with regard to biometric identification and authentication*, 2020. https://www.edps.europa.eu/data-protection/our-work/publications/papers/14-misunderstandings-regard-biometric-identification_en

FHD20. Furnell, Steven and Haskell-Dowland, Paul: *Good guidance or mistaken misdirection: Assessing the quality of password advice.* In Dhillon, G., Demetis, D., and Furnell, S. (editors): *Proceedings of the Annual Information Institute Conference*, Las Vegas, NV, 2020. http://029e2c6.netsolhost.com/II-Proceedings/2020/12.pdf

GFN+17. Grassi, Paul A., Fenton, James L., Newton, Elaine M., Perlner, Ray A., Regenscheid, Andrew R., Burr, William E., Richer, Justin P., Lefkovitz, Naomi B., Danker, Jamie M., Choong, Yee Yin, Greene, Kristen K., and Theofanos, Mary F.: *Digital identity guidelines. authentication and lifecycle management.* Special publication 800-63B, National Institute of Standards and Technology (NIST), June 2017. https://doi.org/10.6028/NIST.SP.800-63b

KM19. Kneuper, Ralf and Macke, Martin: *Rolle der Transportverschlüsselung für die sichere E-Mail-Kommunikation (in German).* DuD Datenschutz und Datensicherheit, 43(2):76–80, 2019. https://link.springer.com/article/10.1007/s11623-019-1067-9

NIS24. NIST: *The NIST Cybersecurity Framework (CSF) 2.0.* Technical report, National Institute of Standards and Technology (NIST), 2024. https://doi.org/10.6028/NIST.CSWP.29

WT99. Whitten, Alma and Tygar, J. D.: *Why Johnny can't encrypt: a usability evaluation of PGP 5.0.* In *Proc. of the 8th Conference on USENIX Security Symposium – Vol. 8*, SSYM'99, page 14, USA, 1999. USENIX Association.

Data Protection Within IT Organisations

8

Abstract

In addition to their role as designers of data protection, software developers and IT employees are also data subjects themselves whose data are collected and processed, for example, in development tools. Cloud-based tools and communities are becoming increasingly important, which may then fall under the requirements for commissioned processing. This chapter therefore provides an overview of the most important systems in which developer and IT employee data may be collected and how it should be handled. This description is supplemented by a summary of the procedure and explanation of the most important measures for implementing data protection within a development or IT organisation.

8.1 Software Developers and IT Considered as Data Subjects

So far, the discussion has focussed on how software development and IT shape data protection for others. However, people working in these areas are also affected by data protection themselves, whose data are collected in development and similar tools and processed in other ways, for example, in document and configuration management systems, ticket systems or a project wiki.

In principle, the same requirements and rules apply here as for other organisations. The following two case studies describe examples of their implementation in software development.

R. Kneuper, *Data Protection for Software Development and IT*, https://doi.org/10.1007/978-3-662-70639-8_8

Case Study 8.1 (Use of a Collaboration Tool in the Software House) The software company intended to use the collaboration tool XY for its development projects and asked its data protection officer for an opinion, with the following result. This assessment took place sometime before the ECJ judgement in July 2020 (Schrems II judgement), in which Privacy Shield was assessed as insufficient, so that this aspect of the assessment would have to be adjusted today.

Since personal data of the employees themselves are processed by XY, and possibly also by others involved in the tasks managed by the tool, the use of this tool falls within the scope of the GDPR.

Tool XY does not run on company's own servers, but on the tool provider's servers in the USA. This means that the relevant personal data are also stored in the USA, i.e. outside the EU, and the legal basis according to the GDPR under which this is possible must be identified. The examination by the data protection officer showed that the tool provider has submitted to the regulations of the *EU-US Privacy Shield*. An adequate level of protection could therefore be assumed under the then-current legal situation, although there was a clear risk that this could change in the foreseeable future (see Sect. 5.4). Therefore, it was recommended to at least check whether a competitor product operated on servers within the EU could be considered as an alternative.

The use of XY is a form of commissioned processing and a corresponding contract needed to be concluded before use (Art. 28, 29 GDPR). In addition, the following points had to be considered from a data protection perspective when introducing and using XY:

- The RoPA must be adapted accordingly for all processing operations concerned to take account of the use of XY.
- The erasure of personal data that are no longer relevant must also be implemented in XY. A corresponding erasure concept should be created from the outset so that processes do not have to be corrected at a later date. The archiving of data offered in XY must also be taken into account, i.e. it must be ensured that data to be deleted are not archived.
- Photos of people (e.g. in their profile page) should only be posted in XY voluntarily and by the persons themselves in order to ensure that the person concerned has given their unambiguous consent.
- In principle, data subjects must be informed about the processing of their data with XY. For employees who work with the tool themselves, this information is automatically provided. If data of other persons, for example, customers, are also processed in XY, it is likely that explicit information of these persons is required.

Case Study 8.2 (Screening of Employees of the Software House) In order to fulfil its own compliance requirements, an important customer of the software company requested screening their employees, including the following checks: identity verification by checking ID; authenticity check of submitted references and certificates; obtaining references from previous employers; submission of a current criminal record, where legally permissible; credit check, where legally permissible; and work permit check. It was requested that the software company checks its employees according to these criteria and confirms to the customer that the check for named employees has taken place and has not revealed any problems. The check was to be carried out once before the start of the employment relationship and subsequently updated as required, and the results should be kept for at least 1 year after the end of the employment relationship.

An assessment of this customer requirement by the DPO led to the following findings:

- Identity checks, document checks and reference checks are generally permitted as long as they are handled restrictively and are limited to essential information that is relevant to the customer.
- Obtaining a criminal record is only an option, if at all, for property offences, but even in this case, it is very doubtful and must also be assessed from a labour law perspective in each individual case.
- A credit check is not permitted but can be replaced to a certain extent by a confirmation from the employee.

In addition, the following general conditions must be taken into account:

- The screening may only be carried out for employees who actually work for this customer, not for all employees. Screening prior to commencement of employment is therefore only possible in special cases.
- Unless the relevant data must already be retained for other reasons, it may only be retained for as long as the respective employee works for this customer (plus a transitional period).
- If screening is carried out, the employees concerned must be informed about the collection of the data as well as its purpose and use.
- It is not legally possible to obtain the consent of the employees concerned, as consent cannot really be given voluntarily under the given circumstances. Instead, legitimate interest is the appropriate legal basis, which however requires an explicit balancing of interests (largely performed by this assessment by the DPO).

(continued)

- Passing on the requested information to the customer leads to a joint responsibility in accordance with Art. 26 GDPR. Therefore, a corresponding agreement on compliance with data protection obligations is required, in particular an obligation on the part of the customer to treat these data confidentially.

8.2   Implementing Data Protection Within an IT Organisation

The following procedure has proven successful in achieving an appropriate implementation of data protection within an IT organisation:

- *Appointment of a data protection officer* who has the necessary expertise in data protection and supports its implementation both within the company and in the systems developed by the organisation. This can be a formally appointed data protection officer as described in Sect. 2.7.8 or, if the appointment of a DPO is not required by law, another employee with a similar area of responsibility.
- *Performing an internal assessment* to clarify the extent to which the relevant requirements have already been met and what gaps remain.
- *Creation of a RoPA.* These records should be created iteratively together with the site assessment in order to clarify and document which procedures exist, which data are processed there and which protective measures have already been implemented.
- *Prioritisation of gaps identified,* depending on the risk for those affected and the visibility to the outside world. For example, data protection deficiencies on a company's Web site are easily visible from the outside, as is the lack of a data protection officer, and should therefore be rectified at very short notice if applicable.
- *Step-by-step elimination* of gaps according to their priority
- *Annual repeat of the internal assessment*

There are a number of further tasks that are particularly important in IT organisations:

Authentication of Support Requesters In support in particular, it is important to ensure that support requesters (via telephone, email, etc.) are correctly authenticated before they can receive personal data (about themselves). Providing name and date of birth or similar information is not sufficient for this purpose since these are easily available to unauthorised third parties.[1]

---

[1] See, for example, https://www.bfdi.bund.de/SharedDocs/Pressemitteilungen/EN/2020/28_Urteil-1und1.html.

Limiting Access to Project Documentation It usually makes sense for different projects within an organisation to exchange experience and knowledge. However, care must be taken to ensure that this free exchange is restricted where personal data are involved, be it customer data, user data or employee data. It is difficult to formulate a generally applicable guideline here, but the principle of data minimisation must always be observed.

Data Protection as a Component of an Integrated Management System As already mentioned in Sect. 7.2, it makes sense to integrate data protection and information security with other management tasks or existing systems to form an integrated management system. In an IT organisation, this typically includes quality management in accordance with ISO 9001 and IT service management in accordance with ISO/IEC 20000. Such an integrated management system makes it possible to jointly develop and utilise important basic functions such as document control, process management, a continuous improvement process (e.g. according to the Plan-Do-Check-Act paradigm (PDCA)) as well as risk management and asset management.

8.3 Protecting Your Own Data

Another important part of implementing data protection within an IT organisation is the protection of your own data. This includes in particular the selection of services that only collect and store the data that is really necessary, for example, for messenger services, scheduling, browsers, search engines, etc. There are widespread services that collect a lot of user data and use it for advertising or political influence or less widespread alternatives that prioritise data minimisation.

Password Vaults Developers typically need many different user accounts for different services. However, different passwords should be used so that the theft of a password for one service does not compromise all of the user's other accounts. To store these different passwords (if you can remember them all, they are probably too simple), the use of a password vault is recommended. A long and secure password is then used for this, but as you only have to remember this one password, it is feasible.

Encryption Tools At the very least, data should be encrypted when storing confidential data on mobile data carriers and devices and when transmitting these data via public networks. This does not only apply to personal data but also to many other types of data that are considered confidential or even business secrets. Well-known open-source programmes for encryption include GnuPG and TrueCrypt/VeraCrypt. However, if several or many users are to be able to access the encrypted data in parallel, or if access to certain data is to be possible in the company without the employees concerned giving out their personal passwords, then commercial tools may be more suitable.

With security products such as password vaults and encryption software, it is of course particularly important that they themselves are secure. Accordingly, care should be taken to ensure that they come from trustworthy providers and, if possible, that they are or have been verified (or certified) by independent bodies.

Excerpts from Important Data Protection Legislation

A

A.1 Charter of Fundamental Rights of the European Union

Article 8: Protection of Personal Data[1]
(1) Everyone has the right to the protection of personal data concerning him or her.
(2) Such data must be processed fairly for specified purposes and on the basis of the consent of the person concerned or some other legitimate basis laid down by law. Everyone has the right of access to data which has been collected concerning him or her, and the right to have it rectified.
(3) Compliance with these rules shall be subject to control by an independent authority.

A.2 General Data Protection Regulation (GDPR)

Article 5: Principles Relating to Processing of Personal Data
(1) Personal data shall be:
  (a) processed lawfully, fairly and in a transparent manner in relation to the data subject ('lawfulness, fairness and transparency');
  (b) collected for specified, explicit and legitimate purposes and not further processed in a manner that is incompatible with those purposes; further processing for archiving purposes in the public interest, scientific or historical research purposes or statistical purposes shall, in accordance with Article 89(1), not be considered to be incompatible with the initial purposes ('purpose limitation');

---

[1] Available from https://eur-lex.europa.eu/legal-content/EN/TXT/?uri=CELEX:12012P/TXT.

    (c) adequate, relevant and limited to what is necessary in relation to the purposes for which they are processed ('data minimisation');

    (d) accurate and, where necessary, kept up to date; every reasonable step must be taken to ensure that personal data that are inaccurate, having regard to the purposes for which they are processed, are erased or rectified without delay ('accuracy');

    (e) kept in a form which permits identification of data subjects for no longer than is necessary for the purposes for which the personal data are processed; personal data may be stored for longer periods insofar as the personal data will be processed solely for archiving purposes in the public interest, scientific or historical research purposes or statistical purposes in accordance with Article 89(1) subject to implementation of the appropriate technical and organisational measures required by this Regulation in order to safeguard the rights and freedoms of the data subject ('storage limitation');

    (f) processed in a manner that ensures appropriate security of the personal data, including protection against unauthorised or unlawful processing and against accidental loss, destruction or damage, using appropriate technical or organisational measures ('integrity and confidentiality').

(2) The controller shall be responsible for, and be able to demonstrate compliance with, paragraph 1 ('accountability').

Article 6: Lawfulness of Processing

(2) Processing shall be lawful only if and to the extent that at least one of the following applies:

    (a) the data subject has given consent to the processing of his or her personal data for one or more specific purposes;

    (b) processing is necessary for the performance of a contract to which the data subject is party or in order to take steps at the request of the data subject prior to entering into a contract;

    (c) processing is necessary for compliance with a legal obligation to which the controller is subject;

    (d) processing is necessary in order to protect the vital interests of the data subject or of another natural person;

    (e) processing is necessary for the performance of a task carried out in the public interest or in the exercise of official authority vested in the controller;

    (f) processing is necessary for the purposes of the legitimate interests pursued by the controller or by a third party, except where such interests are overridden by the interests or fundamental rights and freedoms of the data subject which require protection of personal data, in particular where the data subject is a child.

Point (f) of the first subparagraph shall not apply to processing carried out by public authorities in the performance of their tasks.

(2) ...

(3) ...

(4) Where the processing for a purpose other than that for which the personal data have been collected is not based on the data subject's consent or on a Union or Member State law which constitutes a necessary and proportionate measure in a democratic society to safeguard the objectives referred to in Article 23(1), the controller shall, in order to ascertain whether processing for another purpose is compatible with the purpose for which the personal data are initially collected, take into account, inter alia:
  (a) any link between the purposes for which the personal data have been collected and the purposes of the intended further processing;
  (b) the context in which the personal data have been collected, in particular regarding the relationship between data subjects and the controller;
  (c) the nature of the personal data, in particular whether special categories of personal data are processed, pursuant to Article 9, or whether personal data related to criminal convictions and offences are processed, pursuant to Article 10;
  (d) the possible consequences of the intended further processing for data subjects;
  (e) the existence of appropriate safeguards, which may include encryption or pseudonymisation.

Article 9: Processing of Special Categories of Personal Data
(1) Processing of personal data revealing racial or ethnic origin, political opinions, religious or philosophical beliefs, or trade union membership, and the processing of genetic data, biometric data for the purpose of uniquely identifying a natural person, data concerning health or data concerning a natural person's sex life or sexual orientation shall be prohibited.
(3) Paragraph 1 shall not apply if one of the following applies:
  (a) the data subject has given explicit consent to the processing of those personal data for one or more specified purposes, except where Union or Member State law provide that the prohibition referred to in paragraph 1 may not be lifted by the data subject;
  (b) ...

Article 24: Responsibility of the Controller
(1) Taking into account the nature, scope, context and purposes of processing as well as the risks of varying likelihood and severity for the rights and freedoms of natural persons, the controller shall implement appropriate technical and organisational measures to ensure and to be able to demonstrate that processing is performed in accordance with this Regulation. Those measures shall be reviewed and updated where necessary.
(2) Where proportionate in relation to processing activities, the measures referred to in paragraph 1 shall include the implementation of appropriate data protection policies by the controller.
(3) Adherence to approved codes of conduct as referred to in Article 40 or approved certification mechanisms as referred to in Article 42 may be used as an element by which to demonstrate compliance with the obligations of the controller.

Article 25: Data Protection by Design and by Default

(1) Taking into account the state of the art, the cost of implementation and the nature, scope, context and purposes of processing as well as the risks of varying likelihood and severity for rights and freedoms of natural persons posed by the processing, the controller shall, both at the time of the determination of the means for processing and at the time of the processing itself, implement appropriate technical and organisational measures, such as pseudonymisation, which are designed to implement data-protection principles, such as data minimisation, in an effective manner and to integrate the necessary safeguards into the processing in order to meet the requirements of this Regulation and protect the rights of data subjects.

(2) The controller shall implement appropriate technical and organisational measures for ensuring that, by default, only personal data which are necessary for each specific purpose of the processing are processed. That obligation applies to the amount of personal data collected, the extent of their processing, the period of their storage and their accessibility. In particular, such measures shall ensure that by default personal data are not made accessible without the individual's intervention to an indefinite number of natural persons.

(3) An approved certification mechanism pursuant to Article 42 may be used as an element to demonstrate compliance with the requirements set out in paragraphs 1 and 2 of this Article.

Article 32: Security of Processing

(1) Taking into account the state of the art, the costs of implementation and the nature, scope, context and purposes of processing as well as the risk of varying likelihood and severity for the rights and freedoms of natural persons, the controller and the processor shall implement appropriate technical and organisational measures to ensure a level of security appropriate to the risk, including inter alia as appropriate:

 (a) the pseudonymisation and encryption of personal data;

 (b) the ability to ensure the ongoing confidentiality, integrity, availability and resilience of processing systems and services;

 (c) the ability to restore the availability and access to personal data in a timely manner in the event of a physical or technical incident;

 (d) a process for regularly testing, assessing and evaluating the effectiveness of technical and organisational measures for ensuring the security of the processing.

(2) In assessing the appropriate level of security account shall be taken in particular of the risks that are presented by processing, in particular from accidental or unlawful destruction, loss, alteration, unauthorised disclosure of, or access to personal data transmitted, stored or otherwise processed.

(3) Adherence to an approved code of conduct as referred to in Article 40 or an approved certification mechanism as referred to in Article 42 may be used as an element by which to demonstrate compliance with the requirements set out in paragraph 1 of this Article.

(4) The controller and processor shall take steps to ensure that any natural person acting under the authority of the controller or the processor who has access to personal data does not process them except on instructions from the controller, unless he or she is required to do so by Union or Member State law.

A.3   Links to Relevant Laws and Supervisory Bodies

Link Collections

Data protection and privacy legislation worldwide	
Global Privacy Law and DPA Directory	https://iapp.org/resources/global-privacy-directory/
Data Protection Laws of the World	https://www.dlapiperdataprotection.com/
Data protection and privacy legislation in the EU	
Data Protection Country Overview	https://gdprhub.eu/index.php?title=Category:Country_Overview

European Union

Main data protection law(s)	
Charter of Fundamental Rights of the European Union (in all EU languages)	https://eur-lex.europa.eu/legal-content/EN/TXT/?uri=CELEX:12012P/TXT
General Data Protection Regulation (GDPR) (in all EU languages)	https://eur-lex.europa.eu/legal-content/AUTO/?uri=CELEX:32016R0679&qid=1661354935368&rid=1
Supervisory authority/authorities	
European Data Protection Supervisor (EDPS)	https://edps.europa.eu/
European Data Protection Board (EDPB)	https://edpb.europa.eu/

Glossary

Anonymisation Process by which personally identifiable information (PII) is irreversibly altered in such a way that a PII principal can no longer be identified directly or indirectly, either by the PII controller alone or in collaboration with any other party. (Source: ISO/IEC 29100:2011, Sect. 2.2)

Anonymous information Information which does not relate to an identified or identifiable natural person or to personal data rendered anonymous in such a manner that the data subject is not or no longer identifiable. (Source: Recital 26 GDPR)

Authentication Verifying the identity of a user, process or device, often as a prerequisite to allowing access to resources in an information system. (Source: NIST[2])

Consent Any freely given, specific, informed and unambiguous indication of the data subject's wishes by which he or she, by a statement or by a clear affirmative action, signifies agreement to the processing of personal data relating to him or her. (Source: Art. 4 (11) GDPR)

Controller The natural or legal person, public authority, agency or other body which, alone or jointly with others, determines the purposes and means of the processing of personal data; where the purposes and means of such processing are determined by Union or Member State law, the controller or the specific criteria for its nomination may be provided for by Union or Member State law. (Source: Art. 4 (7) GDPR)

Personal data Any information relating to an identified or identifiable natural person ("data subject"); an identifiable natural person is one who can be identified, directly or indirectly, in particular by reference to an identifier such as a name, an identification number, location data, an online identifier or to one or more factors specific to the physical, physiological, genetic, mental, economic, cultural or social identity of that natural person. (Source: Art. 4 (1) GDPR) Also known as "personally identifiable information" (PII).

---

[2] https://csrc.nist.gov/glossary/term/authentication

© The Author(s), under exclusive license to Springer-Verlag GmbH,
DE, part of Springer Nature 2025
R. Kneuper, *Data Protection for Software Development and IT*,
https://doi.org/10.1007/978-3-662-70639-8

Personal data breach   A breach of security leading to the accidental or unlawful destruction, loss, alteration or unauthorised disclosure of, or access to, personal data transmitted, stored or otherwise processed. (Source: Art. 4 (12) GDPR)

Personal data of special categories   Personal data revealing racial or ethnic origin, political opinions, religious or philosophical beliefs or trade union membership and the processing of genetic data, biometric data for the purpose of uniquely identifying a natural person, data concerning health or data concerning a natural person's sex life or sexual orientation . (Source: Art. 9 GDPR)

Processing   Any operation or set of operations which is performed on personal data or on sets of personal data, whether or not by automated means, such as collection, recording, organisation, structuring, storage, adaptation or alteration, retrieval, consultation, use, disclosure by transmission, dissemination or otherwise making available, alignment or combination, restriction, erasure or destruction. (Source: Art. 4 (2) GDPR)

Processor   A natural or legal person, public authority, agency or other body which processes personal data on behalf of the controller. (Source: Art. 4 (8) GDPR)

Pseudonymisation   The processing of personal data in such a manner that the personal data can no longer be attributed to a specific data subject without the use of additional information, provided that such additional information is kept separately and is subject to technical and organisational measures to ensure that the personal data are not attributed to an identified or identifiable natural person. (Source: Art. 4 (5) GDPR)

Third country   A country which is not party to a certain treaty. In the context of data protection, this term usually applies to a country which is not a member of the EU or the EEA and where the GDPR therefore does not apply directly.

Index

A
Acceptance (life cycle phase), 166
Access restrictions, 103
Access, right of, 46, 108, 110, 138
  See also GDPR, Art. 15)
Accountability, principle of, 45, 51, 104–105
Accuracy, principle of, 43, 92
Adding noise (to data), 150
Adequacy decision, 131
Advertising blacklist, 121
Agile development, 169–171
AI, see Artificial intelligence (AI)
AI Act, 7, 49, 62–64
  roles, 64
Analysis (life cycle phase), 162–163
Andorra (adequacy decision), 131
Anonymisation, 28–34, 91, 143–155, 211
  as substitute for deletion, 94
Anonymity, 43
  models, 150
  threats, 144
Anonymous data/information, 25, 29, 211
Apple, 116
Archiving, 22, 93, 95, 99, 193
  secure, 100
Argentina (adequacy decision), 131
Article 29 Working Party, 60
Artificial intelligence (AI), 5, 7, 49, 55, 62–64,
    76
  bias, 93
  data protection impact assessment, 54
  definition, 63
  development, 173–174

explainable (XAI), 76, 93
  See also AI Act; Machine learning)
ARX (anonymisation tool), 152
Austria, 10
  data protection officer, 58
  minimum age for consent, 39
Authentication, 114, 211
  before consent, 69
  of support requesters, 202
  of users, 164, 182–187
  when exercising data subject's rights, 46,
    112–113
Authorisation, 164, 187
Automated individual decision-making, 49, 123
  See also GDPR, Art. 22)

B
Backup, 99
Bias, 76, 156
Big data, 89
Binding Corporate Rules (BCR), 131
Biometric data, 27, 186
  for authentication, 182, 186
Blockchain, 31, 102–103
Brazil, 14, 89
  Autoridade Nacional de Proteção de Dados
    (ANPD), 60

C
Canada (adequacy decision), 131
Certification, 59
  cloud services, 134

Change control, 169
Charter of Fundamental Rights of the European
        Union, 2, 205
ChatGPT, 93
Children
    consent, 39, 70
    definition, 39
    legitimate interest, 39
China, 16–17
Church, 25
CIA triad, 45, 179
Cloud computing, 156
Cloud services, 51, 128, 134–136
CMDB, *see* Configuration management
        database (CMDB)
CNIL
    PIA tool, 55
    See also France, supervisory authority)
Collaboration tools, 200
Commissioned processing, 51, 128–129
Commitment to confidentiality, 143
Communication (of data breach), 140
Company group, 126, 132
Confidential computing, 75, 156
Configuration management database (CMDB),
        52
Conflict of interest data protection *vs.*
        information security, 167
Conflict of interest data protection *vs.*
        information security, 180
Consent, 68–73, 211
    children (*see* Children, consent)
    legal basis for processing, 37
    refusal, 70
    for special categories of personal data, 26
Consequences of non-conformance, 61
Contact form, 194
Controller, 34, 36, 211
Cookie, 8, 32, 69, 72, 77–78, 114
    as identifier, 29
    lawfulness, 80
    for storing consent, 71
    third-party, 78, 158
Cookie Directive, 8
Credit agency, 47
Criminal convictions, 27
Criminal law
    regarding data protection breaches, 62

Cryptology, 187–192
Customer relationship system (CRM), 108

D
Data, 25
Data analysis, 4, 89
Data backup, 95, 116, 187
Data breach, 139–142
    in IT operations, 167
Data fiduciary, 15
Data minimisation, principle of, 43, 71, 90–91,
        117, 203
Data portability, right to, 48, 119–121
Data privacy vocabulary (DPV), 175
Data protection by default, 50, 160
Data protection by design, 50, 99, 159
Data Protection Directive 95/46/EC, *see* EU
        Data Protection Directive 95/46/EC
Data protection impact assessment (DPIA), 19,
        54–57, 159, 163, 164, 173
Data protection management system (DPMS),
        138
Data protection manager, 57
Data protection officer (DPO), 4, 57–59, 163,
        164
    Brazil, 58
    Germany, 9
Data protection policy
    generators, 175
Data protection policy (for Web sites), 46, 109,
        113
Data protection threats, 4
Data subject, 34, 36
De-anonymisation, *see* Re-identification
Definition of done, 166, 169, 171
Definition of ready, 169
Deletion (of data), 95
Deployer (AI Act), 64
Design (life cycle phase), 163–165
Design pattern, 160
Dev(Sec)Ops, 160, 170
Differential privacy, 152
    local, 154
Direct marketing, 121
Distributed ledger, *see* Blockchain
Do-not-track, 80, 164
DPV, *see* Data privacy vocabulary (DPV)

E
EEA/EFTA, 6, 24, 126
Email, 196
Employee data
  as special categories of personal data, 27
Encryption, 203
  end-to-end, 195
  homomorphic, 34, 135, 155, 156, 191
ePrivacy Directive, 8, 77
ePrivacy Regulation, 8, 73, 77
Erasure, 96
  as processing, 22, 95
  right to, 47, 95, 115–117, 138
    see also GDPR, Art. 17)
Erasure concept, 96
Establishment criterion, 24
Estonia, 11
  data protection for deceased persons, 26
  minimum age for consent, 39
EU Data Protection Directive 95/46/EC, 6
EU directive *vs.* EU regulation, 6
European Court of Justice (ECJ), 69, 84, 133
  Art. 6 *vs.* Art. 9 GDPR, 39
  IP addresses as identifier, 29
  legal basis for cookies, 80
European Data Protection Board (EDPB), 11,
    60, 209
European Data Protection Supervisor (EDPS),
    60, 136, 209
Explainable AI (XAI), *see* Artificial intelligence
    (AI)
Explanation, right to, 49
External specialist services, 130
Extraterritorial applicability
  DPDPA (India), 15
  GDPR, 7, 24
  LGPD (Brazil), 15
  PIPL (China), 16

F
Facebook, 133
Faeroe Islands (adequacy decision), 131
Fair Information Practice Principles (FIPP), 3
Fairness, principle of, 40, 42, 67, 86
Federal Trade Commission (FTC), 13, 42, 89
Federated learning, 75, 158–159
Fines, 61
Fingerprinting, 82

FIPP, *see* Fair Information Practice Principles
    (FIPP)
"forgot password" function, 185–186
Forgotten, right to be, *see* Erasure, right to
France
  supervisory authority CNIL, 60
Free expression of opinion, right to, 24
"Free" services, 79

G
GDPR
  Art. 2, 23
  Art. 3, 12, 23
  Art. 4, 25, 47, 54, 211, 212
  Art. 5, 7, 37, 45, 67, 83, 84, 86, 92, 93, 104,
    205–206
  Art. 6, 37, 42, 48, 67, 68, 73, 83, 84, 87, 121,
    126, 162, 167, 186, 206–207
  Art. 7, 68
  Art. 8, 7, 39, 162
  Art. 9, 26–27, 39, 68, 162, 186, 207, 212
  Art. 10, 26, 27
  Art. 12, 7, 42, 45, 46, 115
  Art. 13, 7, 42, 46, 76, 108
  Art. 14, 7, 42, 46, 76, 108
  Art. 15, 7, 42, 46, 76, 110, 114
  Art. 16, 7, 47, 114
  Art. 17, 7, 47, 94, 115
  Art. 18, 47, 95, 100, 116, 117
  Art. 19, 115, 116
  Art. 20, 48, 119
  Art. 21, 39, 48, 75, 115, 117, 121
  Art. 22, 49, 103, 123
  Art. 24, 49, 104, 137, 143, 207
  Art. 25, 50, 99, 137, 159, 208
  Art. 26, 35, 51, 129, 202
  Art. 28, 35
  Art. 27, 132
  Art. 28, 36, 51, 126, 128, 136
  Art. 30, 52, 138
  Art. 32, 45, 49, 50, 103, 137, 143, 179–181,
    208–209
  Art. 33, 54, 62, 140
  Art. 34, 54, 62, 140
  Art. 35, 54, 164
  Art. 37, 57
  Art. 38, 57, 142
  Art. 40, 208

Art. 42, 18, 59, 208
Art. 43, 59
Art. 44–50, 126, 131, 132
Art. 82, 61
Art. 83, 61
Art. 85, 24, 25
Art. 89, 25, 84, 100, 121, 205, 206
Art. 91, 25
Recital 26, 25
Recital 47, 38
Recital 48, 38
Recital 49, 38
Recital 51, 27
Recital 65, 115
Scope, 23–25
structure, 22
territorial scope, 24
Generalisation (of data), 149, 152
Germany
    data protection officer, 58
    Federal Data Protection Act, 9
Google, 113
    Analytics, 81–82, 149
    FLoC, 158
    RAPPOR, 154
Guernsey (adequacy decision), 131

H
Hash function, 32, 103, 192–193
Haveibeenpwned, 184
Health Insurance Portability and Accountability
        Act (HIPAA), 13
    anonymisation, 148
HIPAA, *see* Health Insurance Portability and
        Accountability Act (HIPAA)
Homomorphic encryption, *see* Encryption,
        homomorphic
http(s) protocol, 77, 168

I
IAB Transparency & Consent Framework, 81,
        164
Iceland, 7, 24
Identifiability, 25, 28–34
Identification (of users), 164, 182
Identifier, 143
Identity fraud, 61

Imbalance of power, 42
IMEI number, 148
Implementation (life cycle phase), 165
India, 15–16
    data protection terminology, 18
    only one class of personal data, 26
Individual decision-making, automated, *see*
        Automated individual decision-
        making
Inference (threat to anonymity), 144
Information *vs.* data, 25
Information security, 44, 78, 134, 167
Information security management system
        (ISMS), 181
Information society service, 70
Information to be provided to data subjects, 46,
        108
Integrated management system, 181, 203
Integrity and confidentiality, principle of, 44,
        47, 103–104
Interests, balancing of, 38
IP address, 31, 34, 79, 148
    anonymisation, 79
Ireland, 10
    supervisory authority, 60, 116
Isle of Man (adequacy decision), 131
ISO/IEC 27001, 17, 18, 104, 181
ISO/IEC 27018, 17, 19, 134
ISO/IEC 27555, 97
ISO/IEC 27701, 17, 18
ISO/IEC 29100, 3, 17–19, 22
ISO/IEC 29134, 17, 19, 55
ISO/IEC 29151, 17, 19
ISO/IEC TS 27560, 72
Israel (adequacy decision), 131
IT operations, v, 95, 167–168

J
Japan
    adequacy decision, 131
    re-identification of anonymised data, 31
Jersey (adequacy decision), 131
Joint controllership, 35, 51, 129–130, 165

K
k-anonymity, 151
Kerckhoff's principle, 189

Korea, Republic of (adequacy decision), 131

L
Law enforcement authorities, 23
Lawfulness, principle of, 37–42, 67–68
i-diversity, 152
Legal obligation (legal basis for processing), 38
Legal person, 2, 26
    Austria, 10
Legitimate interest (legal basis for processing),
        38, 73, 80, 163
    vs. deletion periods, 96
    objection, 48
Libraries, code, 164
Liechtenstein, 7, 24
Linkability (threat to anonymity), 144
Log data, 110
Log files, 28, 167, 180
Long-term protection of personal data, 193

M
Machine learning, 42, 74–75, 89
    accuracy, 92–93
    legal basis, 74
    preventing bias, 156
    prompt, 74, 90, 130
    training data, 15
    See also Artificial intelligence (AI))
Maintenance, 129, 167
Matomo, 82, 132, 149
Metadata, 27–28
Migration testing, 88
MS Office 365, 136
Multi-factor authentication (MFA), 182

N
National Institute of Standards and Technology
        (NIST), 134, 183, 185, 189, 196
Natural person, 2
Necessity of processing, 40
New Zealand (adequacy decision), 131
NIST Cybersecurity Framework (CSF), 181
Non-conformance, consequences, 61
Norway, 7, 11, 24
    minimum age for consent, 39
Notification (of data breach), 140

Notification obligation, 48
    in case of rectification etc., 119
    See also GDPR, Art. 19)
noyb, 69, 81, 93

O
OASIS, 19
Object, right to, 121–123
    See also GDPR, Art. 21)
OECD Privacy Framework, 19
One-way function, 189, 192
Online marketing, 70, 79
    lawfulness, 76
Opening clauses (in GDPR), 7
Opt-in *vs.* opt-out, 80, 160
Opt-out lists (advertising), 123

P
Password
    for authentication, 183
    policy, 183
    vault, 184, 203
PCI-DSS, 32
Perfect forward secrecy, 191, 193
Performance of contract (legal basis for
        processing), 37, 75, 80
Permutation (of data), 150
Person, 2, 26
    deceased, 26
    unborn, 26
Personal data, 22, 25, 211
    special categories, 26–27, 39, 52, 186, 212
Personal data breach, 52, 211
Personal information management system
        (PIMS), 72, 138
Personally identifiable information (PII), 211
PGP, 195
Photo (of a person), 27, 174
PIMS, *see* Privacy information management
        system (PIMS)
planet49 judgement, 80
Platform, *see* Software ecosystem
Plausible deniability, 153
Post-quantum cryptography, 195
Power imbalance, 2, 75
Principles of data protection, 3
    according to GDPR, 37

according to ISO/IEC 29100, 3
accuracy (*see* Accuracy, principle of)
data minimisation (*see* Data minimisation, principle of)
fairness (*see* Fairness, principle of)
integrity and confidentiality (*see* Integrity and confidentiality, principle of)
lawfulness (*see* Lawfulness, principle of)
purpose limitation (*see* Purpose limitation, principle of)
storage limitation (*see* Storage limitation, principle of)
transparency (*see* Transparency, principle of)
Privacy, 4
Privacy by default, 50
Privacy by design, 50, 161
    See also Data protection by design)
Privacy-enhancing technologies (PET), 155, 164
Privacy impact assessment (PIA), *see* Data protection impact assessment (DPIA)
Privacy information management system (PIMS), 18
Privacy Management Reference Model and Methodology (PMRM), 19
Privacy notice, *see* Data protection policy
Privacy paradox, 80
Privacy pattern, 160
Privacy policy, *see* Data protection policy
Privacy Shield, 133
Processing (of data), 22, 212
Processor, 34–36, 212
Profiling, 49
Prohibition of tying, 68
Prohibition with reservation of permission, 7, 37
Prompt, *see* Machine learning, prompt
Provider (AI Act), 64
Pseudonymisation, 28–34, 38, 91, 212
Public interest (legal basis for processing), 38
    objection, 48
Public key encryption, 190
Purpose change, checklist, 84
Purpose compatibility, 83
Purpose limitation, principle of, 42–43, 83–90

Q
Quantum computing, 195

Quasi-identifier, 143, 144

R
Rainbow table, 33
Randomised response, 153
Ransomware, 54
Recitals, 22
Records of processing activities (RoPA), 4, 51–53, 105, 110, 166, 202
    documentation of TOM, 137
Rectification, right to, 47, 114
    See also GDPR, Art. 16)
Referer (in HTTP), 77
Re-identification, 30, 31, 94, 144
Religious community, 25
Remote maintenance, 129
Reporting of personal data breaches, 54
Requirement
    formulation, 19–20
    See also Data protection requirement)
Restriction of processing, right to, 47, 95, 117–119
    See also GDPR, Art. 18)
Retention period, 96
    in the records of processing activities, 52
Rights concept, *see* Role and rights concept
Right to data portability, *see* GDPR, Art. 20
Risk assessment, 181
`robots.txt`, 174
Role and rights concept, 103, 187
Roles in data protection, 34–37, 170
    See also AI Act, roles)
RoPA, *see* Records of processing activities (ROPA)
RSA algorithm, 190, 195, 196

S
Safe Harbor
    agreement for EU-U.S. data transfer, 133
    anonymisation, 148
Schrems II judgement, 60, 133, 200
Schrems, Max, 69, 93, 133
Scraping, 15, 173–174
Screening of employees, 201
SDK, 126, 164
Secure multi-party computation, 157–158
Security objectives, 45

Singling-out (threat to anonymity), 144
Smart contract, 103
S/MIME, 195
Snowden, Edward, 188
Social networks, 70, 121, 139
Software ecosystem, 171–172
Software test
    life cycle phase, 166
    using production data, 85
Special categories of personal data, *see* Personal
        data, special categories
Standard contractual clauses (SCC), 131
Storage limitation, principle of, 43, 47, 93, 95
Supervisory authorities, 4, 9, 60–61
    France (*see* France, supervisory authority)
    Ireland, 60
Suppression (of data), 149, 152
Switzerland
    adequacy decision, 12, 131
    Data Protection Act, 12
    data protection consultant, 58
    legal persons, 26
    Register of Data Collections, 53
    supervisory authority, 60
Synthetic data generation, 75, 156–157

T
Targeting criterion, 24
t-closeness, 152
Technical and organisational measures (TOM),
        49, 137
Terminology overview, 18
Test, *see* Software test
Third country, 12, 108, 109, 212
    data transfer to, 131–133
    definition, 131
TOM, *see* Technical and organisational
        measures (TOM)
Tracking, 77–80, 82
Training on data protection, 142
Trans-Atlantic Data Privacy Framework, 133
Transition (to operations), 166
Transparency, principle of, 42, 67
Transport encryption, 194

Transport Layer Security (TLS), 188, 191, 194
Trusted execution environment (TEE), 156
Two-factor authentication (2FA), 182

U
United Kingdom, 12
    adequacy decision, 13, 131
    data protection officer, 58
    Information Commissioner's Office (ICO),
        60
    re-identification of anonymised data, 31
Unstructured data, 107, 110, 114
Uruguay (adequacy decision), 131
USA, 13–14, 132–133
    adequacy decision, 131
    advertising opt-out lists, 123
    CLOUD Act, 14
    IP address as identifier, 29
    Privacy Shield (*see* Privacy Shield)
    Safe Harbor (*see* Safe Harbor)
User stories, 169

V
Visiting cards, 108
Vital interests (legal basis for processing), 38
Volkszählungsurteil ("census ruling"), 2

W
W3C, 175
Web analytics, 32, 77, 79, 91, 148
Web hosting, 51
Web scraping, *see* Scraping
Web service, 164
Website audit/review, 168
WhatsApp, 23, 195
Withdrawal (life cycle phase), 169

Z
Zero-knowledge proofs, 157
ZIP code, 148

Printed in the United States
by Baker & Taylor Publisher Services